LEARNING
TO BE A
TEACHER

Sara Miller McCune founded SAGE Publishing in 1965 to support the dissemination of usable knowledge and educate a global community. SAGE publishes more than 1000 journals and over 800 new books each year, spanning a wide range of subject areas. Our growing selection of library products includes archives, data, case studies and video. SAGE remains majority owned by our founder and after her lifetime will become owned by a charitable trust that secures the company's continued independence.

Los Angeles | London | New Delhi | Singapore | Washington DC | Melbourne

LEARNING
TO BE A
TEACHER

JOHN LANGE &
SUE BURROUGHS-LANGE

Los Angeles | London | New Delhi
Singapore | Washington DC | Melbourne

Los Angeles | London | New Delhi
Singapore | Washington DC | Melbourne

SAGE Publications Ltd
1 Oliver's Yard
55 City Road
London EC1Y 1SP

SAGE Publications Inc.
2455 Teller Road
Thousand Oaks, California 91320

SAGE Publications India Pvt Ltd
B 1/I 1 Mohan Cooperative Industrial Area
Mathura Road
New Delhi 110 044

SAGE Publications Asia-Pacific Pte Ltd
3 Church Street
#10-04 Samsung Hub
Singapore 049483

Editor: James Clark
Assistant editor: Robert Patterson
Production editor: Jeanette Graham
Copyeditor: Sharon Cawood
Proofreader: Rose Campbell
Indexer: Anne Solamito
Marketing manager: Dilhara Attygalle
Cover design: Sheila Tong
Typeset by: C&M Digitals (P) Ltd, Chennai, India
Printed by: CPI Group (UK) Ltd, Croydon, CR0 4YY

© John Lange & Sue Burroughs-Lange 2017

First published 2017

Library of Congress Control Number: 2016947818

British Library Cataloguing in Publication data

A catalogue record for this book is available from
the British Library

ISBN 978-14739-6033-6
ISBN 978-14739-6034-3 (pbk)

We dedicate this book to the students with whom we've engaged in teacher professional learning over four decades, especially those attending IOE (London) and QUT (Brisbane). They continuously challenged our thinking about how they could learn to be outstanding teachers. It is their successes that are at the heart of this book and now provide readers with the opportunity to develop and extend their capacities in learning to teach and enhancing the lives of many children.

CONTENTS

LIST OF FIGURES

ABOUT THE AUTHORS

Dr John Douglas Lange

John has over 16 years' experience as a classroom teacher and school principal, and has worked as a consultant on the Schools Commission-Innovation programme (Australia). For the last 40 years, he has been a university teacher-educator, programme director and researcher at QUT (Australia), Northern Illinois University (USA) and Institute of Education (London, UK).

His university teaching has included curriculum theory and planning, learning theory, programme planning for school practicum, classroom management and organization. His educational consultancy work has included the development and implementation of a social studies curriculum (Queensland) and external examiner teacher education courses (UK); he has presented at conferences around the world including AERA (USA) and teacher education associations in Australia and New Zealand.

His research and publications have focused on student teacher learning and their acquisition of professional knowledge, the role of mentors in supervisory situations (The Supervision Casebook), innovating teaching of social studies, employing and teaching the qualitative research method and analysis (using NVivo) and course development in teacher education initiatives.

Dr Sue Burroughs-Lange

Sue began a primary teaching career in 1965 and has worked in a variety of consultancy and professional development roles with schools, advising management and teachers, responding to struggling learners and developing resources to support early and experienced teacher learning and mentoring. As a teacher-educator, she has developed and directed masters and doctoral programmes, taught qualitative research and analysis (using NVivo) and has supervised research theses.

She has been an active researcher for over 35 years at QUT (Australia), Northern Illinois University (USA) and the Institute of Education (London, UK), investigating and demonstrating what enables, and quality assures, rapid expansion in educational initiatives and presenting keynote presentations internationally in these areas.

Her most recent published work, *Reading Recovery and Every Child a Reader: History, Policy and Practice* (IOE Press, 2013), typifies her work on the challenge of effecting change in new and experienced educators through professional development, action research and accountability.

ACKNOWLEDGEMENTS

We thank Sage, especially our editor James Clark, whose responses to our questions and earlier drafts provided us with the encouragement and incentive to present our ideas about teacher professional learning in this book.

Sage would like to thank the following reviewers whose comments have helped shape this book:

Chris Baker, Leader of School Direct, Cabot Learning Federation

Martin Husbands, Head of School Direct, Newman University

Susan Marbe, School Direct Leader & Teaching School Director, West Essex Teaching School Alliance

Kriss Turner, Director for Teacher Development, University of Winchester

INTRODUCTION

This book is for:

- the student teacher starting their professional education on a traditional, university-focused, programme with a variety of in-school placements

- those on courses that are predominately school-based with some academic, university-led units of study

- the newly qualified teacher who is responding to an initial school placement

- an end-of-first-year teacher who is assessing whether to, or when and how to, fit into a new career path.

It will also be of interest to and a valuable resource for:

- those education professionals, in colleges and schools, who work closely with these teacher-learners, and early career teachers

- more experienced teachers looking for ways to renew their approaches to teaching and learning and their place within the classroom.

Questions are addressed such as:

- How can I find and use professional learning strategies that will enable me to better understand the complexities of the teaching and learning process?

- How can I learn more about professional learning approaches that might make my work less stressful and more rewarding?

If you are looking for ways to become a proactive and effective professional learner, then the practical strategies and associated theoretical and research content of this book will offer you ways of becoming confident in taking charge of your professional future in teaching.

How does this book do this?

- It will support you in becoming a participant observer, and evaluator of your role.
- It provides you with processes for establishing a conceptual framework for critically analysing, interpreting and theorizing about your teaching and learning environment.
- It shows you examples of how to use embedded professional learning opportunities to take personal control of your learning, through self-regulation and self-monitoring.
- It reviews approaches to planning and preparation for learning. These focus on how to gain greater awareness of teaching models and strategies, together with detailing specific teaching skills to include in your planning process.

How to read this book

Key contributing ideas appear in text boxes throughout the book. They identify the core ideas of that section of the chapter that contribute to your developing awareness, understanding and application of effective professional learning. Collectively, these key ideas map a strong framework for generating your professional growth as an effective, self-improving teacher. These contributing ideas will provide a 'stream of consciousness' about the nature of your professional learning and contribute to building an evaluative framework to ascertain the characteristics of your professional learning. An evaluative format to guide your review of these aspects of your professional learning is provided on the Sage companion website – https://study.sagepub.com/lange

An organizing principle throughout each chapter includes:

- the presentation of a professional learning idea – contributing ideas that focus on your professional learning as a teacher-learner. A conceptual framework is building as these ideas are related to the complexities of the professional learning process against which you can evaluate your awareness and growth
- related explanations and potential application strategies which are presented together, alongside a strategy for how to explore these concepts. This process empowers you to undertake practical investigations and implementation in differing teaching and learning environments. These can be both academic and practice-oriented. You can begin to employ these ideas in your teaching

- an exploration of what we know works – the literature and research that relate to and support the associated key concept or contributing idea are then followed by practical explanation.

This book demonstrates throughout that for professional learning to be meaningful and applicable to you, theoretical and research-based knowledge must be well sourced, understood and recognized. This is critical to establishing the meaningfulness of your practical experiences in the various contexts in which professional learning takes place.

Rationale for this road to success

Wherever you find yourself along this new teacher career path, your interest and goals will converge on how to be the best you can at teaching children and young people how to learn, to thrive and to achieve their potential. Maybe you have just heard that you have a place on a teacher education programme. Perhaps you are about to begin your training year and want to understand the complexities of teaching and learning. You want to be able to cope with the pressures and do well in both your university studies and school experiences. In successfully completing your degree, you have experience of successfully managing extraordinary demands on your time, commitment and intellect to achieve your desired results. But now you find yourself in a learning environment where academic and curriculum preparation tasks can challenge you in a continuous tide of new expectations. This book shows you how to reconsider the enquiry or decision-making strategies that seem to have worked successfully for you in the past. It shows you how to profit from these so that they deliver the insights and build the knowledge that are necessary as you learn to teach.

Consider where you might be in two years' time. With some support from mentors and colleagues, you have been learning how to manage your teaching. You've completed your induction year as a newly qualified teacher (NQT). Are you beginning to wonder about your future in a teaching career? How did you cope with seemingly constant demands on your time and effort? If you are determined to stay and progress within your chosen teaching profession, then are you looking for professional learning approaches that might make your work less stressful and more rewarding?

If you find yourself in any of these early teaching career contexts and want to see yourself firmly as a proactive and effective professional learner, then this book offers proven and alternative ways of thriving and becoming confident to take charge of your own professional future in teaching.

The book includes a conceptual framework for critically analysing, interpreting and theorizing about the complexities of the teaching and learning environment. Importantly, it also includes how to build your understanding, your evolving knowledge and potential to create an effective place for yourself. The development of this insightful teacher awareness relies on a structure for investigation. You can become expert in using a self-assessment framework as a participant-observer and, simultaneously, as the professional responsible for the creation of relevant and responsive learning for your students.

This book also provides practical support for you to develop particular strategies for effective teaching and learning from theoretical material that you meet in your university education studies and educational documents. In this way, you can gradually come to comprehend the interlocking and underpinning nature of theory and practice.

You will find that the term *teacher-learner* is sometimes used in this book. It refers to student teachers during their pre-service programme, beginning teachers who are 'learning in placement' and those full-time teaching in the first years of their career. The alternative term of *neophyte teacher* is also used to refer to new teachers as more enhanced professionals, as they transform their teaching consciousness.

SECTION 1

A LEARNING PERSPECTIVE ON TEACHER DEVELOPMENT

Section 1 consists of two chapters:

Chapter 1 Your professional learning consciousness

Chapter 2 Becoming a self-regulating, autonomous professional

These first two chapters explore how to establish an approach to your professional learning that is self-regulatory and self-monitoring. This approach encourages and empowers you to assume increasing control of your professional knowledge and expertise. Some basic theoretical and research perspectives are also covered.

The *teacher as a learner* is an inquisitive professional who seeks self-awareness (see Feiman-Nemser, 2012). Through focused enquiry and interpretative strategies, you are enabled to assume responsibility for your learning, including when colleague support may not always be available. Input of a mentor or colleague to challenge your evolving professional awareness can also be significant in supporting your early learning for teaching. But with expanding demands on school and university personnel, your professional progress may also depend on your ability to access and enhance your own learning. If you are to develop self-management of your learning, you will need to adopt both organizational and analytical strategies to achieve this. Acquiring the associated language of enquiry and interpretation of professional learning also adds communicative purpose to your learning process.

The professional knowledge and expertise that you will need to acquire during your initial teacher education programme can be placed within three interlocking and reciprocal contexts. These are: the education system (locally and more broadly); the school and classroom; and your individual personal, professional environment. It is within and across these domains that you access and engage with the social and intellectual processes that provide the basis for developing knowledge and understanding of your own learning. Your professional learning is drawn from experiences where you initiate and respond to theoretical and practical dimensions in the classroom, and by a more direct awareness of intellectual processes that support how you can learn effectively and with purpose.

This concept of professional learning relates to two interacting and complementary sets of knowledge, understanding and skills. The first set is the identification and construction of knowledge, and the application of content and pedagogical skills. The second knowledge set is the intellectual ability to investigate, understand and apply the knowledge and skills inherent in your own learning context. The latter conceptualizing process is crucial if you are to fully engage with the complex content knowledge, understanding and application required to successfully engage students in classroom learning activities.

Learning *how* you acquire, modify and create responses for learners, facilitates self-regulation in your control and management of the complexities of teaching and learning. Learning *what* and *how* to teach provides the content context of professional learning; it is *learning how to learn*, its enquiry and interpretative awareness. This provides the unique and major focus of Section 2 of this book.

A special kind of teaching consciousness

Professional learning outcomes usually originate from sources that are both external and internal to the teacher-learner. Evolving ownership of ways of knowing will enhance the possibility of engaging in higher level understanding and in recursive, self-initiated, constructive processes of learning. This places *you* in pivotal control of:

- enquiry strategies that can guide and enhance your own professional learning activities
- processes for implementing and developing aspects of the curriculum
- creating teaching and learning activities in response to both pedagogical and learner needs.

You need to consider the theoretical base for developing an individual learning consciousness that encompasses an awareness of the content and processes of curriculum and pedagogical learning and, more importantly, of the intellectual process that you use to develop professional knowledge and understanding of your role and its associated expertise. At its core, this book provides a number of cognitive strategies to guide you in developing a deeper understanding of your teaching role and to formulate relevant responses to identified professional learning initiatives from teaching and learning episodes. In Section 2, these strategies are placed within a theoretical and research perspective to support you in:

- reviewing teaching initiatives
- focusing on and extending observing and planning skills
- managing the learner and learning process.

The approach to professional learning that is promoted in this book is mirrored in the ways that the teaching and learning process is discussed. The theoretical understanding and articulation of what you are able to do provides a sound platform for individual and authoritative creativity in your professional learning processes. As well as developing effective communication skills with young learners, you want to be able to explain and justify how you are engaging learners, why in this way and for this particular programme.

1
YOUR PROFESSIONAL
LEARNING CONSCIOUSNESS

Having read this chapter, you will have an understanding of how:

- differing contexts you encounter can provide for your knowledge and learning about teaching

- your talk about teaching tells a story – developing a theoretical and practical language of enquiry and interpretation

- you can generate change in yourself through enquiry and self-observation

- to use scaffolding to manage your own tailored learning

- this lift in your cognitive and affective functioning supports you to generate your own responses to teaching and learning challenges

- you can transform your learning though a pattern of awareness, theorizing and interpretation.

The most important feature of this chapter is the individual focus on *your* learning to teach and why and how you can become a self-observing, self-regulating, enquiring, outstanding professional. Let us first consider the particular contexts in which you can develop your teacher self-awareness.

The contexts of your knowledge and learning about teaching

The education system, university and school context

The widest context of professional learning is provided in the teacher education curriculum that is the outcome of both society's and the education system's requirements for the preparation and on-going support and guidance of teacher-learners. The defined curriculum of teacher education is dependent on subject input, both theoretical and research, regarding knowledge acquisition and pedagogical awareness. It is generally provided in partnerships between university and school personnel.

Over recent years in England, the balance between the academic, university-led contribution and time in school settings has changed. According to their particular philosophy, government agencies endeavour to respond to the perceived value of education generally, through university teacher education and the training of individuals who will provide teaching for the children and youth of society.

An emphasis on teaching as learning *what* and *how* to teach, as a practical apprentice-type activity, primarily values time in classrooms. This results in proportionally less time in university settings to explore the pedagogical and research components of any curriculum subject. This constrains teacher education to accessing specific knowledge and understanding of the subject from academics who have made that knowledge discipline the focus of their intellectual lives. You also need to learn the psychology of how knowledge accessed this way can be used to plan learning for students. Knowledge cannot be transferred by osmosis from a subject expert, leaving you, as teacher-learner, to transform it into classroom teaching. Developing as a teacher requires expertise in both content conceptualization and organization; and responsive and relevant pedagogy for your students.

The personal professional learning strategies identified in Section 2 are not particularly concerned with what might be provided by academic subject specialists in the traditional content areas, such as mathematics, science, history, geography, language and literacy, or with the theoretical and research-oriented subjects of educational psychology, philosophy and sociology. Examples are 'how the reading skills of specific learners are to be introduced, maintained and enhanced' or 'how the reading skills of reluctant learners are to be encouraged and reinforced so that they can access other curriculum subjects'. These: (i) would be a component of the pedagogy offered in an English language course in the university, (ii) could prompt an individually focused critical review by you as *teacher-learner*, and (iii) would be further clarified by you in a focus on effective implementation in your classrooms.

School-based requirements may be localized responses to national policy and curriculum statements. You can interrogate and interpret these with a view to integrating them into your range of teaching skills. You can use the professional learning agenda (PLA), set out in Chapter 4, to manage this process. Most primary and secondary schools will have a range of policies and programmes implemented across all classrooms and subject areas, such as the expected requirements of students' behaviour. You will have these strategies available to you to respond directly to off-task incidents with learners and to social behaviour that does not conform to normal expectations.

There will also be classroom curriculum and management patterns, adapted by mentors and teaching colleagues, to which you will initially need to adhere – for example, the development of teaching responses to learners who are exhibiting either significant success in a specific subject area or learners who have demonstrated that they require additional help and support. It is your responsibility not only to know about and to respond to such school initiatives, but also to develop a range of intervention strategies and approaches for use in specific instances with *your* learners that are congruent with stated school policies. An *enquiring, theorizing, interpreting and generating* strategy is useful in developing and extending your approaches. This will become more relevant as you learn to take increasing control of classroom management and teaching. You can ready yourself for these growing responsibilities by observing, interrogating and interpreting individual teacher responses. You can do this through informed listening to colleagues and children, and by generating potential initiatives that you have identified using your enquiry strategy (see Chapter 3, REACT).

The context of the classroom

The classroom environment is a very relevant and potentially productive context for your professional development. It holds the opportunity for you to personalize your knowledge and understanding of teaching and learning. You will want to go beyond being a copier to becoming an implementer who develops ways of responding to teaching and learning episodes; and to move deliberately towards having executive control of your professional development. You will want to investigate and theorize about potential approaches, strategies and skills that best fit your current levels of understanding and individual expertise in working effectively with learners.

What you interpret and understand from the observation of and discussions with informed others, such as colleagues and mentors, can provide a basic framework to which your evolving ideas and responses can be added. Eventually, your deliberations and elaborations will make this conceptual framework into a meaning-making tool or habit for you. An on-going personal agenda for learning how to learn and the associated concepts of what and how to teach, will provide you with a growing intellectual capacity and associated skills to make relevant decisions for yourself and the learners you teach.

The context of *self*

Questions you may ask yourself as you learn to teach include:

- How do I make sense of the order of the classroom?
- What is really happening here?
- Where do I fit comfortably?

- What strategies can support identifying and processing my current professional learning?
- What form of a professional learning agenda could provide a pedagogical resource for supporting my meaning making and my expertise in how to respond?

Some potential answers follow. Though you have spent a considerable proportion of your life in various classrooms, the immediate challenge on a school experience placement or first job appointment is to recognize the duality of your continuing roles in education. The first challenge is accepting the role of teacher, that is, someone who is responsible for creating, organizing and managing the continuing education of a group of learners. We refer to this throughout the book as learning the *what* and the *how* to teach. Your second challenge is to focus on *learning how to learn*, with the varied support of colleagues and course experiences. The enormity and immediacy of taking on these dual roles can seem overwhelming. How will you survive and grow? What content and skills, in planning, resourcing, teaching and behaviour management, will you need to acquire immediately? Once a professional learning approach has been identified and implemented, how might you continue to enhance it? What is there to observe and understand in this classroom? What are other teachers doing? How are the children responding? What makes or encourages the students to act in a certain way?

Observing in a classroom, your first impressions might be students seeming to work quietly and productively with only limited input and interactions by the teacher. Based on the *surface* interactions and engagements, everything seems to be running smoothly. Let us assume that the teacher presents a prepared introduction to the lesson, identifies or reminds students of some rules of how the learning activity is to be conducted, and then the teacher *wanders* around the room to check on individuals and small groups of learners. You see the teacher support learners who need additional help or guide those learners who need to extend the nature and complexity of the learning task. Is this what teaching is really about?

This may look like an easy process to follow, but ask yourself: what did the teacher prepare beforehand to make this classroom run with seeming clockwork precision? Had the management and monitoring of the learners required significant prior training time to achieve? How can you know when to intervene with a learner's task completion, or offer guidance or further support, as the teacher being observed seems to manage so easily? How is this seamless interaction between the teacher's work and the students' learning, and the associated task, arrived at in this classroom? How was trust in engagement in the activity built and maintained between teacher and learner?

At first, the many questions that classroom observation generates, may be confusing. You will become increasingly aware that to understand productive learning in the classroom it is necessary to consider principles and actions that have gone into creating this classroom environment. Your aim as a new teacher is to focus on developing insights, analyses and interpretations through paying direct attention to classroom learning processes. By critically analysing and interpreting these observations, you can to begin to identify some of these *beneath-the-surface* understandings. Learning, through observing and analysing the teaching of more experienced colleagues, can therefore become meaningful. In the analogy of a swan moving apparently effortlessly across a still pond, the water surface is calm with no visible disruption from the effort of energetic propulsion occurring below the surface.

In order to gather relevant information and make sense of complex classroom situations, you will need to develop a range of interpersonal psychological functions. These include listening and attending, discriminating, observing, recording, collating and acquiring describing skills to articulate what you observe. These are an *investigative set* of research skills which underpin *learning how to learn* in the social domain. As well as information gathering and organizational cognitive skills, you will want to apply higher-level intellectual processes of critical analysis in order to interpret, interrogate, restructure, critique, predict and synthesize your findings. In this book, the term *critical analysis set* is used to describe these enquiry and interpretive skills operating in the intra-psychological domain (see Vygotsky, 1978). Both of these sets of exploratory skills apply within the *syntactic* orientation of the professional learning curriculum, further explored in Chapter 2. These terms are used to represent each of these sets of professional learning skills. In this book, you will learn how to use these social and cognitive skills to create your evolving understanding of your teaching role.

To formulate relevant responses to teaching and learning episodes, you need to employ systematic, enquiry-focused and self-generating learning frameworks. By using these frameworks, you can create potential initiatives to be trialled, evaluated for possible modification, and tentatively included in your repertoire of teaching strategies. Such strategies for observing, analysing, enquiring, theorizing, interpreting, and the creation of the associated professional learning agenda, are covered in the chapters in Section 2 of this book.

Developing theoretical and practical language for professional learning

There is a perception in education that teachers, and by implication, *teacher-learners* and their mentors and colleagues, feel uneasy using theoretical language for describing the practical functioning of classrooms (Campbell & Neill, 1994; Hancock, 1997; Marchel & Green, 2014). As professionals, we need to feel comfortable in describing and justifying, in theoretical terms, the practices and conventions of the educative process. To do this we use the language of enquiry and interpretation, and the application of scientific concepts that allow us to define, describe and theorize about the teaching and learning process, and the ways that our students learn. The terms we use must be precise enough for significant understanding to be interpreted, developed and communicated – for example, the range of skills in the investigative set of interpersonal, psychological functions that you will need for information gathering and meaning making in the classroom. These cognitive functions are an interrelated cluster of social, inter-psychological skills, and a number of these include observation and discrimination. They become the organizing foci for exploration in the following chapters. As a brief introduction to what is intended, let's consider *observing* as a task you undertake as a teacher and learner. Aids to observation and the associated processes will be found more fully in Chapters 3 and 4.

Observing in schools and classrooms is seen as a legitimate activity for *teacher-learners* to engage in. You want to feel prepared to make insightful and meaningful observations within the very busy classroom environment. You need to develop observation techniques so that you can accurately identify, describe and interpret the significant characteristics and connections. This observation process is not a skill that everyone possesses. You need to employ a level of analytical enquiry and interpretation that allows you to develop appropriate understandings about what you are actually seeing.

Recent constructivist approaches to teacher education emphasize observing and reflecting (after Schön, 1987; Crichton & Valdera, 2015). How can you listen attentively and discriminate between and among the characteristics and conditions that exist in the classroom? Skills of listening, discriminating, recording and describing form a cluster of pre-requisite skills for enhancing your higher intellectual processes.

Skills in critical analysis and interpretation are referred to here as the critical analysis set. They are also fundamental to developing effective understanding of the complex teaching and learning process. Your critique underpins discrimination between characteristics that, on the surface, may seem very similar. This critical analysis allows you to thoughtfully review your own involvement.

We need to be alert to the adequacy, for our professional purposes, of some concepts in everyday usage. One example is over-use of the labels *reflecting* and *reflection* for defining complex theoretical ideas and investigation of teachers' work. The concept of critical awareness we talk about here is a more inclusive and detailed representation of the term *reflection* used by Dewey (1933). Later, Schön's (1991) description of the *reflective* practitioner entailed analysis, discrimination, interrogation, interpretation and evaluation. To better understand reflection, we want to be able to articulate and explore the constituent parts of the critical awareness needed. In this case, we want, and need, to know more about what our observed *teacher swans* do, to propel the learning of their students.

Generating cognitive change through enquiry

Higher-order intellectual processes within the individual domain include critiquing, re-framing, critical review and evaluation. These four processes are specifically described by their sub-set of intellectual processes. Critiquing, for example, involves the associated intellectual skills of analysing, interrogating, interpreting, synthesizing, inferring and generalizing. You learn to use these processes as you articulate, understand, interpret and theorize about your own involvement in professional learning activities in classroom and study contexts. Engaging with these cognitive functions provides you with complex and supportive enquiry schema. The concept of schemata is taken from Piaget (1952) who defined schema as cognitive or knowledge structures or mental maps. Later research by McVee and colleagues (2005) focused on Piaget's schema as a pattern of repeatable behaviour where experiences are assimilated. The resultant structure and connections lead to higher-order cognitive levels and more influential and authoritative states. The schema can be characterized as a basic building block of intelligent behaviour, a way of organizing knowledge that increases in number and complexity as an individual learns in a particular content domain.

You can maintain, extend and contextualize your professional learning as schemata as you seek underlying reasons and meanings from observed incidents in the learning environment. To find personal relevance in professional learning situations, you need to be directly involved in both the generation and control of your learning contexts, and the intellectual skills that you bring to this process. This is a personal recognition of the intellectual worth that you bring to teaching, and growing confidence in your ability to respond creatively to the education of your students.

In proposing a shift of control in learning from the provision of structured learning tasks to a strategy of conscious understanding and control by the learner, Bruner (1983) considers the concept of *scaffolding*, a concept which you can readily apply to your own professional learning. The metaphor of a scaffold is used to describe both the structure of the social interaction of the professional learning process, and the content and process of the professional learning experience (Wood et al., 1976). Here the scaffold is in the form of the sequencing of the strategic processes that you learn to use. If a mentor or colleague is involved in a supporting role, then the strategic enquiry may be carried out in collaboration. Use of the professional learning agenda pro-forma (PLA in Chapter 4) provides the scaffold for considering your role in self-directing learning and understanding (much more on this practical tool later). When another teacher is available and involved, these concepts exist in the social and content interactions of the zone of proximal development (ZPD) (Vygotsky, 1978). An emphasis on involvement in, and management of, your own professional learning requires a change in the traditional way of working with an *informed other* (a mentor or colleague). Together these play a more supportive role in a collegial approach to interaction and communication in considering the scaffolding process. You should aim to establish a scaffolding framework of self-initiating and self-regulating learning strategies so that you are becoming the initiator and controller of a significant proportion of your own learning.

CONTRIBUTING IDEAS 1.1

Establishing a framework for self-initiating and self-regulating strategies enables you, the teacher-learner, to initiate, collaborate and control your professional learning.

Learning to become a critical inquirer and a self-regulating practitioner requires you to clinically and comprehensively review the conditions and characteristics that influence your engagement in both simple and complex learning situations. Your aim is to store knowledge in *propositional* form, rather than rely on experiential memory of encounters and strategic responses stored in the form of a case repertoire. As you progress, useful and applicable propositional knowledge derived from many situations can be analysed, interpreted and then synthesized into a description that defines a relevant teaching response to a situation. This current understanding will also represent your progress in applying the specific characteristics of critical review, and the perceived validity of your responses to the situation.

You are learning from studying real and relevant practical situations that are problematic, complex and open to a variety of interpretations from different perspectives. A pedagogy of learning and enquiry to enhance your professional learning is focused on experiences where you can develop the attributes of critical analysis and interpretation, self-monitoring of your personal judgements and responses, and the ability to consider a situation from a variety of theoretical and practical perspectives. You are required to translate ways of thinking that are usually characteristic of one location of professional learning into another setting, and to 'particularize abstract theories and to abstract principles from particulars' (Leinhardt et al., 1995: 403).

Implications for understanding professional learning

The integration and transformation of the various types and aspects of professional knowledge require you to engage in systematic and focused observation, including self-observation. Thus, you come to perceive, articulate and theorize about the connections between these theoretical and practical perspectives of professional understanding. This awareness lifts your perception of both practical and theoretical relevance for your on-going learning and expertise.

For systematic self-observation together with critical analyses, you need to identify and develop enquiry strategies and associated intellectual skills. These *investigative* and *critical analysis* skill-sets qualify your evolving understanding of teaching and learning. You are driven to perceive the effect of theory on practice, and practice on theory. Using the framework of interpretative and theorizing learning processes facilitates your construction of responsive, integrated and generative professional knowledge.

CONTRIBUTING IDEAS 1.2

Using interpretative and theorizing frameworks brings structure to your responsive, integrated and generative professional knowledge.

You are refining the analytical and generative strategies that you can employ to develop responses to classroom encounters (Biggs, 1996; Vermunt & Vermetten, 2004). Your confidence as a teacher will build as you strive for a secure awareness of the contribution that you can make to your own knowledge and understanding of the teaching and learning environment. This awareness is founded on recognition of personal, self-generated successes in planning and teaching, rather than a less effective imitation of others' programme and teaching responses.

CONTRIBUTING IDEAS 1.3

Teaching confidence is more likely to be built on personal, self-generated successes rather than from copying another's teaching.

The nature of teacher learning explored in later chapters parallels the features of learning development that were first theorized by Vygotsky (1978) in his socio-historical theory of intellectual development. The features of neophyte teacher learning are similar to the characteristics, conditions and processes that Vygotsky described as mediated activities of a zone of proximal development (ZPD). Most (but not all) of Vygotsky's ideas and theoretical perspectives are helpful in understanding and investigating the similar connections of the concepts and processes inherent in the teacher learning model in this book. These activities for your professional learning are found in later chapters that refer to the self-monitoring (REACT) process, the professional learning agenda (PLA) and critical review strategies (see Section 2).

Generative responses in professional learning

Over time, there has been a movement away from the idea of 'one grand theory of teaching and learning' that could be generalized across a variety of contexts and associated conditions (Biggs, 1996). The shift has been towards the articulation of a set of generalizations based on bottom to top, theorizing from research carried out within the context of teacher education. A conceptual framework is proposed for interpreting and extending understanding of the nature of the teaching and learning process. This framework endeavours to describe, order and characterize interpretative understandings of how *you* might learn to become an effective, responsible and responsive professional. Your professional learning programme needs to start with you, the teacher-learner, rather than from a set curriculum. Once you have been led into identifying and evaluating your individual, antecedent, current and potential professional learning, then a responsive agenda can begin to take account of each individual's needs and abilities (Darling-Hammond et al., 1995). Hence, self-regulation is a most desirable characteristic to develop and engage in as you gain executive control of your current and future professional learning (Manning & Payne, 1993). It is the application of a higher-order psychological process that will enable you to go beyond a superficial awareness of the contextual characteristics of your teaching. You will see how cognitive and affective self-regulation also includes self-questioning, self-coping and self-reinforcing strategies. In self-regulating your learning, you will explore how new cognitive and affective behaviours can enhance a particular learning situation. You come to perceive the application of your newly-learned behaviours to anticipated future contexts. Your analysis of these learning episodes, contexts and outcomes feeds into subsequent action and responses, and in this way you can continually use your enquiry processes to focus on professional learning and improvement.

So, how might you use these enquiry, interpretative and generative processes? Consider 'learning through play' as an example? From your, possibly confusing, observations of learners engaged in open-ended play activities, you realize your assumptions about any learning directions for responding to learner behaviour should draw on a theoretical understanding of *how* students learn through play. Let's assume that your research and interpretation incline you to recognize the value of different play activities. So your subsequent planning needs to be enriched by juxtaposing theoretical and practical understandings in creating your lesson plans. You introduce a sequence of pedagogical responses to this professional learning initiative, over time. You develop critical review and interpretations to ascertain the relative effectiveness in matching play activities with students' involvement in learning. Your introduction of a changed learning environment is proving sensitive to both sequence and learner ability. You could substitute role play, scientific investigation, problem solving, and so on, for 'play'.

In a cyclical process, you identify – from differing teaching situations, professional learning initiatives, contexts and outcomes – and go on to develop behavioural responses (O'Brien & Hart, 1999). In doing so, you feel a positive motivational awareness through recognizing your need to know about, understand and apply processes of effective learning.

In summary, such cognitive and affective functioning can be identified in the inter- and intra-psychological phases (Vygotsky, 1978, 1986, 1987) of your development of a professional learning consciousness. In this way, your social (inter-psychological) and individual (intra-psychological) learning is interactional. It is within these interactions that you can seek and establish a scaffold of the teaching and learning schema and relationships for initiating your professional learning. As the professional development process moves forward, scaffolding support is not provided directly by an external source, such as a mentor or colleague, but rather by the conceptual frameworks that you are tentatively evolving and trialling. To acquire these interactive frameworks, the content, knowledge and skills patterns of these mediated strategic activities must be well structured.

Your critical enquiry skills are continually being honed through focusing on real classroom incidents. However, you should not expect to transfer responses directly from one classroom teaching event to the next. These insights are the tenets inherent in the enquiry strategy of the professional learning agenda (PLA, Section 2). This analytical process should convince you that teacher learning is multi-faceted; that you will need to build complex conceptualizations for your on-going professional development; and that you make connections between the activities and processes, theoretical and practical, of your teaching.

Learner-focused teacher development

Darling-Hammond (2000, 2006) writes of a need to respond to the call for reform in the education of all learners (children and teachers) to achieve higher levels of intellectual functioning and committed performance. Effective student learning requires skilled teachers who understand and apply the processes of learning to the strategies and skills of effective teaching.

To achieve these intellectual gains, teacher-learners need to:

- develop the learning and enquiry strategies to appraise and modify their own actions
- evaluate, anticipate and control the behaviours of learners
- differentiate the learning responses required to meet the learning abilities and needs of their learners. (Darling-Hammond, 1994)

Though the second and third points are significant foci for teacher learning, it is the initial proposition that has guided the development of the practical and researched strategies underpinning this book. Teachers need to know about and to incorporate new credible theories and research findings into their practice, and be aware that underlying theoretical support exists for their planning and preparation. You aim to possess, or acquire, the intellectual skills and understandings needed to enable you to articulate your planned teaching and to communicate your actions to others, including fellow professionals. In becoming an *inquisitive teacher*, you will be increasingly aware of new and theoretically grounded conceptual frameworks (or schemata) for thinking about and implementing these teaching and learning processes. These forms of knowledge and enquiry systems are developed through individual critical enquiry and in collaborative professional relationships for collegial problem solving.

To self-regulate your professional learning, you will need to learn how to evaluate, and be supported in evaluating, both your intellectual and practical involvement with learners and the learning process, including understanding and extending what you are finding out from both theoretical and practical perspectives.

The key issue in engaging in your learning experiences involves more than the transformation of learning. Your learning experiences should involve collaborative interactions and empowerment of your actions and responses to the complexities of the teaching and learning processes that reinforce the concept of the professional as a learner. This is a concept of *learning how to learn* that can support teachers from the start of their teacher education and throughout their careers.

For example, purposeful observations can help to clarify the reasoning underlying any classroom activity. It is relevant to your critical review process for you to offer tentative suggestions about how you might have responded to observed incidents and to test your initial understandings in a follow-up discussion with the colleague you have observed (Wood et al., 1976).

Consider the following questions to support an observation process:

- How will the observation be recorded?
- What should you be attending to as the scope and sequence of the learning activity unfolds?
- How could you add interpretative comments during the recording? (This is an example of probing for clarification that goes beyond description, in considering the intensity and timing of an observed lesson.)
- In identifying the time frame of each section of the lesson, ask: is the timing or the pace of the lesson's sequencing particular to this group of learners and individuals at this specific phase of their learning?
- Is a concept of pace or keeping to an exact time sequence transferable to another learning context or is it directly dependent on the learning abilities and needs of the given group?
- Is it necessary to observe and record the lesson in its entirety or is it more appropriate to concentrate on specific sections of the lesson for closer focused attention?
- How should your observations be detailed for later interrogation and interpretation to enable your on-going adaptation and application?
- How could observations be modified and reframed to benefit *your* future teaching experiences?
- What or whose purposes were being served?
- Would the observation of specific, identified and relevant segments of the lesson focus, help in later discussions between you and a colleague, for example your mentor?

- What does it mean to critically review?
- How is it possible to understand, interpret and evaluate your review outcomes?
- What is the purpose of discussions of school organization and procedures with school administrative and teaching personnel?

Addressing the list of questions above may challenge you in identifying the significant learning that you encounter in an observed practical situation. This list focuses primarily on being able to *see* how colleagues operate with their learners, whereas in Chapter 3 (REACT) the emphasis is on self-observation. It may be interesting for you to juxtapose these different types of observation to develop more insightful information-gathering processes.

You need to be able to relate these observation skills to the academic component of your teacher education. Your experiences on university-based courses and in schools can support the careful scaffolding and articulation of relevant, interconnected knowledge and understanding through critical enquiry. There have been increasing initiatives during the last two decades to help you make connections to alternative models of teacher education that have an enquiry focus or are research based (see, for example, Goodlad, 1990; Holmes Group, 1990; Reid & O'Donoghue, 2004; Williamson & Morgan, 2009). The value for you in understanding your teaching and learning comes from this occurring as enquiry-focused experiences in both school and university contexts.

It is only after you are proficient and committed to your application of such cognitive processing that you will feel free to seek more involvement in the decision making associated with professional learning. You will still appreciate and be mindful of the support and guidance offered by informed others, but importantly you will also recognize your evolving expertise in self-managing and self-regulating your professional learning, which can subsequently support your early teaching years.

So, what do you need to succeed in becoming a self-regulating and self-coping teacher during your initial teacher education programme and thereafter? The traditional focus of beginning teacher learning has been on the acquisition of subject-specific knowledge and skills. You are required to plan, initiate, teach, manage and assess learning programmes that are responsive to learners' abilities and needs within your planned classroom placements. However, knowledge and understanding of the complexities that exist in the teaching and learning process still need to be acquired. What has not been regularly featured, or is perceived as being incidental to those teaching and learning activities, is the enquiry-focused learning necessary to function as a self-initiating learner.

However, if new teachers are to carry increasing responsibility for their own professional education, then it will be necessary to acquire the knowledge and skills to do so effectively and relevantly early on in their professional development. So, during your teacher education programme you should aim to develop the intellectual tools that you need to identify, plan, interpret, monitor and reframe your own personal educational learning needs and potentials (McKay & Kember, 1997). The subsequent executive control that develops as you are involved in such processes enhances the possibility of this level of self-directedness being transformed or re-created in future learning opportunities.

When practical and theoretical experiences are associated with significant learning, these need to be mindfully managed in provocative, though supportive ways. It is not sufficient to simply equate experience with learning or that learning or development can be expected to derive readily from it without focused instruction and guidance. You need to characterize your professional development process as one of on-going and expanding empowerment. Your professional learning, when perceived in this way, is a self-monitored enhancement, rather than continually dependent on the role of a facilitator, be that person a mentor teacher, a member of university faculty or, ultimately, your school management team.

CONTRIBUTING IDEAS 1.4

Acquiring intellectual tools to interpret, monitor and reframe your personal educational potential will empower you now and throughout your career.

Your accumulated teacher-learner consciousness and your continuing confidence to be able to identify, articulate and respond appropriately to the specific teaching and learning issues, powers your evolving understanding, expertise and application.

It is difficult for informed others (teacher educators, mentors or peers) to understand all the relevant antecedent experiences and knowledge you have and are acquiring as a teacher-learner. Therefore, it is important that you undertake a comprehensive inventory of these pre-requisites of your professional knowledge and current expertise. Doing so will focus your expanding awareness of what you know and can apply in the classroom. Effective professional learning can take place when you are developing an attitude towards openness, and a cluster of interrelated cognitive processing skills that will enable authoritative analysis, interpretation, self-evaluation and self-generation of teaching and learning responses.

The five-phase self-monitoring process (REACT, Chapter 3) and the professional learning agenda (PLA, Chapters 4–6) with its associated enquiry-focusing and response-generating questions, have been created and researched to support these processes. Be aware though that what you already know, or believe, can have a biasing effect on your acceptance of *new* information or learning experiences. Try to see the existing conceptual framework where your knowledge and skills are considered as being a tentative representation at that developmental point in your professional learning journey. This pre-existing knowledge and understanding can be interrogated so that the ways in which they may influence future learning responses can be recognized, reframed and utilized. This applies to your awareness of curriculum and pedagogy that made sense earlier but now provides useful foundational bases for deriving alternative pathways of individual enquiry and interpretation.

Transforming learning: the social and intellectual planes of your teacher-learner consciousness

Though the primary objective of this book is to provide you with personal strategies for engaging your professional learning, you may be collaborating with a university or school mentor or colleague. This may create situations of critical learning dissonance or incongruity between what you have learnt previously and what is currently the focus of the learning environment or situation. Initially, this may seem confusing, but this dissonance may be an appropriate context for creating analytical processes for interrogating and interpreting your individual perspectives and pedagogical practices (Lange & Burroughs-Lange, 1994). Transformation of your learning occurs as your knowledge and understanding move from the social, inter-psychological phase of consciousness, to the individual, intra-psychological plane. Initially, you use these learning skills to identify, collect, organize, categorize, critically review and interpret. Subsequently, you come to use the acquired theoretical and practical knowledge and understanding within an expanding realm of *teaching consciousness*. You are moving through enquiry processes from the social to the interpretative, intellectual domain of your teacher learning.

If the fundamental objective of the school experience placements, within the teacher education curriculum, is to support the transformation of teacher-learners' learning, then enquiry activities that will guide the neophyte teacher to develop theoretical understandings about the associated practice of teaching need to be developed. Such activities will demonstrate and clarify the theoretical or conceptual frameworks that teacher-learners use to understand and extend their own knowledge and related practice. They may also be closely associated with the educative dialogical interactions that may be engaged between the teacher-learner and an informed other. So, let us continue with a discussion of the transformation of such learning if, on some occasions, other professionals are available to this educative process. It is important that you are aware of the tentative and evolving nature of these conceptual, interpretative and generative frameworks so that you continue to have an open mind to encourage further interrogation and enhancement. Your professional learning depends on detailing a personal agenda that identifies initiatives around individual strengths and weaknesses in knowledge and skill development. You need to be precise regarding the terms that you use to describe and theorize about the interpretations of your and others' practice and the related explanations. The preciseness of your articulation, using a shared *language of enquiry and interpretation*, is a significant factor in expressing this professional learning agenda.

The characteristics, patterns and actions of the ZPD-like interactions within your teacher learning will provide both the content and processes by which you will transform your understanding and internalize from the inter-psychological to the intra-psychological planes of learning consciousness. Getting to recognize your stage of development, *knowing where you're at*, will mean, at some times, together with your tutors and colleagues, that you will want to try and determine whether you are using syncretic, complexive or conceptual descriptions to illustrate your knowledge and understanding. Higher-order psychological functions that you are coming to know and able to use to, for example, enumerate, interrogate, interpret, create and respond, conceptually support the enhancement of your understanding. These functions operate within the internalization and integrating processes of the intra-psychological, the intellectual phase of consciousness. The patterns of awareness and theorizing that exist between these two levels of social and intellectual functioning support your development and articulation of professional learning and understanding.

You want to be able to verbalize your thoughts and feelings about your involvement in the teaching and learning process and present these openly for scrutiny by fellow professionals. It is thought-provoking activities of this nature that will heighten your awareness of the meta-cognitive processes that you use to initiate, guide and verbalize personal enquiry. Both the five-phase self-monitoring process with its focused questioning at each of the phases, and the individual critical analyses, re-construction and focused responses of the professional learning agenda, are intended to provide the learning framework for the critical awareness processes articulated above. They each provide the intellectual structure and scaffolding for your teacher learning within a meta-cognitive orientation (see Chapters 3–6).

You can develop such meta-cognitive learning skills while engaged in individually focused, enquiry and response, generating strategies, but also in dialogical interactions with a colleague or mentor as learning ideas and situations are analysed, interpreted and theorized about. Then you can use conceptual and experiential frameworks for interrogating, interpreting and applying concepts and processes in the future review of your own teaching and learning behaviours and interactions in the classroom.

Your unifying experiences that are based on theorizing, generative and self-regulated principles, are not seen as only occurring at the time of a school experience placement, nor focused only on learning activities that might take place in this context. You should seek opportunities for the application of associated enquiry strategies when accessing and developing knowledge and skills within your university-based courses. The notion that teaching and learning responses are multi-faceted and not knowledge-domain-specific should be reinforced as a condition of learning at all stages of *your* professional development and within all your learning contexts. Therefore, you should continue to search for ways of linking elements in these processes of your teacher learning more widely.

This exploration of a teaching consciousness has endeavoured to provide insights into how knowledge might be acquired, with understanding of your own cognitive processes and the variety of ways that learning can be enhanced. You must respond to your own meaning making from within your own teaching behaviour through the framing of problems and the identification, integration and synthesis of information and active enquiry. This requires a professional learning agenda in which activities are engaged in challenging ZPD-like processes that enable you to be increasingly involved in the structuring and development of your personal professional learning process.

The teaching and learning process can be conceived as being reciprocal, complex and contingent (Darling-Hammond et al., 1995). Teacher learning is reciprocal in that it is intimately linked to being responsive to your current abilities and professional needs, as well as to being appreciative of potential areas for development. Professional learning is complex in its content and processes as it is dependent on many knowledge bases, such as subject content, subject pedagogy and general pedagogy (Shulman, 1986). Professional outcomes can be accomplished by seizing 'opportunities for directing one's own learning, being receptive to inquiry, and challenging one's own ideas to construct new knowledge' (Darling-Hammond et al., 1995: 220). This research literature reflects the components and interrelatedness of the learning framework, proposed by Darling-Hammond et al. (1995) and extended by Biggs (1996). These researchers prompted the authors' development of and research into the use of the tools in this book.

The tools have their foundation in self-regulation, multi-dimensional enquiry and the potential for dialoguing with like-minded colleagues. They encompass a learning process that must be multi-dimensional, not linear. The emphasis here is on the teacher-learner's self-regulation of their professional learning. The role of colleagues, school or university-based, is also valued to support and guide the teacher-learner in constructing understanding that makes it transformative, rather than just transferring what might be perceived as *correct* understanding and techniques. You will be in control of a learning approach that is both responsible to the needs of society and the profession, and responsive to your individual learning agenda now and in the future (Edwards, 1995).

The above discussion has identified learning perspectives divergent from an approach that insists on the tabula rasa nature of the teacher-learner's experience that may be based in behavioural theory and the notion of transfer of knowledge. This book acknowledges that the social context contributes to learning (Hansman, 2001). Situated learning – in this case, the classroom and school environment – emphasizes the specific setting and the mediated activity as dialectically integrating you, the techniques and strategies of enquiring and interpreting, and the context within a professional learning episode. Proponents of situated cognition (Lave & Wenger, 1991; Rogoff, 1995; Lave, 1996; Korthagen, 2010) suggest that learning does not happen in independent isolation or just inside the mind, but instead is shaped by the context, culture and strategies in the learning situation. Brandt et al. (1993) gave us the concept of a *cognitive apprenticeship* in professional learning. This accords with the focus of this book, where the emphasis on your teacher learning, in both university and school settings, will have equipped you to continue to transform the content and processes of your teaching and learning through observation, interrogation, interpretation, critical analysis and generative response. We believe that you will be better prepared to theorize about and regenerate your practice rather than merely hoping to survive when you first enter the classroom. The generation of critical knowledge bases that are robust and symbiotic will promote you as a prospective teacher through all the professional learning experiences. This belief is in accord with Doll (1989) who suggested that a postmodern *teacher as learner* is one who considers the complex, chaotic and finite world of contemporary teaching and learning ideas and practices. Doll (1989: 250) conceptualized this as a process of development, in which the principles of enquiry, interpretation and creativity take over the direction and scope of the programme design process.

Earlier in this chapter, we explored the professional language of interpreting, interrogating and investigating teaching and learning, and the 'scientific' concepts that are used in academic learning environments to provide the content and meaning pathways that can be internalized by the teacher-learner (Vygotsky, 1978, 1986, 1987). The learning activities that engage the phases of consciousness included models, collaborations, observations (including self-observations), dialogues, challenges and self-questioning. A number of these activities benefit from the application of a language of enquiry and interpretation, that is, with pedagogy. The preciseness of an acceptable language of learning will provide professional legitimacy to your educational endeavour, for your self-managed coping in the theoretical and practical complexities of classrooms, and in effectively communicating these understandings with authority to other professionals and policy makers.

So, there is a constant need to focus your professional learning through conceptualizing learning strategies and challenging questioning to create situations of professional uncertainty that will require you to seek thoughtful resolution (Lange & Burroughs-Lange, 1994). The levels of your teacher-learner understanding and development are dependent on your control and on the complexity and intensity of the challenging teaching and learning initiatives to which you respond (Feiman-Nemser, 2012).

The literature associated with the concepts of dissonance and psychological distancing may also be explored in identifying and explaining the conditions and the characteristics of challenging learning episodes and the initiatives that can be derived from them (Festinger, 1957; Cooper, 2007). Understanding the sequencing of challenging learning experiences is an essential professional pre-requisite for teacher-learners who are attempting to move their understanding and expertise from a comfort zone of operating with limited thought, towards challenge and application at an individual's level of potential development and relevance. A number of questions to help us think about the extent of this personal enriching process include:

- How can you develop the knowledge and understanding for selecting and sequencing procedures as you engage in school, classroom and university experiences?
- Should you, as one who is assuming increasing control of your professional learning, also develop selecting and sequencing skills for identifying and engaging with developmental strategies?
- Is it important for you to comprehend the description of the optimal behaviour to be achieved by you?
- What role does learning dissonance play in achieving your cognitive change?
- How does the structure of the learning experience increase the potential for your success in meaning making? (On these last two questions, see the *what* and the *why* of the PLA process, in Section 2.)

- If the complexity of the learning sequence is targeted beyond your potential developmental level, can any worthwhile learning be achieved? This is relevant if the teacher-learner overreaches their ability to comprehend.

The answers to these questions might only provide a limited understanding of the role that challenging learning situations and activities might play in the enhancement of your meaningful learning. But they might provide you with further opportunities to delineate the selecting and sequencing processes for developing well-structured and challenging professional learning strategies. The engagement of the ZPD-like process for focusing on a particular initiative of professional learning establishes an investigative orientation that accepts rather than rejects difficult learning experiences and situations, and so values the construction of a set of idiosyncratic responses to a perceived professional learning issue. The descriptions above regarding pedagogical conversations, self-dialogue and critical dialogues with colleagues, including mentors, have been further enhanced by linking the discussion to the conceptions of *critical dissonance* and *collaborative resonance* offered by Cochran-Smith (1991).

Through the discussions in this chapter, it would seem that in learning to teach, practice may *not* make perfect, if it merely reproduces a set of teaching practices that are founded on somewhat limited conceptions of learning and cognition. Learning to teach needs you to discard concerns about fitting in, or copying existing practices unchallenged. More importantly, the emphasis turns to the *transformative* rather than a *reproductive* nature of practice. As the quality and expertise of your teacher-learning change, so too does the context because you have changed. The converse would also be true, but much less profitably for that professional.

Professional learning characterizes knowledge as an interactional phenomenon between the individual and the situation, and as enquiry strategies through which this interaction contributes to the reorganization and reinterpretation of both. In this way, the notions of learner and learning that are situated within a particular context can also be recognized as part of that context. As you learn, so the context of learning changes and so do your learner identity and social and intellectual characteristics. In this interactive relationship, learning may be considered as being intricately and completely dependent on the context rather than as the outcome of direct causal and linear conditions and directions. Davis and Sumara (1997), in drawing ideas from Bateson (1987) and Varela et al. (1991: 105), have called such a relationship of learner, context and learning, an 'enactivist theory of cognition' (see also Davis & Sumara, 2002). There are clear implications for neophyte learning:

this notion helps us to rethink what it means to teach and to interpret the difficulties of enacting alternative conceptions of teaching. The oft-noted problems of taking on teaching actions that are known to be inappropriate and, of coping with tacit pressures to behave in particular ways can, for us, be better understood through ecological rather than a monological basis of action. (Davis & Sumara, 1997: 112)

Davis and Sumara's enactivist theory of cognition tends towards a hermeneutic perspective (Habermas, 1987) that favours a more holistic, all-at-once, co-emergent programme of learning that may be defined by the circumstances of multiple realities and serendipity, rather than being responsive to pre-determined learning objectives.

From this perspective, cognition is thus understood as a process of organizing and re-organizing one's own subjective world of experience, involving the simultaneous revision, re-organization and re-interpretation of past, present and anticipated actions and perceptions (Davis & Sumara, 1997: 109).

Cognitive change is engaged in this manner because 'teaching, like any other collectively situated experience, occurs in wholly embodied contexts that in some way must cohere' (Davis & Sumara, 1997: 113). Relationships existing among the supporting functions of cognitive change, the process of teaching in the creation and maintenance of cultural perspectives, and learning were identified earlier by Bruner (1986). Bruner suggested that in order to understand the relationships between concepts and processes of teaching and learning as pervasive, co-emergent and evolving practices within a culture's self-renewal and self-organizing procedures, it might be necessary to blur the defined boundaries between schools and universities. Therefore, he believes in a collaborative, educative, cultural environment where the teacher-learner uses self-enquiry strategies to understand the social milieu of the teaching and learning process. Within this book, the focus is on the processes of self-observation, analysis, interpretation and generation of responses, and we endeavour to provide enquiry skills for these purposes.

If you are empowered in the ways presented in this book, you will be protected from what Richardson (1990: 16) has fears of becoming: 'victims of their personal biographies, systematic political demands, and ecological conditions, rather than making use of them in developing and sustaining worthwhile and significant change'. You have an opportunity not only to begin your own teaching career, but also to be part of significant change in the education of young people in your charge and the school institutions in which you work and lead. Look to the long term as well as to the immediate challenge of learning to teach.

FURTHER READING

Korthagen, F. (2010) Situated learning theory and the pedagogy of teacher education: towards an integration view of teacher behavior and teacher learning. *Teaching and Teacher Education*, 26(1): 98–106.

Korthagen provides a three-level model of learning that can be used to analyse the friction between teacher behaviour in practice and the intention to ground teachers' practice in theory (Lave & Wenger, 1991). It reconciles the situated learning perspective with traditional cognitive theory and leads to concrete implications for the pedagogy of teacher education.

McKay, J. and Kember, D. (1997) Spoon feeding leads to regurgitation: a better diet can result in more digestible learning outcomes. *Higher Education Research and Development*, 16(1): 55–67.

A case study of a course which originally relied on memorization but was altered in order to incorporate more clinical reasoning, problem solving and analytical judgement, through the use of case studies, role play and student-led seminars.

Williamson, D. and Morgan, J. (2009) Educational reform, enquiry-based learning and the re-professionalisation of teachers. *The Curriculum Journal*, 20(3): 287–304.

The implications for teacher education and continuous professional development of enquiry-based learning are explored. It is suggested that adopting enquiry-based practices is partly influenced by teachers' own narrative pathways, and by professional biographies. The focus is on teacher re-professionalization in the context of enquiry learning.

2

BECOMING A SELF-REGULATING, AUTONOMOUS PROFESSIONAL

Having read this chapter, you will have an understanding of:

- your professional learning, where the locus of control is changing
- how self-regulation will influence your learning
- the critical conditions that will enhance your self-regulation
- a conceptual model for exploring your professional learning
- the enquiry and interpretative strategies for exploring your professional learning initiatives.

Introduction

This chapter is concerned with developing an awareness of your place in your continuing professional learning and how, through processes of self-regulation, you can begin to gain executive control of your learning. The initial focus in this chapter is on the relevant literature; then on identifying processes for managing and theorizing about your professional learning. Finally, this chapter shows how you might critically review episodes from your classroom teaching. The chapter explores how to identify a professional learning initiative from your early teaching experiences and then how to analyse and interpret these episodes, using the professional learning strategy processes in this text. You will then be able to create potential responses to your specific professional learning initiatives and develop more comprehensive answers to apply to your teaching progress.

Many of these concepts about learning, developing knowledge and understanding, and creating thinking strategies, will also have application in the teaching programmes that you develop for your learners. As you seek relevance of these in your professional learning context, also look for ways of adaptation and application for your classroom. To start this awareness process, we review one of the significant concepts that you will need to understand and apply in developing self-regulated autonomy in your own professional learning.

Making sense of the school and the classroom

You have already spent a considerable proportion of your life in various classrooms, from primary or elementary school through secondary school to university. Now, as a teacher-learner, or a newly appointed teacher, the immediate challenge for you in entering your school placement is to recognize the duality of your new role in education. You are a teacher who is responsible for organizing and managing the learning of a group of students, and also a participant-learner focused not only on learning *what* and *how* to teach, but also learning *how* to learn and developing an awareness of your routes to self-improvement. This can seem overwhelming, as the complexity and immediacy of how this can possibly be accomplished is brought into your immediate focus.

How will you survive and cope initially with the complexities and demands of your professional life? How will you manage your day-to-day involvement in the school's academic and social life, together with the learning programme for your assigned group of young learners? There is an anticipation that you will respond positively and creatively to the demands and expectations of colleagues. The school's administrative team will require you to demonstrate resilience, a high degree of commitment and expert time management. The culture shock can seem stressful for the neophyte teacher. Later in this chapter, the discussion draws on the work of theorists who have considered the processes and strategies that are used by an individual who is learning their way into a cultural group – *the schooling phenomena*.

Recent reports have shown that 40% of potential young teachers decide not to take up a position after graduating, or they leave their teaching role after the first year on the job (Bousted, 2015). This represents a considerable waste of personal and state funding aimed at enhancing the teaching profession; a financial burden on new graduates; and, moreover, is disruptive of the professional life of those who take this exit route. This statistic also suggests that very early in starting their new career, despite the reduction in class load and the on-going support they receive as a newly qualified teacher (NQT), new teachers are finding that they are inadequately prepared for the environmental and professional expectations. How is it then that despite 60–80% of the time in their initial teacher education being spent at the coal-face, many teacher-learners do not develop an earlier understanding of whether teaching is the right career for them? What are the significant reasons for this apparent mismatch among the student selection process, teacher preparation, expectations of the teacher-learner and the reality of being in individual control of the learning pro-grammes and the success of a class group of learners? How can you ensure that this doesn't happen to you and that you will go on to succeed as an experienced teacher professional?

The pre-service teacher education curricula, that university and school personnel provide, seem to take the form of significant and helpful sup-port to carry new teachers through the requirements and standards to achieve qualified teacher status. Could part of the problem be the nature of support – a mother hen approach – where the new teacher chicks are guided and protected on their journey across and within the farmyard of the school curriculum and its pedagogical processes? Is the neophyte's professional learning oriented to rely too closely on informed others, on mentors in school and university? Is there sufficient opportunity and expectation for teacher-learners to develop for themselves the relevant and purposeful, conceptual, theoretical, practical, interpretative and genera-tive frameworks for creating their individual purpose and process for knowing, understanding and extending their own professional learning? What is perceived as the priority in one-year pre-service courses, whether they are university guided or school-led?

'There is so much subject knowledge and pedagogy to be covered and I have so much to tell them', might be the guiding expert's response. That is, there is a need to ensure that the teacher-learner has time to absorb the col-lective knowledge of the education team. Is there an underlying belief that as the teacher-learner has experienced 12 or 13 years of primary and sec-ondary education, together with three years or more of tertiary discipline studies at a university, there is no need to teach them how to learn? The enquiry and interpretative strategies explored through examples in the fol-lowing chapters will help you to develop an independent ability to learn how to learn as a professional.

As evidence suggests that personal learning awareness may not have developed in those earlier years of tertiary education, you now need to know how to initiate, develop, modify and assess the strategies you need to use independently to succeed as a teacher (Brew & Boud, 1995; Biggs & Tang, 2011). It is critical to your personal and professional well-being that you become aware of, and are able to focus on, those critical enquiry strategies that will provide support in developing this self-awareness and self-regulation. Without this individual critical awareness, the classroom can become a confusing and overly stressful working environment. New teach-ers can have difficulty in coping and managing, which creates stress and ill-health, and risks an early exit from the profession. If you are able to achieve a level of critical awareness of your place in the classroom, then you will be more effective in understanding and creatively responding to questions such as the following:

What knowledge and skills, in selecting and using teaching strategies, content selection and sequencing in planning, and behaviour management, will you need to acquire immediately? What do you observe in this classroom? What is your colleague teacher doing? How are the students responding? What makes or encourages them to act in this way? How can you come to an understanding as a result of your enquiries?

Your first impressions may be that the students seem to be working quietly and productively with only initial, minimal input from the teacher. Is it really just explaining the learning task to the group of learners and then monitoring their achievements or difficulties? You want to be able to identify and adopt strategies that can focus your investigation, to interpret and plan informed teaching and learning responses for your students to achieve success.

CONTRIBUTING IDEAS 2.1

You will need to identify and adopt investigative strategies for interpreting and creating teaching and learning responses.

You are involved in making meaning of the complex context of the classroom. You need a range of social inter-psychological and internal intra-psychological skills to develop a strategy for creating critical enquiry and interpretative understanding as an evolving agenda for your personal, professional learning.

This chapter provides you with a theoretical and research basis for the development of enquiring, interpretative and generative strategies. A five-phase self-monitoring process (adopting the REACT acronym: rehearse, enact, analyse, critique, transform) and the professional learning agenda (PLA) represent action-research formulae. You use these strategies for identifying and guiding the relevance and comprehensiveness of learning *what* and *how* to teach through a learning *how* to learn perspective.

The five-phase self-monitoring (REACT) process provides the structure and questioning patterns for identifying and engaging in initial analyses of your professional learning initiatives. This way you can learn to isolate them from the earlier critical review of teaching and learning episodes (see Chapter 3). You select an initiative because of its significance for your individual continuing professional learning. This is then available to you for more critical analysis, interrogation, interpretation and response generation to enter into your professional learning agenda (see Chapters 4–6). The PLA has a structure and a range of speculative, diagnostic and investigative questions to help you to understand and theorize about your involvement in the complexities of your teaching and learning environment.

Establishing 'self-regulatory' behaviours

To achieve a controlling role in personal professional learning, an outstanding teacher-learner needs to acquire high levels of cognitive processing (that is, intellectual abilities) in interpreting, transforming and evaluating the teaching and learning process. Importantly, they also need to demonstrate a commitment to the further enhancement of their professional learning and expertise to meet the teaching and learning demands of the particular educational contexts in which they are engaged. The outstanding teacher-learner is a focused and engaged critical enquirer who can anticipate and generate an innovative curriculum for learners with relevant teaching and learning responses. They value the quality of their involvement in challenging educational settings, and so become more comfortable and confident with their self-managing and self-regulating abilities.

Learning consciousness and control of professional learning

As introduced in Chapter 1, professional learning outcomes originate from sources that are both external and internal to the individual. What appears to be essential to this interaction between external and internal sources, and the individual learner, is the planned introduction of learning strategies and situations that will maximize the likelihood of you taking personal initiatives within your teacher education programme. Again, it is important that you acquire a holistic and comprehensive understanding of the components of your teacher education curriculum and the ways that these contribute and relate not only to each other but also to your professional learning.

CONTRIBUTING IDEAS 2.2

It is essential to acquire a comprehensive understanding of the interconnections between the content and processes of your teacher education curriculum.

It is interesting to note that despite all the university and school personnel involved in the theoretical and practical dimensions of your teacher education, it really comes down to you – you are experiencing the 'whole thing' and therefore are uniquely able to conceptualize the comprehensive nature of your programme. In most instances, it is your intellectual responsibility to seek out and theorize about, and apply the inherent connections that are evident in the content and pedagogical structures of the programme.

These internal and external sources were discussed in Chapter 1. They consist of three interlocking and reciprocal domain contexts: the education system (national and local), the classroom, and the individual. It is within these domains that you access the social and intellectual processes that provide the basis for knowing and understanding your learning.

A theoretical perspective of self-regulation

What does self-regulation mean in this context? Some insight can be drawn from the theorizing of Vygotsky (1978, 1981, 1986), who perceived self-regulation not as a single trait or even a combination of traits, but rather as critical developmental phases that signal the emergence, for the individual learner, of unique sets of competencies of higher intellectual functioning with an associated commitment to self-learning and heightened understanding. A perception of self-awareness that is associated with the enhancement and application of higher-order cognitive skills fits well with the notion of you, the teacher-learner, acquiring an informed and referenced conceptualization of your place in the controlled development of your professional learning (Lave & Wenger, 1991). Your evolving understanding signals a change in levels of support and guidance within a mentoring process, as you enhance the quality of your own professional knowledge and expertise. The application of a growing, informed understanding in responding appropriately to a range of classroom learning situations, provides you with an authoritative confidence in your awareness of yourself as an effective and inquisitive practitioner and lessens your reliance on others. Engagement in mentoring and collegial support relationships can contribute to your professional learning development but should be conceived as an initial contributing phase in enabling your self-management of this growth.

Reviewing the 'locus of control' in the professional learning process

Vygotsky (1978) described these self-regulatory competencies as 'deliberate, intentional, or volitional behaviours' that enable the learner to experience increasing control over their growth and development. Through these competencies for enhancing your enquiry and analytical thinking skills, you can reach a critical transitional stage of learning development where you move from being controlled by others and the context, to becoming the initiator of your own behaviour. You are doing this in a context where well-structured enquiry and interpretative strategies can support you in generating relevant curriculum and teaching responses. Assuming executive control of your evolving professional learning, and identifying the relevant contexts and cognitive strategies, enables such learning to occur. In the context of your professional learning, these learning environments and situated strategic awareness can be identified in both university and school settings. These intellectual strategies are your professional learning tools for gathering, organizing and conceptualizing ideas and processes that are provided in these interconnecting but also inseparable professional learning contexts. The self-controlling awareness of your self-regulation encourages the acquisition of specific cultural awareness tools for use within the education community. These also include language and other symbolic systems that can be used to gain control over your individual physical, emotional and cognitive functioning. For operating in these complex educational environments, the cultural awareness tools involve:

- the scientific, sometimes referred to as the theoretical, language of education, including concepts from psychology, sociology, philosophy and pedagogy, which are used to identify and clarify the complexities that are embedded in the teaching and learning process
- the identification, assessment and acceptance of knowledge, strategies and skills in observing and/or engaging with colleagues, mentors or learners, and the relevant teaching and learning processes
- the critical analysis and interpretation of the varied individual and group teaching and learning interactions, and the curriculum situations that require intellectual processes for understanding, analysing, interrogating, interpreting, transforming, synthesizing and generating, together with informative evaluative review.

You need to acquire these practical and theoretical skills for understanding and generalizing theory to practice (and practice to theory) within the educational culture. This educational language, alongside the intellectual functions of observing, self-observing, understanding, interpreting and responding to specific classroom situations that are representative of your teaching behaviours, enables you to be increasingly involved in generating meaning-making responses in the educational environments of both university and school settings.

CONTRIBUTING IDEAS 2.3

Acquiring the language symbols and tools of the educational context, both practical and theoretical, enables you to understand and generalize about these aspects of your involvement.

For all higher intellectual functions, learners' self-regulatory abilities originate in complex social interactions. It is only later, after careful critical review, analysis and interpretation, that these abilities become internalized within your evolving interpretative, theorizing and generative cognitive frameworks. This leads to your independent use of these functions, where applicable, in practical settings (Vygotsky, 1978). However, self-regulation does not emerge spontaneously. It is created, managed and nurtured, formally or informally, within a social context, for example in self-enquiry situations, as well as within the culture of mentoring and collegial support processes in university or school settings.

With anticipated support from your university and school mentors and, wherever possible, peers, you will identify, design, sequentially plan and resource your professional learning situations and related cognitive strategies. These contexts and processes will enable you, with appropriate discussion and questioning for scaffolding, to achieve higher cognitive functioning of, and commitment to, the role of a self-monitoring participant in your own teacher educational curriculum. Your professional learning resides in the intrapersonal and scaffolded interactions that are embedded in the structure of the planned and challenging professional learning activities, as exemplified in this book. These experiences can be engaged within either university or school-based components of your teacher education (Wood et al., 1976; Holton & Clarke, 2006).

Let us now consider the content and contexts of the *investigative process skills* and the *critical analysis process skills* of the self-regulatory approach to professional learning that is theorized about in this chapter. In some instances, the sub-set *label* is used to represent the specific thinking skills in each of the skill areas. Occasionally, the full list is used and amplified as appropriate to the discussion.

SELF-REGULATION

Investigative process skills

- inter-psychological, inter-intellectual, outside the individual
- operating in the social interactive environment outside, though including the individual and focused by observation, self-observation, questioning, explaining, dialogical attentive listening, interactive discussions and collegial feed-forward
- involving a process of identifying, isolating, clarifying, organizing and interpreting.

Critical analysis process skills

- intra-psychological, intra-intellectual, operating within the conceptual understanding of the individual
- involves the application of interpretative, theorizing and generative conceptual frameworks of knowledge and thinking skills
- thinking skills inherent in critical analysis – analysing, interrogating, critiquing, transforming, synthesizing and generating – that are applied to the identified initiatives of the investigative process skills strategy.

You will find how to use these information processes and the creative skills of the self-regulation process in the REACT and PLA professional learning strategies (Chapters 3–6).

Critical conditions for the development of self-regulation

A number of critical conditions and associated perspectives are needed for the development of self-regulatory behaviours for teacher-learners so that they may develop higher-order intellectual functions in the individual intellectual plane – this is what Vygotsky refers to as the intra-psychological (1978, 1981).

Though the central focus of this book is on the management of your personal professional learning, we also need to consider the implications for self-monitoring when an informed other (a mentor, colleague or peer) is available as a listening and clarifying participant, an external influence who can provide challenging responses to your discussion of the complexities of the teaching and learning process. Throughout this book, the term *informed other* is used to refer to school or university personnel who are aware of and support the enquiry and interpretative process, as well as the self-regulatory emphasis in this approach to professional learning. They are not seen as a content and pedagogical master teacher but rather as someone who knows and understands the self-regulating strategies and contexts in which you, as a self-guiding teacher, are acquiring knowledge and adapting it for your specific purposes. If you have the chance to work with a supportive informed other, then they may take on the challenging, scaffolding activity alongside the processes of your own *inquisitive self.* If collegial support is available, then this can be conceptualized and developed, as discussed below. The review process involving the informed other will lead effectively into your self-concept as the inquisitive self. In a sense, you are creating another internal voice that in some ways represents thoughts from the social context. Sometimes, external interactions from the informed other will trigger the internal speech of your inquisitive self. This voice will become the powerful enquiry-focusing tool of your professional learning. Let us now look at some specific critical conditions for developing self-regulation.

1. Accessing the intellectual processes of self-regulation

A necessary condition for the emergence of self-regulation is the acquisition of individual thinking skills that develop cognitive capacities to theorize about and use self-regulatory behaviours independently. Among the first such tools that you might acquire is self-talk or 'internal speech' (Vygotsky, 1987). In Chapter 3, the concept of self-talk is explored within the theme of *rehearsal* as the pre-implementation phase of a lesson. The rehearsal phase of self-monitoring as a context for self-talk refers to the cognitive techniques you will use to assist in recalling, then projecting, information and experiences as these are represented in the lesson's actual implementation. Self-talk enables you to focus more specifically on the perception, conceptualizing and categorizing of stimuli that provide insights and awareness in your classroom. This inner speech, through the creation of vivid mental representations of your intentions and through preview, provides a rehearsal for anticipating cognitively and experientially how the content and pedagogical features of the proposed lesson might occur.

You can engage in internal speech at varying levels of focus and intensity as you consider the potential responses to professional learning initiatives that you have articulated, for example by thinking through a perplexing episode in which you were involved as a significant participant. Internal speech also relates to the development of a language of enquiry and interpretation for you to use in theorizing about the regulation of behaviour within learning environments. These techniques are now readily available to you for guiding the purposes of your self-regulation (for further consideration of these concepts, see Mead, 1934; Kremer-Hayon & Tilleman, 1999; Daniels, 2001: Van Eekelen et al., 2005).

Strategic knowledge or the metacognition of how you focus and use your own thinking processes are also relevant in seeking an understanding of how to self-regulate practical and theoretical learning strategies and tasks. As Chapter 3 highlights, strategic knowledge involves planning that is entered into before your purposeful involvement in a cognitive activity and includes the subsequent assessment of the effectiveness and appropriateness of this cognitive activity in responding to your stated intentions. Your use of this metacognition is a key factor in learning, problem solving, decision making and the self-monitoring of your evolving professional understanding.

2. An individually focused critical approach

Another condition becomes evident as you engage in situated learning episodes that provide a focus for your critical analysis and interpretative processes. When well designed, these can include the evaluation of observations of others, and comprehensive reviews of involvement and contributions within the classroom. This contextualizes what may have earlier been the focus of your internal speech within a rehearsal activity. It is the internal processing of these observations, of others and yourself, reviews and the subsequent creation of teaching and learning responses, that provides opportunities for your professional learning. It allows you to perfect the self-regulatory components of multiple intellectual functioning that you have acquired through your investigations of teaching and learning contexts and in collegial interactions with other professionals, mentors and colleagues (Mead, 1934; Vygotsky, 1978).

The notion of 'double-loop' learning proposed by Argyris and Schön (1978) also adds authority to your use of self-focused and self-regulated activities. Double-loop learning is evident when the participant is questioning the activity variables, for example goals, values, plans and rules. In doing so, you are looking for potential alterations to these controlling variables so that there can be a shift in your thinking about other potential strategies, and possible consequences that might be formed. For Argyris and Schön, double-loop learning occurs when error is detected and corrected in ways that involve the modification of an organization's underlying norms, policies or objectives (1978: 2–3). They hold that it is important, for resolution of your professional learning concern, to question the influential variables that impact on a context and to subject them to critical scrutiny rather than to jump immediately to another strategy. Questioning the variables in the classroom might require you to refocus your consideration of the antecedent and contextual conditions and influences affecting the identified incident of concern. Subsequently, you might isolate a professional learning initiative for yourself from this episode (see Chapters 4–6 for examples and questioning sequences of how the PLA strategy guides this recursive learning process).

This questioning is critical for you, as it shifts the ways in which strategies and outcomes are framed, analysed, reframed and synthesized. This perspective suggests that the deeper and more comprehensive direction your critical review process takes, the greater the support for your theorizing and generalizing. This is a powerful way to seek clarity and guidance from the confusion and dissonance that is sometimes encountered when your focus is on trying to understand the complexities of classroom teaching and your place within it (Lange & Burroughs-Lange, 1994).

3. The role of the 'informed other' and collegial interaction

If an informed other is able to participate in the focusing and clarification of your professional learning, then the following is worth considering together. The *informed* element here relates to the knowledge and commitment that the other holds for the stance of enquiry, generated individually, for the self-regulation of professional learning that is emphasized in this book. An informed other is *not* simply a fellow professional that is perceived as having greater content or pedagogical awareness than your own.

You may be able to recall a time when you've had a supportive and productive interaction with someone that has made a difference in how equipped or confident you felt to take a risk and try something that you thought may work for that situation. What made the interaction work that way for you? Can you recall how this support and guidance impacted on the task or skill that you were engaged with, and how were you and they specifically involved? What can you take from this experience? Can you apply your understanding of this to your current role? Think about having experienced this on the shared plane (that is, Vygotsky's reference to the social components of the inter-psychological). Mentoring experiences are ideally managed and resourced in a supportive learning environment of mutual trust and respect. You work collaboratively with participants and the informed other to become comfortable in the social interaction. You want to reach an openness of dialogue that enables your current professional knowledge and understandings to be proposed, questioned and interrogated without a focus on getting to the correct response. Prepare yourself for this discussion by imagining yourself in the role of the other, predicting questioning sequences and preparing your likely responses. You will find this preparation useful in your efforts to clarify your intentions and responses.

In the early phases of your acquisition of new knowledge and skills, you want to present a positive face to the informed other that you are relying on for collegial guidance. Goffman (1959) proposed that when coming into contact with others, an individual will attempt to guide the initial impression that they might make by modifying their presentation style and their manner of demonstrating knowledge and understanding. You need to be comfortable and confident that the comments and responses you are offering to the learning situation will be accepted by colleagues as relevant to, and representative of, the current stage of your professional growth.

4. The emergence of the inquisitive self

As you engage with a sequence of collegial partnerships, you will find yourself getting in front of the critical discussion and increasingly able to anticipate the next probing question that may be asked to challenge your on-going professional knowledge and understanding. Inquisitiveness, as characterized for teacher-learners in this text, is founded within the constructivist perspective (Piaget, 1964; Bruner, 1966; Vygosky, 1978; Wood, 1998). This is defined as an eagerness for knowledge, being intellectually curious, being given to enquiry and research, and applying a scrutinizing, penetrating perspective. Or, as Albert Einstein is quoted as saying, 'I have no special talents. I am passionately curious'. The real challenge may be to stimulate your natural curiosity or inquisitiveness that a couple of decades of traditional formal education may have partly obscured. You will need to develop your talent for curiosity and inquisitiveness.

The first phase in developing your inquisitive self might be dealing with the uncertainty that sometimes seems paralysing when attempting to introduce a new strategy or teaching skill into an existing repertoire. Adopt the approach of 'Yes, I understand the fundamental characteristics of this technique and am now going to have a go at using it'. Why? Because 'I know that if I introduce this change effectively, it will be enjoyable for the learners and myself'. The second phase of becoming your 'inquisitive self' is the realization that there is no single correct procedure choice. Why? 'Because of the uniqueness of this particular learning environment, for these learners and me'. If you engage in self-directed reasoning and improvisation through the teaching and learning experience and take full responsibility for your involvement and that of your learners in the activity, then you will gain a sense of personal achievement. If this process also involves critical analysis and interpretation of the teaching and learning outcomes achieved, with the potential for future adjustments in both content and process, then you will be acquiring significant learning. As proposed by Bruner, 'develop the best pedagogy that you can. See how well you can do. Then analyse the nature of what you did that worked' (1960: 618). Doing so will provide you with the freedom and opportunity to control and construct your on-going professional learning experiences.

CONTRIBUTING IDEAS 2.4

Teacher-learner inquisitiveness involves an eagerness for knowledge, intellectual curiosity, the application of enquiry and research, and an evolving penetrating perspective on one's work.

Aim to continually revisit questions such as 'What am I intellectually curious about in my teaching and how does this lead to my creative responses in thought and action?' This will stimulate your focused professional learning enquiry. An investigative approach where you use and adapt an intentionally open-ended process of self-conversation of critical analysis and interpretation will also need to accommodate your own levels of skill and confidence. In the context of pressure from higher accountability, greater compliance to the official curriculum and the intensity of everyday work in classrooms, teacher-learners may feel that they are not readily able to engage in quality, on-going, critical analysis and interpretation for enhancing learning. But Hatcher (2011) warns: 'In order for professional learning to generate new practices by teachers, not simply the replication of imported practices, it requires not just procedural and performance knowledge – "practical knowledge" – but also theoretical knowledge' (p. 404).

In response to such warnings, enquiry-focused professional learning strategies need to consider the integrative potential of theory and practice in embracing the diversity of interpretation and planned change. It is also worth emphasizing that the response to expectation of higher accountability may reside in your ability to bring authoritative theoretical relevance to your explanations of your practice of classroom teaching. There is a definitive need to bring a language of enquiry and interpretation into your investigative work as a teacher.

You will see that the five-phase self-monitoring process (REACT) and the professional learning agenda (PLA) enquiry strategies are not solely concerned with directing intensive thinking about practice but are also intended to challenge you to engage in analytical and synthesizing thinking processes. These strategies can also provide authoritative responses on how to represent your practice in theoretical descriptions. By creating a cognitive dimension of inquisitiveness in providing information to fulfil a pedagogical or content need, these processes also promote a more sustainable scrutiny that is grounded in an open-ended and varied enquiry setting.

This represents a different focus on practice and in so doing offers the potential for a diversity of generated responses.

This inquisitive approach to professional learning requires you to uncover new insights in your critical enquiry. This is achieved by engaging an effective dynamic in making what is familiar strange and, conversely, making what is strange a more familiar element in the teaching and learning context. This is drawn from an ethnographic perspective where a researcher, when engaged with a study environment, endeavours to make what is familiar and possibly well known to them *anthropologically strange* (Spiro, 1992). Therefore, in your critical analyses of your operating in the classroom, challenge your taken-for-granted assumptions about the learning environment and what takes place within it. You are urged not to take events, behaviours or ideas at face value or to think about them as you have previously known them. See such characteristics as strange and endeavour to enquire and interpret from a totally new and unbiased perspective. Remember, you have spent many years in classrooms and there may be some un-learning required of what you accept as normal (see Smith, 1967; Frank, 1999). This dynamic tension, strange and familiar, is established so that the complexity of teaching and learning becomes significant, by creating opportunities for you to be Janus-like in seeking understandings within and outside of practice, and so fostering purposeful and challenging encounters with definition and adaptability.

CONTRIBUTING IDEAS 2.5

Consider *all* observed teaching and learning activities as anthropologically strange and interpret them from an unbiased perspective.

In accordance with Hatcher (2011), if the uncertainty of inexperience is to become more manageable, then you must recognize that more complex learning and new practices are not only the result of acquiring knowledge but also come about by generating innovative experience. Though there is recognition that time-poor teacher-learners may seek certainty and simplicity in the face of increasing curriculum pressures and new reporting systems, this perception needs to be considered alongside educational processes and practices that 'tend to be characterized by non-linearity and unpredictability and a fundamental gap between *input* (teaching, curriculum, pedagogy) and *output* (learning)' (Biesta, 2010: 6). So, it will be important that you use your time in reviewing classroom practices diligently and effectively. Ensure that you have the available time for enquiry and interpretative strategies that will do this for you. It remains imperative that you are exposed to, and are comfortable with, enquiry and interpretive strategies that enable the development of anticipatory awareness of what can be identified as *unpredictability*. This is an inquisitiveness that prepares you for responding to the uncertainty of the classroom. So, be your best possible inquisitive self as you assume the role, and make your professional learning unique to you.

As well as consideration of these critical conditions and associated perspectives for establishing your self-regulatory approach, be aware that in any teaching and learning situation or professional learning initiative, there are likely to be many legitimate responses, of varying degrees of sophistication of discussion and action, in terms of both practice and theory. The identification and application of a professional learning initiative as the focus for professional development activities is introduced in the later parts of this chapter.

The five-phase self-monitoring review process (REACT), explored in the next chapter, highlights that a significant aim of the professional learning process is to provide opportunities to create tentative, interpretative, theorizing and generative conceptualizing platforms of knowledge and skills. These platforms or frameworks need to be appropriately referenced by access to relevant theory, research and practice, for continuing investigation and critical review. Be assured that during the early phases of developing a teaching and learning consciousness, your thoughts about and responses to any facet of your professional learning will be valuable at varying levels of sophistication or comprehensiveness. There is no sense of a single right response, just a supported exploration that some theoretical and practical ideas may be more relevant and applicable than others, within the particular context of a given professional learning initiative. You can become comfortable with the notion that significantly more useful responses will be generated as you acquire more knowledge and understanding of the interlocking relationship between referenced research and theory, and with your decisions about what practice to use. Further enhancement of your enquiry and interpretative skills, and a broadening of experience and tentative applications, will make these more acceptable and relevant to your growing expertise.

Within all co-operative professional learning interactions with others or internally with your inquisitive self, your 'response-in-development' in the context of the on-going personal creation of knowledge and expertise is significant. You know this will be challenged for further refinement and application during later learning experiences.

Chapter 1 discussed how Vygotsky's ideas of a zone of proximal development (ZPD) can be useful in understanding how interactions between you and informed others can be managed and enhanced in the professional learning support process. A critical questioning approach adopted by the informed other needs to avoid 'telling' or 'instructing', or even 'do as I do as it works for me' suggestions. Without becoming dependent on any fixed ideas, you can reach a level of professional awareness that is consistent with, though sometimes challenged by, your current conceptual frameworks. As already discussed, the tentativeness and openness of your frameworks for professional interactions are essential in enabling you to assimilate or accommodate new and challenging learning (Piaget, 1972).

A summary of self-regulatory perspectives

To develop self-regulatory behaviours, socially as well as cognitively, you will initially need opportunities to engage in other-regulation interactional learning situations. Other-regulation implies that you will engage as both a subject of another person's regulatory behaviours, as happens in many interactions with mentor colleagues, and as an actor in regulating another person's behaviour, as might happen in interactions with peers or students. The regulation by others when employed by experienced mentors, goes beyond telling and creates an analytical and interpretative orientation where you are required to theorize about the knowledge and practical experience that underpin your understanding of a particular teaching and learning episode and encourage you to generate possible responses to introduce and trial in future teaching.

Working in this way, informed others (and, increasingly, your inquisitive self) should aim to be open, collegial and also challenging of the assumptions and interpretations of any identified teaching response. Professional support is not required to provide the perfect solution to any learning incident or initiative, but rather to evoke your critical awareness of what you know, why and how it is known, and to offer potential responses based in your current understanding and contextual awareness.

In a similar way, a teacher-learner paired with a peer or colleague can benefit from opportunities for questioning and from exchanging understandings of professional learning episodes as you both move tentatively towards critically analysing and interpreting them. These supportive relationships can provide teaching colleagues with an opportunity, and the expectation, to consider the professional learning initiative from a questioning and responsive perspective. The asking of probing questions requiring analytical and generative responses from the teacher-learner, also requires the questioner to formulate their own likely response that they can then contrast with that of the teacher-learner. This is a thought-provoking process for both parties in this shared professional learning experience.

Consider how you share interpretative, theoretical and practically focused professional knowledge with a colleague who may be at a similar stage of developing a teaching consciousness. In this partnership on some occasions, you will engage in other-regulation that serves to enhance your individual strategies for initiating and refining your regulatory skills and processes. These opportunities can occur during school experience or during briefing and debriefing sessions in the university classroom. These co-operative learning interactions could be extended to university-based units of study where opportunities to facilitate and clarify your developing knowledge and understanding are juxtaposed with the meaning making that is being arrived at by the other participants. An open perspective on where and how professional learning can occur challenges the notion that it is mainly through working with a group of learners in the classroom that one becomes a teacher. Can the adage that *more practice makes perfect* be relied on to work in the complexity of teaching or is *perfecting practice* also necessary?

Your professional learning goal

This review of how you might engage in self-regulating behaviours empha-sizes the need to identify and create sequences of planned and managed opportunities to acquire, review and assess your own professional develop-ment. In this way, professional learning comes under your control in servicing the goal of achieving outstanding levels of professional expertise and integrity that will continue throughout your teaching career. This sec-tion has identified and explored a number of theoretical tenets and perspectives for evaluating self-regulatory approaches for engagement of your inquisitive self and your professional learning with others. Chapters 3–6 explore this approach and the availability of self-regulating strategies for challenging and guiding your critical reviews and interpretative pro-cesses within a systematic awareness of professional learning. These strategies can be used to widen and deepen your knowledge and under-standing of your evolving teacher expertise in responding to both the curriculum and learners' needs and abilities. But how can these profes-sional learning processes be conceived and explained?

A conceptual model for exploring a self-regulatory professional learning process

Figure 2.1 represents the interlocking and interactive relationships between two identified domains of a teacher-learner's involvement in their profes-sional learning. It represents the idiosyncratic professional learning curriculum of the teacher-learner.

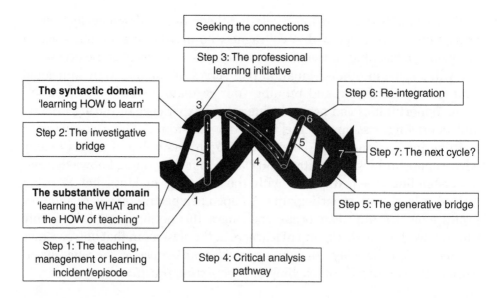

Figure 2.1   Professional learning curriculum: interlocking interpretative pathways

The model shows the two closely related domains of the professional learning curriculum: the substantive (learning *what* and *how* to teach) and the syntactic (learning *how* to learn). It illustrates the professional growth that evolves from interactions between these substantive and syntactic pathways. The model draws from concepts of curriculum design and adapts its conceptual understanding from the theorizing of curriculum knowledge and pedagogy of Schwab (1978) and Shulman (1987). Schwab (1978) described such dimensions of a subject discipline as the:

(a) *substantive*, which represents the statements of facts, concepts, propositions and principles that are constructed as an outcome of *discipline* investigations and so become the *content* of a curriculum
(b) *syntactic* or procedural knowledge of conducting a discipline enquiry, or the *know-how* pedagogy of a curriculum.

In this book, the teacher professional learning programme is represented by curriculum design features and applies Schwab's (1978) theory to the discipline of teacher development (see Figure 2.1). The substantive strand of the conceptual model represents the curriculum of the teacher education programme that you are engaging with, and therefore includes all content, pedagogical and foundational educational disciplines, such as psychology, philosophy, sociology, and so forth. From this perspective, the substantive

domain includes both the substantive and syntactic elements of the practical and theoretical subject domains of the teacher education curriculum.

For example, a university-based educational sociology unit of study, as
well as organizing concepts of social change, conflict theory, structural
function, equality, sustainability and globalization, will also include the
study of information-gathering and justifying strategies such as ethnogra-
phy. So, the teacher-learner is acquiring both the substantive content and
the syntactic process of the subject domain. Figure 2.1 represents these
relevant curriculum design features.

On the other hand, the syntactic domain of the conceptual model represents the social and cognitive enquiry skills that the teacher-learner uses in
investigating the subject components of the teacher education curriculum.
It includes your involvement with, and subsequent application of, the
knowledge and understanding gained from your experiences within this
programme. These social and cognitive analytical processes (explored in
detail in Chapters 3 and 4) include identifying, collecting and organizing
information from your classroom experience, and operate in the substantive
domain of the curriculum. Some elements of the episode may be isolated as
an initiative that has direct relevance to your professional learning. The
professional learning initiative (PLI) is then critically analysed, interrogated and interpreted within this syntactic emphasis. Teaching and learning
responses are generated to feed-forward into your on-going teaching and
learning repertoire (the analytical and interpretative treatment of the PLI
is detailed in Chapters 4–6).

The professional learning initiative (step 3 of the model) is identified in
the substantive domain of your professional learning by using the knowledge bases and structures that are within the content and pedagogy of your
teacher education curriculum. The initiative is intellectually scrutinized
and refined, along the *critical analysis pathway* within the syntactic
domain (step 4), with the relevant responses included at a later stage of
your professional knowledge and understanding, through the *generative
bridge* (step 5). You will note how these steps are placed in a developmental sequence in the model. This is a forward-moving cycle where the
initiative for professional learning is identified and critically reviewed.
Your resultant responses are placed back into the substantive strand for
further application within your teaching and learning programme. Each of
these stages is labelled in Figure 2.1, with directional arrows showing how
the analytical, interpretative and generative processes are enacted.

Continue to see incidents and responses of your professional learning
from a curriculum design perspective where the *what* and the *how* are
always scrutinized through your enquiry and interpretative language, and

associated processes. Professional learning perceived in this way may seem complex, but it is through your manipulation of the syntactic processes and the content of the substantive domain that you make meaning from your involvement in the teaching and learning process. Although each of these strands could be perceived and analysed separately, it is only when they are considered as integrating processes, happening concurrently and informing each other, that enlightened and generative professional learning takes place. It is your ability to identify and relate the integrative and generative nature of this process that enables you to take increasing control over your professional learning and to self-regulate your identified responses through these *coming to know* (substantive) or *meaning-making* (syntactic) processes.

The orientation and relatedness of each domain

The expanding double-helix model (Figure 2.1) represents how each of these orientations interrelate and support both the acquiring of professional content and process knowledge of the curriculum and teaching, and how, as an inquisitive teacher-learner, you can comprehend, justify and enhance your learning to be an effective teacher. As the diagram illustrates through the placement of bridging, and critical analysis pathways, the double-helix model conceptualizes the relationship that is perceived as existing between the substantive and syntactic domains of the professional learning curriculum. What are the ways in which these two orientations are connected and complement the learning process? Let us briefly review the distinction between the different types of knowing within professional teacher learning.

In Shulman's (1986) mental map (also found in Shulman and Grossman, 1988), and in Schwab (1978), there is this clear distinction between substantive and syntactic knowledge. Substantive knowledge encompasses the key concepts, generalizations, principles, structures, facts and explanatory conceptual frameworks within a content domain – in teacher education, this relates to its curriculum and learning environments. The syntactic understanding is concerned with the rules of evidence and confirmation, statements of fact, the nature of enquiry within the domain, and how new knowledge and understanding are introduced and accepted. In short, this conceptual understanding is how to find out, with the heuristics of enquiry being central to the creation and extension of the anticipated meaning. In this text, the theorization, generation and acceptance of 'new' knowledge within your professional responsibilities and development provide the varied foci of the enquiry process. What is the nature of these orientations to the professional learning process and how are they diagrammatically represented?

The substantive domain: 'learning what and how to teach'

Learning '*what* and *how* to teach' encompasses all of the content knowledge, in the form of concepts, generalizations and facts, skills, both social and academic, thinking processes, and attitudes and values, its scope and sequencing, and associated pedagogical applications, and the theoretical input that a teacher-learner is engaged with when working in their chosen subjects of their teacher education programme. These domains will exist in the units of study of your teacher education course in both the university and school learning environments. This orientation endeavours to transfer from university and school personnel to teacher-learners the accumulated practical and theoretical knowledge and understandings required to teach effectively. So, the substantive orientation, as represented in this model, is the complete content and units of study generally found in a teacher educa-tion curriculum, together with the practical knowledge held by the professionals running your course. Related information and advice are also available, in curriculum documents, at both local and national level, and through associated in-service professional development experiences, in your first and subsequent years of teaching. It is both the subject content and the associated pedagogical process that you will access in the substan-tive component of your preparation courses and beyond. Therefore, the specific subject content and pedagogical courses of study, together with the theoretical and research information of foundational disciplines, provide you with both the content and process of a comprehensive curriculum. Such a curriculum process would recognize that practical and theoretical support would be provided by *all* participating teacher education personnel, whether they were based at university or school.

In order to be sure of the reciprocal nature of theory and practice, and of your professional learning process, it is essential that, together with such education personnel, you recognize the need to articulate all guidance as being represented in both theory and practice, and its relationship with all aspects of professional learning. This should debunk the notion that univer-sity is the place that you learn the theory and school is the place where you learn the more important practical responses. This is not the case. Effective teaching needs to be seen as being dependent on both these learning envi-ronments so that relevance and consistency are brought to the teaching and learning process. Relevant learning strategies and pedagogy can be effec-tively understood and further enhanced when the underlying theoretical principles of how and why they are sequenced and applied in particular ways are supported by practical experience.

It is the emphasis on the *professional expert* component of professional learning that enables you to become self-regulating. This develops further through internal control as you challenge and renew your planning, pedagogy and evaluative procedures and enhance your theoretical understanding. Teachers who manage teaching and learning in this way become increasingly confident in their ability to formulate relevant curricular responses to the learning uncertainty that they recognize in the classroom and in their prepared teaching. There are many voices that the teacher has to attend to in their classroom that will guide them in creating responsive interactions with the learners and their planned teaching. These learner voices (as well as their own inner voice), with their associated actions, provide significant information for the teacher in developing individually focused responses. For such sensitive attention, these teachers have both a theoretical knowledge of and an attitude to enquiry, as well as potential generative strategies available to them, that encourage them to attend to, rather than evade, the challenges or uncertainties that arise.

As teaching can involve unpredictable interactions within a complex interactional setting, it is essential that you acquire cognitive strategies to identify, interrogate and resolve the issues and conditions that might occur. It is also important to remember that your considered response in recognizing the potential for advancing learning in such challenging situations, will provide the incentive for you to seek a more lasting and transformative teaching style. These disruptive speed bumps can create opportunities, for you and your learners, to advance knowledge and understanding.

The following section describes the positioning of the higher-order cognitive processes that you need to master and apply if you are to make sense of the complexities of the classroom's learning environment. This is where the interventions and teaching and learning responses of the *what* and the *how* of teaching reside and can become accessible.

The syntactic domain: learning how to learn

The focus of this strand is dependent on you developing, maintaining, engaging and evaluating your tentative conceptual frameworks to interact with information that has been drawn from your involvement with the teaching and learning process. By doing so, you come to appreciate how professional learning can be personally constructed, and then implemented as required. This on-going conceptual consciousness is tentative in nature so as to enable changes to be introduced, clarified and then subsequently modified as new practical and theoretical knowledge and experiences are encountered. This is the developmental characteristic of professional learning where ways of responding in teaching and learning situations are continually under scrutiny and being generated.

Similar theoretical tenets were proposed by Piaget (1977) in his explanation of the processes of an intellectual schema being able to assimilate new information into a conceptual understanding, or the existing schema needing to be modified to accommodate this new challenging input. Thus, it is essential that the conceptual framework is perceived as tentative in promoting an interpretative integrity that is open to accepting newly encountered experiences or ideas. Focused and persistent reasoning, initiated by 'what if?' questioning, will challenge you to seek conceptually more demanding explanations and predictions of your work.

As you increase your knowledge of the specific articulation of a challenging idea or initiative, your own well-structured enquiry and interpretation processes and your understanding and identification of potential responses become more sophisticated, complex and transformable. The professional initiative is then reliably assimilated into the current conceptual framework or a modified, updated version of it. A healthy realization should develop that a final conceptual framework for interpreting and reacting to teaching and learning initiatives may never be reached, but will continually undergo review and refinement.

The interlocking and interactive representation of the model (Figure 2.1) endeavours to show the reciprocal relationship that is found when these two orientations of 'learning *what* and *how* to teach' and 'learning *how* to learn' are applied when you attend to a teaching and learning concern and its relevant initiative. When these perspectives are juxtaposed in this way, meaning making and resolution generation are engendered. The double-helix model represents both the content and your professional process of the enquiry-based regenerative experience. Thus, it characterizes both the identified single instance – that is, the professional learning initiative derived from a teaching incident – and the initiative's antecedent and contextual influences, and an explanation of the developmental and continuous nature of acquiring such learning.

As identified in Figure 2.1, the initial *investigative bridge* (step 2 in the diagram) for each reviewed classroom episode (step 1) is isolated and identified through the inter-psychological social awareness processes of observing and discussing. This allows you to collect, collate, clarify, organize and manage information so that a professional learning initiative can be identified (step 3). The initiative is then taken into, and critically analysed within, the syntactic domain, through the intra-psychological skills of critical analysis, interrogation and interpretation along the critical analysis pathway (step 4). This takes place in the conceptual frameworks of the syntactic orientation so that potential responses can be eventually generated (the *generative bridge* – step 5), and then re-integrated back into the stream of teaching and learning activities of the substantive strand (step 6). This 'cycling-forward loop' process represents how you make sense of, and continually enhance, your professional learning. The boxed sequence shows how the steps of the double-helix model can be engaged with.

Step 1 Identifies the incident or teaching and learning episode that contains the potential professional learning initiative (PLI).

Step 2 Identifies the investigative bridge. The bridge is created in the syntactic orientation and provides for the application of the inter-psychological processes of the social context to isolate the initiative for further critical review.

Step 3 The PLI is brought into the syntactic domain for categorizing and articulation.

Step 4 The critical analysis pathway will take professional learning time as the PLI is analysed, interrogated, interpreted and theorized about. This is where your intra-psychological intellectual skills will be engaged for critical analysis, with potential teaching and learning responses identified.

Step 5 The generative bridge is where these potential teaching and learning responses are refined and transformed for feed-forward placement into the substantive domain.

Step 6 This represents re-entry of the selected generated teaching and learning response back into the teacher-learner's repertoire.

Step 7 Labelled 'the next cycle?' on the model, this step demonstrates the on-going nature of this professional learning process by identifying another episode and therefore a new PLI that requires your attention.

(*Note*: As you develop enhanced competence and confidence in executing this sequence, a number of cycling-forward processes will be happening simultaneously.)

Let us review what has been proposed above by using an example of how a professional learning initiative might be isolated from the context of a teaching episode. For example, a PLI relating to the 'management of teacher questioning' is identified from a teaching episode. This resides in the substantive knowledge of the first strand of the helix. The initiative can be analysed, interpreted, theorized about and re-contextualized through critical enquiry associated with a professional learning strategy of the syntactic focus of the second strand. The processes of identifying and contextualizing and the subsequent enquiry process are perceived as residing in the two intertwining threads of the double helix that represent the curriculum of professional learning. Here, practical learning based in the classroom, 'managing questioning' and the theorizing and generative domains of theory and research, coalesce and form your individually constructed enquiry strategy for initiating, developing and restructuring personal professional learning processes.

The professional learning objective, for you, is to see connections among what is known, what is to be known, and ways of focusing and conceptualizing this knowing. Coming to see these critical connections represents a continuing sophistication and complexity around the theorizing and generating processes associated with a classroom incident and its identified professional learning initiative. These processes provide the potential for subsequent change in the broader conceptual framework of your professional learning. The bridges or pathways shown on the double-helix model represent the interconnectedness between the professional learning episode and its theoretical and practical contexts and the enquiry processes you have used to understand the initiative. The model also illustrates the critical analysis processes and strategies for clarifying, understanding and responding that can enhance the teaching behaviours associated with the initiative.

The professional learning strategy's conceptual processes of understanding, analysing, interrogating, interpreting, transforming, synthesizing, generating and evaluating, support valuable yet tentative responses and outcomes from this one cycle of learning. The initiative, 'managing questioning', might be cycled forward through this enquiry and generative process a number of times as you acquire increasing executive control over potential responses generated for the initiative.

CONTRIBUTING IDEAS 2.6

Seeking enquiry strategies and connections among 'what is known', 'what is to be known' and 'ways of focusing and conceptualizing this knowing' is critical to developing professional understanding.

Though the connective bridging in the helix model represents this cycle-forward of learning, it also shows the way that carefully considered and created responses can be introduced into your teaching repertoire in subsequent planning and teaching. These responses will be subject to review and regeneration through continuing application in a variety of teaching and learning episodes and investigative cycles, as with the questioning sequences or goals.

You are engaging in a cycle of professional learning that is continually seeking to create learning outcomes beyond the immediate context, and provide you with initiatives and future opportunities for added clarification and growth. The cycle-forward process is moving on and gathering complexity and cohesiveness as it collects and clarifies new practical and theoretical experiences from your classroom teaching and related professional learning activity.

Initiating a critical enquiry awareness

What does this tentative conceptual framework need in order to operate effectively in advancing the teaching consciousness of your professional learning? First, there needs to be a set of well-defined and structured strategies for identifying, describing, interrogating, interpreting and synthesizing. You use these for understanding and responding to a teaching and learning episode from which you can form a professional learning initiative. This is an initiative for developing the specific teaching behaviour or skill that you had extracted from a teaching and learning episode, in the school or university classroom.

So, in the first instance, you select a teaching episode that will provide a simple and clear focus, an initiative, for your critical enquiry and generate a response, or responses, that will further enhance your professional expertise (described in more detail in Figure 4.1 in Chapter 4). This focus needs to be presented with clarity and purpose. It becomes the *what* – the professional learning initiative that focuses the self-regulating process of the professional learning agenda.

Second, there is a need to gather strategies for accessing knowledge that is relevant to the identified professional learning initiative or that needs to be resourced if the process is to generate relevant teaching responses. For example, what are the pedagogical, practical or theoretical understandings that can be drawn from the psychological and sociological tenets which are inherent in or underpin the identified initiative? You abstract the initiative from a teaching episode that has challenged you in some way. Your processes of knowing and reasoning enable you to respond in such situations. Processes for accessing critical understandings are needed, which might be derived through analysis and interpretation of a range of available information. Therefore, the ability is required to sort, categorize and analyse these understandings and your potential responses, for relevance and subsequent application.

Third, you access or develop strategies that can be introduced into your classroom to meet your teaching and learning responses to the professional learning initiative. In this phase of the response process, you will use or raise your awareness of teaching models, strategies and skills. You will collect and focus on illustrative resources that will enrich your teaching or classroom management. Chapter 7 provides details about this pedagogy and how creative and relevant responses might be introduced into your preparation and planning.

This is also the time to consider how the implementation of these generative responses might be evaluated. Evaluative understanding can be significant if a decision is being made about the new strategy's permanent introduction to, or rejection from, your evolving expertise. If applicable and meaningful responses have not yet been found to meet the pedagogical need of your initiative, then it is necessary to review it and refocus on the *why* phase of the professional learning agenda process. This is in order to redefine and extend your understanding of why proposed changes in your teaching approach are needed to effect relevant learning for the class group. This is a refocusing of the legitimacy of your enquiry- and response-generating processes (Chapters 4–6 have more on this).

A review of the model of professional learning

Let's review and re-emphasize how the two orientations ('learning *what* and *how* to teach' and 'learning *how* to learn') are related and interlock within the professional learning frameworks that you develop as you acquire the knowledge and skills of teaching. This organization represents critical understandings that you need to acquire to place yourself within a personal professional learning curriculum where the syntactic component enables you to take control and direction of your teaching and learning knowledge for more effective engagement in the classroom. It is a holistic perspective that emphasizes your abilities as a self-regulating, autonomous teacher-learner.

Conceptualization of a professional learning initiative is most likely to occur if there is a structural and conceptual binding of the episode in which the initiative is embedded within an identified known response that can be attributed to your critical analysis and interpretation or as an associated theoretical explanation. You will find that the PLA self-regulatory processes will guide and support this learning for you. It is these processes that form the interpretative and analytical connections that bridge across the conceptual strands of the double-helix model. The syntactic and substantive strands of the model are conceptualized as complementary professional awareness processes: the REACT self-monitoring process (Chapter 3) and the self-regulatory strategies of the professional learning agenda (Chapters 4–6). Once the initiative has been explored and critically reviewed, the resultant responses are 'fed forward' into an enhanced teaching and learning strategy that explores the *what* and the *how* to teach. The double helix represents the process by which a given initiative's structure or functionality is appropriately identified, described, sequenced, structured and so connected to the theoretical and practical dimensions of the 'learning *what* and *how* to teach' domain (that is, the content and pedagogical processes of the curriculum). It is the sequencing that determines the pattern of connectivity within the overall structure of this conceptual framework of your professional learning. The interrogation and interpretation of the initiative occur within the context of your theoretical and practical understandings of the discipline content and processes of the substantive strand. The critical analysis, theorizing, interpreting and generating of your enquiry strategy of the syntactic strand is applied within the connections presented in the model – the bridges and pathways between the two strands.

Being attentive to incidents that can generate professional learning initiatives represents capturing a moment in time or taking a snapshot of your teaching and learning. It enables you to focus on and respond inquisitively to your developing professional practice. Listening for, and then attending to, these brief moments in the flow of a classroom activity, through focused analyses, interpretations and the generation of responses, can create *leaping-off* points or *triggers* for significant professional learning experiences that are uniquely focused on your development. To enable this identification and clarification of professional learning, it is essential that the created initiative is defined succinctly in generic terms. Suggestions about the nature of this initial defining of the professional learning initiative will be considered through examples from a professional learning agenda format, in Chapters 4–6.

So, where to from here?

After decades of teacher education reform, policy makers and university educators are realizing that what students learn in school is directly related to what and how teachers teach, and so, inherently, how they learnt to be a teacher: 'What and how teachers teach depends on the knowledge, skills and commitments they bring to their teaching and the opportunities that they have to continue learning in and from their practice' (Feiman-Nemser, 2001: 1013).

If education policy guidance from authorities, districts and schools (and maybe textbooks?) wants teachers to produce more powerful learning by student learners, then it is important that teachers, especially those considered as initial teacher-learners, engage with more powerful and challenging learning strategies and opportunities (Feiman-Nemser, 2001; see also Young, 2014). Ball and Cohen (1999) add that unless teachers have access to complex and sustained learning opportunities at all stages of their career path, there is little likelihood that they will engage their learners in, similarly planned and implemented, demanding learning events (also supported by Young, 2014).

We concur with these teacher educators. Through the use and application of self-regulating observational and enquiry strategies, teacher-learners can be challenged to develop carefully articulated and complex learning that can initiate and extend their capacity to operate in ways that enable them to enhance their teaching expertise.

The strategies in this text have been developed in direct response to questions like that proposed by Feiman-Nemser (2001), for instance: What are the central tasks of teacher learning in the early stages of learning to teach? It is essential that you acquire and become practised in strategies that trigger intellectual habits and skills, including self-observation, interpretation and analysis in developing and improving your practice. For this, you need well-designed opportunities to link practice and theory, to develop higher-order cognitive skills and strategies, and to cultivate habits of analysis, interpretation and creativity through focused observation and critical enquiry in identifying that a place to learn to teach may be in the school classroom. That is a place where you understand and respond with focused research and theorizing capacities.

In other words, you can use your practice as a setting for enquiry (Ball & Cohen, 1999). This requires you to refocus any confusion and uncertainty on questions, trialling a newly acquired skill and assessing the effects; then framing new questions and learning initiatives to modify and extend your knowledge and understanding of practical and theoretical influences.

Your involvement requires the development of skills of observation, both of yourself and others, analysis and interpretation, together with an openness to challenge existing ways and to be receptive to differing opinions and interpretations. You will need to develop a self-belief that recognizes that knowledge and understanding formed in this way will be tentative, right for this point in time, but always available for continuing clarification and refinement.

On-going metacognition and enhancement of teaching can be difficult to accomplish. The specific self-regulating strategies, available in this text, will provide you with both purpose and self-monitoring and self-regulating strategies so that this state of professional learning might be accomplished. Though a self-controlling approach is intended in this text, the involvement of others can contribute purposefully when available. Because of the isolated nature of teaching, you will need opportunities to talk with others about your teaching, your analysis and projections of this, to co-examine common issues and problems and to seek alternative explanations and potential actions. As you learn to talk with clarity and authority about specific practices in theoretical and practical constructs, and seek clarification and guidance in the sharing of uncertainties, and to anticipate help, you are further developing and consolidating the tentative conceptual frameworks for critical scrutiny of your on-going professional learning. You will, through such interactions, be consolidating the knowledge, understanding and actions of your inquisitive self.

CHAPTER SUMMARY

For the most part, teaching is a highly personal and, in most settings, private activity. Teachers work alone in their classrooms, generally out of sight of other colleagues and cocooned by standards and contexts of limited autonomy and non-interference. So, seek out teacher education programmes, initial and extending, that take new teachers seriously as competent learners who should be challenged on all practical and theoretical fronts and should respond to issues in an inquisitive and analytical way. The strategies of this text recognize your potential to be a self-motivating and self-regulatory professional in finding your own solutions to the concerns that challenge you. Using this text and its activities will serve you well in arriving at your own tested solutions and, even more potently, at a position where you are ready to move on to the next challenge.

FURTHER READING

Holton, D. and Clarke, D. (2006) Scaffolding and metacognition. *Journal of Mathematics Education and Technology*, 37(2): 127–43.

This article proposes an expanded conception of scaffolding with four key elements: scaffolding agency, the scaffolding domain, the identification of self-scaffolding with metacognition, and the identification of six zones of scaffolding activity. These key elements are illustrated with empirical examples drawn from a variety of research studies.

Shulman, L. (1987) Knowledge and teaching: foundations of the new reform. *Harvard Educational Review*, 57(1): 1–22.

Shulman proposes an idea of teaching that emphasizes comprehension and reasoning, transformation and reflection. Shulman responds to four questions: What are the sources of the knowledge base for teaching? In what terms can these sources be conceptualized? What are the processes of pedagogical reasoning and action? And what are the implications for teaching policy and educational reform? Though produced 30 years ago, this article provides a seminal discussion still very relevant today.

Van Eekelen, M., Boshuizen, H. and Vermunt, J. (2005) Self-regulation in higher education. *Higher Education*, 50 (3): 447–71.

Various studies have focused on the self-regulated student learner, with little attention paid to such processes in teacher learning. This study aims to discover whether teachers actively self-regulate their learning experiences.

SECTION 2
PROFESSIONAL LEARNING STRATEGIES

Section 2 consists of five related chapters:

Chapter 3 Self-monitoring teaching and learning

Chapter 4 The self-regulation of professional learning – the professional learning agenda

Chapter 5 Advancing your professional learning

Chapter 6 Refining professional learning through review and interpretation

Chapter 7 The planning process

Section 2 introduces you to focused strategies for identifying, interrogating, interpreting and responding creatively to components of professional learning. These critical enquiry cycles equip you to take control of your professional learning. They also include ways in which an informed other, such as a mentor, colleague or peer, can provide an insightful contribution to this learning process.

The pattern for exploring these strategies focuses on their usefulness, with further suggestions about how other professionals may be able to provide support. Teachers can often feel that they operate in an isolated environment, where the support and confidence of colleagues is not imme-diately available. Interactions with those who might be experiencing similar professional issues are important for both your emotional and intellectual awareness.

As you become comfortable in using the professional learning strategies of this text, you will discover that such external support can be heard with a more focused relevance within the extended knowledge and skill domains of their and your inquisitive selves.

In the chapters in this section, although the emphasis is on self-observation as a self-regulatory approach to learning to be a teacher, guidance is also provided about how you can introduce and maximize the support of like-minded professionals. This guidance appears as sub-sections, usually at the end of each phase description of the professional learning agenda. In the context of these phases, such involvement from others can enhance understanding of your professional learning process. This development can occur more effectively when the professional learning agenda is generated from your own critical awareness as a teacher-learner who is actively seeking knowledge and understanding of your role within the complexities of the teaching and learning environment. Responsibility for the learning focus is still initiated by you from the personal investigative role of the inquisitive self. As the inquisitive self, you will find yourself asking clarifying questions regarding your intended action and associated thoughts that mirror those normally coming from a mentor/colleague. In this sense, you are enhancing the effectiveness of your self-monitoring persona.

Your professional learning starts from your own critical analyses and interpretations, and might be further enhanced by contributions from others, but it is essential that you remain in control of your evolving professional awareness. This self-monitoring strategy is first introduced by considering some of the concepts and processes that have provided the theoretical context of this particular strategy. Although theoretical and research information here is directed at providing an understanding of this specific aspect for your professional learning, you will also find that these understandings will extend your insights into how your own students learn. The learning theory that is applicable to your continuing professional development can be used or adapted in the context of supporting students' learning.

3

SELF-MONITORING TEACHING AND LEARNING

Having read this chapter, you should:

- have a detailed understanding of the five phases of the self-monitoring strategy, its purpose and potential application in defining your professional learning outcomes

- be increasingly aware of the knowledge and skill domains that provide an interpretative framework for your observation and analyses, and subsequent professional learning initiatives

- develop the intellectual ability to visualize and make images of your curriculum content knowledge and the associated pedagogical skills in rehearsing before teaching

- be able to critically analyse and interpret the theoretical and practical implications of your observations

- be able to identify professional learning initiatives that can be introduced into your professional learning agenda (PLA) strategy, for continuing review and implementation in subsequent lessons

- be able to create relevant, differentiated learning programmes for your teaching group

- be developing a critically informed and comprehensive understanding of yourself as a teacher-learner.

Introduction

The concept of self-monitoring, as used in this chapter, is defined as the intellectual ability to attend, examine, appraise and judge the quality and focus of one's own cognitive involvement while engaged in doing it (Bandura, 1991; Kleitman & Stankov, 2001; Koch, 2001). The individual learner's capacity to monitor cognitive processes effectively in achieving their optimal learning skills can enhance their use of learning strategies and achieve a higher awareness to recognize, adapt and correct their inadequate knowledge bases (Karabenick, 1996; Chen & Kuo, 2009).

So, how will this self-regulatory process impact on your professional learning? In Section 1, professional competence was conceived as your evolving ability to identify and apply qualities of decision making and judgements to the construction of intelligent responses to novel and unpredictable situations. So, how can you achieve these competencies?

Teacher as learner

A significant goal of teacher preparation is analysing your own knowledge and beliefs about learning and yourself as a learner. Gaining this perception of what teaching involves allows you to create a framework for your teaching experiences that enables a revised professional awareness to emerge.

> Prospective teachers need opportunities to critically examine their taken-for-granted, often deeply entrenched beliefs so that these beliefs can be developed or amended. Teacher candidates must also form visions of what is possible and desirable in teaching to inspire and guide their professional learning and practice. Such visions connect important values and goals to concrete classroom practices. (Feiman-Nemser, 2001: 1017)

Such a critical awareness of your own beliefs about student learning and the effect that these will have on your teaching experiences provides a crucial framework for subsequent preparation and learning. Oosterheert and Vermunt (2001) proposed that a transition into being a teacher typically involves moving from a focus on yourself to issues about the teaching process, and finally to a concern about students' involvement in the teaching and learning process (see also Fuller, 1969).

In order to explicitly model an effective and challenging learning process, it is important that, as teachers, we understand and view ourselves as proactive, self-aware and strategic learners who are competent in selecting and engaging processes and curriculum content that will enable students to reach their planned learning intentions. Teachers need to identify professional intentions, monitor their evolving knowledge and understanding about the teaching and learning process, engage in critical reviews and adapt to varying teaching requirements. This is because they are creating an increasing collection of learning strategies to apply in differing teaching and learning environments. In this way, teacher-learners who engage in their own professional learning processes are acting as self-regulating (Cleary & Zimmerman, 2002) and meaning-making learners (Vermunt & Vermetten, 2004).

To support your professional development of self-regulating and personal knowledge creation, your teacher education programmes introduce learning strategies that will 'develop and change their existing frame of reference in accordance with current understanding of what constitutes good teaching and learning' (Oosterheert & Vermunt, 2001: 134).

However, Weinberger and McCombs (2003) have suggested that few pedagogical techniques exist for supporting teacher-learners to critically review themselves as learners, and the ways that they can come to comprehend and extend their teaching practices with respect to their own and students' learning.

The professional learning strategies that are provided in this book should provide you with ways of recognizing and exploring your motivational beliefs, and your strategies about learning, and thus support your own learning to teach (Beijaard et al., 1999; Feiman-Nemser, 2001; Kelaher-Young & Carver, 2013).

Introduction to the five-phase self-monitoring strategy (REACT)

THE REACT STRATEGY FOR MONITORING YOUR TEACHING, AND THE LEARNING PROCESS

Phase 1: Rehearse – pre-teaching rehearsal and clarification of content and pedagogical sequences; this includes the reviewing of the specific professional learning initiative (15 minutes)

Phase 2: Enact – self-observation of teaching – identifying and capturing the teaching, learning and management aspects of the lesson as you enact the content and pedagogical schemata of the rehearsal phase (~60 minutes during the lesson)

Phase 3: Analyse – the immediate post-teaching review; personal professional initial analysis and interpretation of focused observations (after the lesson 10–15 minutes)

Phase 4: Critique – identifying, analysing, interpreting and theorizing about your observational content of Phases 1, 2 and 3 (45 minutes)

Phase 5: Transform – re-conceptualizing the outcomes of your critique and generating and justifying initiatives for on-going development of your professional learning agenda (PLA) (15 minutes).

This strategy is focused on supporting and guiding you in assuming increasing executive control of your knowledge and understanding. This comes from the analysis, interpretation and theorizing of your professional learning as you engage in school-based activities of planning, managing, teaching and assessing learners. A time frame has been suggested for each phase. You will understand that your involvement time in all aspects of your professional duties is valuable so it is important to maximize your focus for each of these phases.

The five-phase strategy (REACT) draws its theoretical support from a number of key areas pertinent to how professional learning can be conceptualized, organized and focused. First, this is research-based and draws from the tenets of action research (for example, Lewin, 1946; Denscombe, 2010; Ponte, 2010), in conceptualizing and adapting the professional learning foci. Your analysis, interpretation and subsequent action-responses as a teacher-learner participant, engage you in a critical review and planning process for understanding and responding thoughtfully and creatively to your place in that teaching and learning environment.

This is a process by which you identify and clarify initiatives for guiding professional learning. Subsequently, this steers your development of expertise and a repertoire of effective strategies, in providing relevant and challenging learning responses for your students. These initiatives are identified and described within a contextual framework of theoretical and practical understanding. The focused responses that you create from these initiatives are formulated and introduced, and then evaluated, within a variety of learning contexts. This action research and associated action learning is an ever-expanding, spiralling process of identifying, understanding, interpreting, theorizing, implementing, evaluating and renewing. You are situated in the action context of your learning, as you endeavour to apply enquiry processes to gain increasingly higher cognitive levels of professional knowledge and understanding. Through this, you are assuming increased executive control over not only your expanding knowledge and expertise but also the critical enquiry processes that enable you to find meaning in and enhancement of your involvement in learning interactions. The key professional learning focus of your self-observation lies in your enhanced conceptualization of the knowledge and understanding of what it means to be an aware and responsive teacher, engaging with learners in the complexities of the teaching and learning environment.

CONTRIBUTING IDEAS 3.1

Professional learning is initiated by your critical analyses and interpretations. It is essential that you remain in control of your evolving professional awareness.

The five-phase strategy (REACT) places specific emphasis on what is described in the literature as 'learning how to learn', 'double loop learning', 'legitimate learner self-direction' and 'self-evaluation' (for example, Argyris et al., 1985; Habermas, 1987; Torbert, 1991; Mezirow, 2003). Here, the emphasis is on the self-enhancement of your conceptual skills in learning how to learn, as well as learning about planning, teaching, managing and assessing competencies, and their application within the classroom. In earlier chapters, these two conceptual processes were explored as the substantive and syntactic elements of our double-helix model of professional learning (see Figure 2.1 in Chapter 2).

Such self-determined learning draws on recent research and application. Learning is considered as an integrative experience where a change in behaviour, knowledge or understanding is incorporated into an individual teacher-learner's repertoire of planning and teaching behaviours. An evolving conceptual frame of reference enables your professional growth beyond your immediate needs, allowing you to formulate initiatives for professional learning. Programmatic and teaching responses are a result of this interpretative awareness. It is the continual testing, challenging and re-defining of these interpretative conceptual frameworks that enables you to progressively know, interpret, understand and act on the educational environment of the classroom as a contributing, inquisitive and purposeful participant (Kolb, 1984; Bandura, 1986; Luckner & Nadler, 1997; Mezirow, 2000).

Though this higher level of self-directed learning provides the ultimate goal in teacher learning, in the early stages the role and guiding contributions of an appropriate self-monitoring strategy are crucial if you are to be challenged to evolve in a developmentally astute manner. How others may also provide guided support to this development is explored later in this chapter.

In the following, each of the five phases of the self-monitoring strategy is provided together with a theoretical explanation and a set of questions to focus your personal enquiry into the associated theoretical and practical responses of your own teaching. Comprehensive details are provided on the first phase, that of rehearsal and clarification. The processes of rehearsal (self-talk, visualization and mental imagery) and content organization in preparing for success in your planning and teaching, are reviewed and applied in this phase of the professional learning strategy. Though these processes are introduced here, you will also become aware of their influence on your metacognitive enquiry in each of the subsequent phases of the strategy.

The questioning sequences are provided for use in the planning, teaching, managing and evaluating components of a teaching episode evolved from curriculum planning documents. These questions are wide-ranging and provide a guiding framework of possible enquiry pathways rather than a detailed script to be followed. You will find these questioning sequences readily applicable to your self-assessment of specific lessons and the professional learning initiatives that you may have identified. Your own on-going critical reviews of your teaching may be complemented by the analyses and supportive interactions of peers, colleagues or mentors who have observed your lessons. Comments that relate to involvement by others are provided in each section below, in an explanatory discussion box.

Phase 1: Rehearsal – pre-teaching lesson rehearsal and clarification

This phase is dedicated to rehearsing and previewing of the prepared lesson's curriculum content and processes; the pedagogical procedures to be used; and your specific professional learning initiative.

This is the rehearsal of lesson preparation and implementation, and is appropriate for the one or two key lessons that are likely to focus and structure the learning day. You should take approximately 15 minutes for this review process so that you become confident with the content and pedagogical processes of the lesson and comfortable with the security of your conceptual knowledge of the subject area. As you become more competent in this review process, you will find that less time may be needed. You need to identify these key lessons in your planning, as a significant anchor or challenging stages for your students' learning. They may be introducing or changing the emphasis on learning of activities that you have previously identified as essential conceptual stages for student learning.

As is discussed in more detail in the preparation and planning section of Chapter 7, you will have created content structures, schemas or webs that guide the scope and sequencing of the curriculum content. It is important to remember that curriculum content is not just about knowledge but also includes aspects of skill development, thinking processes and attitudinal or affective emphases. For knowledge content, these schemata or conceptual structures identify the interrelatedness of the concepts, generalizations and specific facts that you have prepared for your lesson. Your knowledge and understanding of the sequence and structure of the content provide the model of learning that anticipates what your students will acquire from this lesson. This rehearsal phase enables you to review and consolidate the selected content schema as well as the scope and sequence of the teaching strategy that you have acquired, or modified, to best fit with the nature of the selected content.

Let's consider that you have selected a specific cognitive content sample because of its developmental relevance for your learning group and which could be well supported by a range of visual and enactive resources. There will be a number of available content samples of activities and support materials you could choose from.

For example in a primary classroom, if a mathematics lesson is focused on extending the student learners' knowledge and understanding of the operations of number, then the schema that you have conceptualized will recognize that:

(i) number is a key organizing concept in mathematics
(ii) there are four operations to consider in the development of this concept (addition, subtraction, multiplication and division)
(iii) the specific facts to be included in the lesson will be consistent with the level of mathematical knowledge and understanding of the learning group
(iv) there is a reciprocal relationship between the number of attributes which are to be emphasized, for example addition and subtraction. If the learning group is new to these relationships in the operations of number, the cognitive content (schema) of this specific lesson might be restricted to facts relating to numbers from one to ten. On the other hand, if the learning group was in an early secondary classroom, the content sample of number might involve decimals, proper fractions or mixed numbers.

The content schema is representative of the learning process undertaken by the learners as their understanding moves from the acquisition of facts about number, such as integers, fractions or decimals, to the investigation and application of the operation, leading these learners to a more comprehensive and applicable knowledge and understanding of the concept. Your content schema might be represented both deductively, from the planning and teaching perspective, and inductively, from the perspective and learning pathways of the students. The former perspective emphasizes the fact that teachers plan and prepare for teaching deductively by starting their processes at an understanding of the most complex and abstract idea, in this case the concept of number. After identifying associated minor concepts and attributes, the teacher selects a content sample of factual knowledge that provides the specific content for their students' learning. The students then access these content facts during the lesson's activities, and so acquire another layer of cognitive understanding of the relevant concept. The students are, in a sense, progressing their learning in a reverse process along the learning pathway from specific facts to generalizations, minor concepts and the conceptualization of the key idea, the concept (of number). They are, therefore, learning inductively in acquiring more complex knowledge and understanding of the activity that you have planned deductively.

These ideas and content schemata as *knowledge structures* that organize curriculum content are considered later in the chapter. Here the foci are on the mental imaging process within the rehearsal phase, including knowledge categorization and the subsequent detailing of a framework for application in the review process. Discussion of these attributes is crucial in the rehearsal phase as the attributes have significant influence on the ways in which complex learning situations are recognized and interpreted. These knowledge structures, as the fundamental unit of curriculum content, are considered in more detail in Chapter 7. In the example that follows, a teaching behaviour or skill that can provide the pedagogical initiative in the lesson has been interrogated and explained.

CONTRIBUTING IDEAS 3.2

The complexity and interrelatedness of your knowledge structures (content and skill schemata) provide the foundation on which to build your planning and teaching expertise.

Example: rehearsal of a planned lesson sequence – teaching skill

Let's consider an example of how you might undertake a rehearsal event that is expected to form part of your upcoming lesson. In critiquing your latest lesson with this group, you noted that your presentation of explanations and modelling was worth close scrutiny. So, in your current planning documentation you will identify a teaching segment where you are going to explain attributes of a concept that provides the content that you, the teacher, need to know. It is not necessary for you to focus on a lesson in the same subject area in which, previously, this professional learning intention had been identified, as this is a generic teaching procedure rather than being concerned with the exploration of a subject-specific attribute or idea. Your planned ways of explaining and modelling this content will be your professional teaching and learning strategy. You can rehearse in mental images the steps that you will follow in making explanations. You can draw from your conceptual schema or representations of this content sequence and include any written or diagrammatic resources that you will use, for example details on the interactive white board or wall charts.

As well as the descriptions and modelling processes, you can also foresee the qualifying and enhancing questions you plan to ask, and preview where you might direct these questioning sequences. You can also predict likely learner responses to your questions with the opportunity to hear those that provide the emphases and directions to your discussion sequence. Visualize yourself referring to prepared teaching aids and moving around the classroom to monitor more closely the verbal interactions that you are engaging in with the learners. Be aware that your teaching and learning process needs to link to the associated learning elements within the developing scope and sequence of the lesson. In both the rehearsal and implementation phases of the lesson, you should continually seek sensory input into your perception and conceptual schemata of your teaching. Aim to make the rehearsal phase imagery as live as your teaching performance (see de Beni & Moe, 2003).

Because of the security of your curriculum knowledge base of content reference, this rehearsal will prepare you in the actual implementation to identify responses from yourself and the learners that are relevant to the pedagogical questioning and response sequences as they happen. You could consider projecting into this rehearsal sequence a teaching and learning mini-process that you have been working on. Substitute a questioning, organizing or management event within your imaging and rehearsal enactment that provides a professional learning initiative for you at this time. The more often you are able to practise these processes, the more efficient and proactive you will become in responding to intended and unpredictable instances in the teaching and learning process.

As well as providing a focus on the content and pedagogical components of the planned lesson, the above example demonstrates how this critical review phase allows you time to intellectually consider your own professional learning. At this stage of your professional development, you are identifying, through the analyses and interpretations of your own teaching, a number of significant teacher objectives that can allow you to extend your teacher expertise. You are taking a moment to review and consider how you will engage and learn from the responses that you are introducing into your pedagogical sequencing of the lesson. In this way, you are setting up the foundations for self-assessment through metacognitive processes, as both a teacher and a learner. It is always important that you engage with an assessment of both students' and your own learning within the teaching sequence. This preparation, implementation, assessment and further preparation form a cyclical process of self-regulation. You should be slightly uncertain about what you currently know and, through these processes, be continually seeking to grow your professional expertise. You should not be overly concerned about instances of dissonance and confusion; instead, see them as significant trigger opportunities for resolving any teaching challenges that you are experiencing. Being uncertain about where you are professionally can lead to the eventual resolution of challenges that can support your development (Lange & Burroughs-Lange, 1994).

CONTRIBUTING IDEAS 3.3

Both your students' and your own learning need to be assessed within the teaching sequence.

The following is a critique of theoretical and practical aspects of the rehearsal phase. The emphasis is on how you identify the cognitive imagery to focus on during the rehearsal process. This is underpinned by understanding how knowledge may be classified. It is these knowledge categories that create the perceptual, representative frameworks that you will use to focus and guide your developing cognitive awareness of your learning environment. We will come back to this discussion of knowledge organization later on in this chapter. Principles for establishing your personal perceiving and conceptualizing framework provide the summary of this discussion.

Rehearsal through imagery and self-talk

The concept of rehearsal as used here refers to cognitive techniques to assist in the recall and projection of information and experience. These characteristics, of the review of both teacher and student learning, are known as *elaborative rehearsal* (Carroll & Bandura, 1985; Dudley, 2013) – that is, a rehearsal process that covers a number of conceptual frames of reference with connections being identified and extended. In the self-monitoring strategy, this involves the association of new material, both curriculum content and pedagogy, which exists in the preview, preparation and planning of lesson sequences for a particular group of learners.

Elaborative strategies that engage you in understanding lesson components and their inter-connectedness are useful for both storing and retrieving information. They also enable you to focus more directly on the perception, conceptualization and categorization of stimuli or cues that are available for investigation in the classroom. This is a significant application of conceptualizing schemata to support your growing understanding of the complexities of teaching and learning.

In a further enhancement of the elaborating processes, you may also use projected images from the conceptual schemata where you might visualize interactions between yourself and learners at the various stages of the lesson sequence. As suggested earlier, you will progressively evolve a number of perceptive and cognitive frameworks, at differing levels of sophistication and complexity, on which to hang your personal observations of what is occurring as a response to the teaching sequence.

You can develop your cognitive imagery to create vivid mental representations of your intentions, and the anticipated behaviours and responses that are expected in the classroom. In doing so, you are substituting the language of content, pedagogical organization and response that you used in your written preparation, with visual representations of what might be observed in the teaching episode. This will guide the effectiveness of your rehearsal and review of the significant content and pedagogical features of the proposed lesson, and how these aspects might be demonstrated as overt behaviours from both you and the learners. Employing imagery may also help you to alleviate stress and anxiety, improve your self-confidence, assist you in visualizing a successful lesson and further enhance your ability to transform your planning into practice. Imagery allows you to answer *what if* or predictive questions by making explicit and accessible the likely consequences of various classroom situations or when performing a specific action, such as asking questions requiring a prediction from a learner (Wheatley et al., 1987; Deshier & Lenz, 1989).

As you rehearse the learning sequence and your involvement in this process, it will help you foster a state of inner absorption or focused attention on what you perceive as likely observable stimuli of the predicted situation or action. Research shows that consciousness responds to engaging in vivid imagery almost as a real experience. When an event is imagined visually, the visual cortex is active, just as the auditory cortex is engaged when a conversation or verbal exchange is imagined (Marks, 1999; Thomas, 1999; Baars & Franklin, 2003).

Focusing the imagery of the rehearsal phase

Your imagery will focus on the various knowledge structures that you are developing as you heighten your understanding of how you engage with learners, the curriculum and the learning environment. These domains of content and teaching and learning knowledge provide perceptual and cognitive frameworks for your imagery. Knowledge can be classified in a variety of ways. For example, it can be designated as domain-specific (the content and processes of a particular subject area) and general knowledge. Cognitive theorists (Shulman, 1987; Weber, 2001; Gruber, 2013) have identified various types of knowledge that are relevant for new teachers and that can be applied during a self-monitoring strategy.

These are:

(i) declarative knowledge of concepts, facts and principles that are known in any domain of knowledge
(ii) procedural knowledge that involves knowing how to undertake various cognitive processes, and action (Berliner, 1988)

(iii) strategic knowledge or metacognition which is an individual's aware-
      ness of their own thinking processes and can therefore be used to
      complete professional learning tasks of self-monitoring and self-
      regulating cognitive and practical understandings.

You will recall in earlier chapters that this collective declarative and procedural knowledge was included in the articulation of the substantive
knowledge component of professional learning, while strategic knowledge
or metacognition was identified as the syntactic orientation that provided a
process of gaining insights into your thinking in learning contexts. Strategic
knowledge involves:

- the planning that is engaged before purposeful involvement in an intellectual activity
- the regulation and organization of thinking strategies within the activity,
  and then
- subsequently, the evaluation of the appropriateness of such thinking in
  responding to the intention of the activity.

In our professional learning activities, metacognition includes intellectual
strategies such as: advanced planning, self-monitoring, self-reviewing and
interpreting, questioning, summarizing, predicting, hypothesizing, generating potential responses, and evaluating such conceptual learning.

In supporting the significance of metacognition as a key factor in learning, problem solving and decision making, Brown (1978) proposed that
having the ability to monitor one's own understanding is an essential pre-
requisite for all problem-solving ability, and might also include a notion of
pre-planning for such cognitive learning to be initiated and subsequently
engaged in.

The social cognitive theory of Bandura (1986, 1997) supports such
observational or interactional learning in the classroom environment,
where it is recognized as 'largely an information processing activity in which
information about the structure of behaviour and about environmental
events is transformed into symbolic representations that serve as guides for
action' (Bandura, 1986: 51). Later, Bandura reaffirmed such relationships
in social cognitive theory by confirming that observational learning results
in 'knowledge structures representing the rules and strategies of effective
action' that effectively 'serve as cognitive guides for the construction of complex modes of behaviour' (Bandura, 1997: 34).

It seems that these cognitive guides, or schemata, are representative of
the significant role that knowledge structures provide for rehearsal imagery.
These are mediating mechanisms between observational transactional

learning in the classroom and professional learning outcomes for the teacher-learner. Social cognitive theory specifically articulates the formulation of knowledge structures at various levels of sophistication and complexity as a central mechanism in regulating observational learning (Bandura, 1986, 1997). This emphasis is consistent with the identification and engagement of the detailed self-monitoring strategy in this book.

The importance of knowledge structures is reinforced by the literature on expertise, learning and skill acquisition (for example, Glaser, 1990; Eichenbaum, 1997; May & Kahnweiler, 2000). A developmental view is proposed where knowledge proceeds from an explicit declarative form, resulting from being aware of the structure and application of a concept or skill. Finally, it moves to the gathering of procedural representation that may be characteristic of enhanced understanding and performance. In this way, the early stages of knowledge acquisition are characterized by steady and effortful information processing, whereas the later stages of involvement are characterized by relatively smooth, automatic and seemingly effortless performance. Throughout this process of knowledge structuring, specific elements of knowledge that may be acquired by sensory input, seeing and hearing, can be interpreted and theorized to become increasingly interconnected and organized into tentative knowledge structures. These can be described as tentative in nature as the later introduction of other similar information may challenge the existing structures. Cognitive maps or schemata provide the content of the mental images that are initiated in the rehearsal phase, and further clarified, adapted or applied in the later stages of this self-monitoring strategy (Glaser, 1990; Aarts & Dijksterhuis, 2001).

In the context of the above theoretical explanations, you may find the following principles helpful to create clear visual representations of your teaching. Remember, it is these representations that formulate the insights that you create about your planning and teaching. In early pre-lesson rehearsals, you may find that the imagery process relates to your professional learning initiative and that you are perceiving the stages of the lesson sequence that you anticipate will go well, or which may present difficulties or challenges to the learners. Although these professional issues are significant for you, it is important to review the subject content structures and activity that your learners are engaging with. It may be the sequencing of the content, rather than engagement with the activity, that is not being readily assimilated by the learners. So, look to both these aspects before deciding which characteristic to modify.

When you review explanations and insights that you have made about the teaching and learning environment, it is important to be explicit in describing them so that they can be used as objectives for the learning activity. This is especially relevant when identifying any skill or learning behaviour that is your professional learning initiative. At first, you may consider these foci during the preparation phase of the planning, but they will become more applicable to the immediate rehearsal of the lesson, before implementation. Consider the following explanations alongside the rehearsal questions provided for phase 1.

The following framework may help you to organize your developing understanding of your role in the teaching and learning process, as you ask questions about significant elements of your preparation for teaching and the sequence of imagery that you juxtapose with your observations and interpretations. The framework provides a bridging awareness between your pre-lesson rehearsal and the perceptions and interpretations derived as you question your planning preparation. Using the framework will heighten your observational foci and prepare you to accept such input in an organized and cognitive manner. So, consider this framework as a process for placing your responses to the question sequences into the developmental context of your professional learning and your metacognitive investigations of this.

An organizing and conceptualizing framework

- With your professional learning initiative in mind, predict how its underlying principles can be adopted to achieve a successful outcome for you. What will you be doing and how will the learners interact or react? See yourself successfully engaged with and responding to such interactions and this sequencing of the initiative.
- Use a multi-sensory approach, seeing, hearing, sensing as well as moving, as you engage with the learners and the teaching and learning process. Again, feel confident about your ability to respond to all actions and conditions, and imagine creative responses to challenging issues that you may foresee.
- Focus your rehearsal imagery on anticipated overt changes in learners and their learning environment. These might include verbal interactions with learners, your introduction of resources and teaching aids, the ways that you utilize the involvement of other classroom adults, your patterns of movement around the classroom and your anticipated verbal and action responses to what may be offered by the learners.
- Also be self-aware of your covert cognitive behaviours (i.e. the intra-psychological processes of metacognition) as you perceive what is being introduced into the lesson flow by you or by the learners. Can you see yourself effectively predicting, synthesizing and evaluating the process and outcomes of your intervention? How will you conceptualize a response and be confident in your intellectual and pedagogical ability to guide the activities and interactions of the learning process in relevant ways? You may find that you are making mental notes (and possibly written notes on

your planning documents as well) about likely responses that will be attended to later in the learning sequence. These will become elements of your mental imagery and cognitive schemata. Being able to predict responses to your teaching will be an essential element of your investigative, evaluative processes. Be aware that some learner responses might not be directly relevant to the current state of conceptual exploration, but may be useful at a later stage of the development of their conceptual understanding. Such 'not-relevant-at-this-time' contributions could be re-introduced into the future planning and implementation sequence.

- During your imagery rehearsal, identify possible disruptors to how you perceive the lesson sequence being engaged in by the learners. Be aware of how you will respond to and modify your control of the teaching and learning process. See such disruptions in the lesson flow as offering positive challenges to your evolving expertise and layered experience that may require *critique-in-action* and creative re-construction of your intended lesson sequence, or a widening of the learning context in which the key concepts and skills of the lesson are embedded.

- Value and enjoy the rehearsal phase as well as the perceived successful implementation of the activity with your learners. The complementary cognitive activity represents you as a learner as you focus your metacognitive processes on developing your teacher consciousness and professional competencies. In this way, you are educating yourself in developing a positive attitude to your perceived and observed ability to be prepared, insightful and responsive.

- It may also be helpful if you are able to record the outcome of your imagery rehearsal, as demonstrated through the unfolding of the lesson sequence. This will be explored when we discuss phase 2 of the self-monitoring strategy.

Let us consider the following set of questions that you might draw on during your rehearsal self-evaluation. You can select enquiry questions from this set that you perceive are of direct relevance to you. It is equally probable that you will also find other relevant probing questions to use. The question set is not a list to be covered but rather an enquiry framework that you can adapt for your own personal learning.

Enquiry-directing questioning sequences

(i) Focusing on the content and processes of the lesson to be taught

- What do I want the learners to achieve by the end of this lesson? What knowledge, skills or attitudes will this involve for the learners? How will I recognize that such learning is progressing? What cues am I expecting to receive to help me decide when to move the lesson sequence on? What responses from the learners will indicate this for me? Am I confident of the relevance of the prepared resources?

- What will be the sequence of this learning? Do I need to identify intermediate steps for the students in acquiring this learning? Have I worked through the teaching and learning examples of the topic to ensure that they are appropriate to the learning process and outcome? What do I think is the strength of this lesson? Are there aspects that may need more focused thought?
- What has been provided for the learners on this topic in earlier lessons? What do I anticipate will be covered on this topic in subsequent lessons? How will I assess the learning being achieved during the lesson?
- Are there any concerns that I have about this lesson? What do I think will be the challenges for these student learners? In what parts of the content and processes of the lesson might some students experience some difficulties? What will I recognize from the learners' interaction with the activity that will indicate this to me? How might I respond to these potential difficulties? What relevant activities have I prepared in readiness for such eventualities?
- What resources have I provided to support all students' learning? How am I providing support for the range of learning levels of the students? In what ways have I differentiated both the content sequence and the nature of the activity to respond to these identified differences?
- Why have I decided to group, or pair, the learners in this particular way for this activity segment of the lesson? How will I ensure that all learners are able to be involved in the activity as I intend? How will I ensure that all the student participants make the intended learning progress?
- I have decided to work with group X. Why have I planned my involvement in this way? Why this particular group? How will I monitor the on-task engagement by other groups?
- How have I prepared for the involvement of other adults in the learning process?
- What safety aspects have I taken into account? For example, supervision of students, and what would happen if ...?

(ii) Focusing on your professional learning initiative

Rehearse the nature of my teacher objective to focus my professional learning during this lesson activity:

- Why have I decided to focus on this initiative in this lesson?
- How will I identify my, and the students', responses to this initiative?
- What am I looking for as responses from the learners?
- What cues will provide me with positive feed-forward responses?
- So what will I need to specifically attend to in the lesson?
- How have I responded to this initiative in past experiences? What have I introduced that is different today?

If you have the opportunity to involve a peer, colleague or mentor in this professional monitoring strategy, they become another set of eyes for you. They can be asked to provide insights into how learners engage with the teaching and learning process. Remember, you are still taking the lead in this process. The other professional is responding to your directions. Consider them asking you:

- What do you specifically want me to focus on during the lesson? Do you want me to record such observations in a particular way?

- You have listed in your lesson plan the teacher objective that will be introduced into your repertoire in today's lesson. Why have you decided to focus on this professional learning initiative during the lesson? In what ways is this initiative linked to your developing expertise in this strategy and its knowledge base? How will you identify learner responses to this?

- Do you require me to identify any questions that I might have about the scope and sequence of the content, and the various teaching, resourcing and management skills, and learners' engagement with the activity that you include in the lesson?

Phase 1 summary

Let us review your professional learning intention for phase 1. It was to respond, in an organized manner, to the ideas that you formed through the imagery implicit in rehearsal. The questioning sequences will help you consolidate and enhance the frames of reference that you are establishing. They can provide relevance not only to your planning of curriculum content and pedagogy, but also to your conceptualization of your own thinking process. How you use these to interpret, interrogate, analyse and generate both conceptual and practical responses to your self-awareness, will provide on-going foci for your professional attention.

The rehearsal phase is therefore laying down conscious cognitive foundations to provide you with significant and relevant reference points for your evolving professional competence. Comprehensiveness and consistency in developing such knowledge patterns and processes are crucial to this learning process. The sensing of the relevance and linking of observable patterns of knowledge, understandings, skills, attitudes and behaviours will further encourage you to successfully negotiate and modify learning situations as required.

Your evolving competence in recognizing the interrelatedness of these elements of your professional learning is a dynamic concept; the process of acquiring this is unending and entirely idiosyncratic to your knowledge and experience. The level of competence can be recognized by reference to the more knowledgeable and sophisticated states of understanding that you bring to your learning. The key to any stage of a competent performance lies specifically in the complex nature of the organization of your knowledge. Due to their organization of memory into 'clusters of knowing', more experienced professionals possess a wide-ranging knowledge base that is seemingly organized into extensive and integrated structures as schemata (Piaget, 1926). New teachers possess less knowledge and understanding that may not yet be coherently organized, and so there is a professional learning requirement to focus attention on strategies that identify and consolidate frames of knowledge.

Schema theory

Let's take a moment to review and consolidate our earlier discussion of knowledge organization and schema theory. Understanding the organization of knowledge is based on schema theory (Bruner, 1966; Vygotsky, 1978; Shulman, 1987), which proposes that unconscious mental structuring underlies all human conceptual understanding. The abstracted generic knowledge that you have organized and referenced into new qualitative knowledge structures, enables you to situate your meaning making about the information that you are receiving from your involvement in the teaching and learning environment. The processes that you use in handling this new knowledge can be framed by accommodating and assimilating processes in attaining the knowing and understanding equilibrium that is the foundation of Piagetian theory.

The possession of extensive, readily focused, knowledge structures seems to have a significant influence on the ways in which complex learning situations are perceived and conceptualized. The classroom is such a complex context.

Briefly stated, knowledge structures (schemata):

- influence the focus, quality and quantity of attention to the sensory input that is available in complex social interactions
- serve as a framework of memory organizations of knowledge and understanding for the clarification, modification or acceptance of knowledge newly acquired. The existing knowledge structure or schema interacts

with the new information to form conceptual representations that may be a combination of old and revised structures. Such knowledge is experiential in nature and available for recall and application, and modification if appropriate

- facilitate maintenance and application in accessing the information, both from the memory structures and the multi-sensory environment that is being attended to
- develop in complexity, adaptability and applicability in securing new knowledge input, so ensuring that such cognitive structures are kept under constant review.

It seems that, in addition to having better organized, conceptual schema, more intellectually advanced teacher-learners are able to use and apply their knowledge to create cognitive representations of the social situations or problems that confront them. Such causal representational models also support these advanced learners in predicting, problem solving, decision making, explaining and justifying their interactions with others and the social situation.

Attaining levels of high expertise depends very much on the procedures that are selected in order to perceive and attend, intellectually, to a problem or otherwise challenging information. Those with enhanced expertise and access to a range of relevant experiences have engaged in many opportunities to test their problem-solving skills, and to develop a more substantive and applicable knowledge base. This more clearly defined knowledge base enables these teacher-learners to focus on smaller, more manageable segments of any problem and its influencing context. They are able to focus on the constituent parts as well as the whole and can process and use information that is more directly associated with the relevant knowledge structure. Therefore, they are more likely to resolve the learning issue that has challenged both them and the professional learning concern and its context.

As a new teacher, you will have more limited experience and a less robust knowledge base than an experienced educator. As such, you may find it difficult to discriminate between relevant and irrelevant information. Consequently, you will be challenged to reduce the size of any problem and its context. You may feel that many of the conditions, challenging or otherwise, of a focused area of study are unique to you. Significant problem-solving time and effort can be distracted by irrelevant information, and this can lessen your ability to make meaningful appropriate decisions. What is not immediately available to newer critical reviewers is the ability to sort relevant from less relevant information. To do this, you need deliberate strategies to help you focus on such categorizing skills, including effective use of the self-monitoring strategy. This will give you a process for purposefully applying your knowledge and skills schemata in seeking and selecting appropriate information, to accurately interpret and classify that information, and to manage and direct your actions through informed preparation and planning.

Phase 2: *Enact* – together with the self-observation of the teaching episode

During your teaching, you should be endeavouring to observe your engagement with learners and the learning environment. In doing so, you will be reviewing the content and pedagogical schemata of your rehearsal phase and how you used the rehearsal to understand your role in the learning process. Not only will you be aware of the cognitive demand that you are placing on your students' learning, but you will also be involved in higher-order metacognitive processes as you develop an intellectual understanding of yourself as you learn how to teach. You will be organizing your awareness as an insightful teacher-learner.

Focusing personal observations

One significant, yet complex, self-monitoring skill that you might develop is the ability to quickly read and interpret a situation in the classroom. You want to be able to come up with an explanation (or theory-in-action) of why something is happening, as well as identifying ways of responding. This requires an ability to raise your awareness level so that you can pay attention to the barely visible or hidden interactions that take place in the classroom. Your attention to such behavioural details of students' learning and interaction depends substantially on the focus and filtering of your listening skills. More discussion on attentive listening follows later, and further examples and strategies for developing listening skills can be found in Chapter 7.

You will find that many of the listening strategies that you can develop with your learners will also be helpful for your own teaching skill set. Development of the critical cycle of higher-order cognitive skills, including analysis, prediction, theorizing, hypothesizing, evaluating and synthesizing, needs to be based on effective attention-focusing awareness and the ability to be responsive to sensory input from listening and seeing. Listening is not just hearing the noise of speech interactions; it is attending to the meanings inherent in the verbal commentary. So listen attentively and use your content and pedagogical schemata as filters. It is important that they are not overly prescriptive and do not block out meaning generated by other aspects in the teaching and learning environment. Use your schemata but ensure that you use them in ways that allow you to still perceive unexpected, but possibly relevant, information.

Effective and insightful observation of your students operating in complex teaching and learning situations is an incredibly valuable skill to develop. It provides you with the ability to notice subtle cues and behaviours during explanations, discussions and questioning that may prompt you to re-conceptualize your approach, and respond accordingly. This becomes easier to apply over time, during your teaching, as you raise your perceptive and conceptual consciousness. You can identify and apply the perception and cognitive schemata that you are tentatively establishing. They provide ways of focusing your understanding of your role and the teaching and learning process.

CONTRIBUTING IDEAS 3.4

Effective and insightful observation of your students operating in complex teaching and learning situations is an incredibly valuable skill to develop.

When immersed in the teaching and learning process, it may seem that there is no time to pay focused attention to what is occurring in a busy classroom. You still need to ask, 'Why is that happening there?', 'What has caused this behaviour, or situation, to happen?'

Is your teaching habit to 'get on with the lesson' and 'get the immediate task completed'? Is this due to nervousness or not being completely sure about the content or pedagogy that you are implementing? If so, then you already recognize the need to prioritize your involvement and to cultivate habits of slowing down your delivery, developing your listening and seeing, and focusing your attention on how learners are involved *with* you in the lesson sequence. An initial action might be to pause and pay more attention to what is happening in front of you. This sense of needing to keep going so as to cover what has been planned can be a distracting influence on your increasing awareness in your immediate environment. Be conscious that this can happen and that you need to respond appropriately. The development of an attentive awareness will require you to gradually work this pedagogic habit into each day's involvement with students and could be included as reference notes in your lesson planning. Consistent use of attention-guiding strategies will enable you to be more inclusive in your involvement.

Gradually encourage yourself to develop a consciousness of your perceptive schemata about the elements of the teaching and learning process, and take notice of small details in your planning and teaching environment that relate to these. In this way, you are using theoretical and practical filters that can offer meaningful insights that can inform effective professional judgements within your classroom. By doing this, you will start to notice more instances that seem to make pedagogical sense and others that don't seem to fit into your planned teaching. Consider putting these seemingly irrelevant incidents aside for more detailed consideration during subsequent planning sessions. You can critically examine these incidents at a later time for their relevance and applicability to your evolving expertise. How might you extend the habit of attending to your planning and teaching environment? As part of your daily tasks as a teacher, you develop teaching plans and programmes for engaging learners with the content and processes of the curriculum. Are there ways that you can strategically use these to focus your evolving professional awareness?

In exploring rehearsal as the first phase of the self-monitoring strategy, you have begun an inquisitive journey by considering both your students' and your own learning processes. These may be similar in some ways. Your professional learning schemata and frames of reference for teaching, although tentative, have been initiated and are available for further refinement and sophistication. You will have supported this strategic awareness by introducing written notes into your documentation before your teaching session. Continue this *noticing and noting* during the lesson and shortly after its conclusion. As you did in the rehearsal stage, you will continue to identify ideas and questions, from your various schemata, that will focus your attention on the guiding aspects of the lesson sequence. You have already raised your awareness of any part of the sequence where learners might struggle to understand or apply what they have learnt. Your notes will help you to attend to the more relevant features and disregard those you identify as less salient. It helps to write descriptions, offer theoretical and practical clarifications, and make pictures and diagrams to represent what you know conceptually. This output will also provide reference points when you review your self-observations in later phases of the self-monitoring strategy, comparing them against your rehearsal thinking and developing perceptual awareness.

During the lesson, when you have a few minutes where you are not directly involved with learners, look around the learning environment and note what you see. Think critically about what has just happened in the lesson, review a couple of observations and make brief notes on what you have seen or remembered. Carry a pen and Post-it pad with you as you move around the classroom during the lesson. Make coded notes and stick the Post-it to your planning documentation as you pass your desk. If you are able to manage this immediately after the implementation of your planned professional learning initiative, and on other occasions during the lesson, you will find that you have identified sufficient information to trigger critical analyses in the later phases of this strategy. Just a couple of bullet points would work at this stage. Soon after the completion of the lesson, repeat and extend the recording of the process.

As you establish a mindset for succinct descriptive observations, you will find that you are paying more attention to what you may have considered in the past as insignificant details. Initially, your note-taking need only be very brief, maybe only a couple of words, to aid the critical analysis, interpretation and interrogation processes essentially being applied in later phases. Your observations in social situations outside of the classroom can help here too – for example, being as inconspicuous as you can, watch a colleague who is working at their computer; observe others while enjoying a cup of coffee in a cafe; or note the reactions of someone talking on their phone on a train journey. You may also consider the actions of someone window-shopping, of parents overseeing children's activities at the playground, of interactions in the school staffroom, and so on. Where possible, commit your thoughts on such interactions to paper and then later endeavour to make predictive sense of your observations. It is the focused and attending processes that are important here, not whether your predictions were accurate. Through activities of this nature, you are raising your awareness levels, and you may be surprised at how your immediate environment is packed with interesting events. You could also make up similar attention-focusing activities for your learners as you encourage them to be more attentive to others. More of these activities will be highlighted in Chapter 7.

You might also consider how meditation, another area of mindfulness training, may teach you to pay attention to yourself and what is going through your head as you are engaged in an activity or are observing others' involvement. Meditation doesn't mean running off to be a monk, but rather taking the time to re-focus your mind. Consider allocating a quiet time to take stock of what you have accomplished during the day. Consider the positive thoughts and interactions that you experienced and that gave you a good feeling about what you were doing. Your professional learning focus on positive outcomes is considered in phases 3 and 4 of this self-monitoring strategy. The other, not so positive, occasions tend to come readily to mind without too much encouragement!

You will find that as you continue to pay attention to what is happening in the classroom you will start conceptualizing these observations and the associated critical awareness into ideas or theories that will give content and guidance to your thinking. This can include theory-generating foci and the creative practical responses that could follow. In this way, you are increasing your ability to isolate potential learning triggers as well as enhancing your critical thinking. In teaching yourself to think critically, the set of enquiry questions of this and other phases will support an intellectual processing of issues that arise from your focused observations. You are monitoring yourself to critically analyse everything that appears to have exerted an influence on your planning and teaching as you assimilate and accommodate new learning and new ways of responding.

Throughout this book, you are encouraged to ask questions such as:

- What is this issue, concern or challenge that I have identified?
- How will I develop an understanding of this?
- Why is this important?
- Why do I want to be able to understand and apply it?
- In what ways could I use or adapt this learning initiative?
- How does this connect with content, skills or strategies that I already know?
- How will I be able to use this information or process later?

During this enquiry focus, you are building networks of knowledge of curriculum and pedagogy, and developing cognitive and meta-cognitive processes to make connections among 'what and how you know', 'how you find out about such elements and their connections' and 'what potential it holds for my continuing professional learning'. It is not the isolated portions of knowledge that you have acquired but rather your intellectual ability to see and apply connections and relationships that integrate and accommodate these knowledge elements into a useful theory or approach for your teaching.

Although gathering knowledge and processes about teaching and learning are directly relevant to your engagement in the classroom, it is vitally important that your perceptions and critical thinking are increased so that the connections you identify can be maintained, challenged and modified where necessary. You will start to appreciate your world as an entire network of possible connections as you build a 'mind map' of knowledge and processes. Mind map techniques, as they relate to your cognitive and skill schema, are also useful when you are making notes, as they move your critical thinking onwards from simply recording factual information. You can achieve becomes a more sophisticated level of critical consciousness as you bring an added iconic definition to your verbal and symbolic perspectives.

You must also consider the breadth of your knowledge base, so that you are able to go beyond one area of specialization and stay open to ideas from another content or process domain. The adaptation of a skill or concept from another domain comes with your increasing powers of deduction and critical thinking.

Be positive and inquisitive in seeking out incidents and the associated initiatives that will support your continuing growth. Think smart rather than thinking yourself in circles. Have a plan for logical thinking based on focused questioning. Look for the road map of critical thinking routes for an applicable and adaptable teaching consciousness. Remember, you have created these schemata and inquisitive frameworks while involved in the planning and rehearsal phases of preparing for teaching. You are starting to know expressive ranges of essential content and pedagogical knowledge, so make conscious plans to use these heightened levels of understanding and application in all aspects of the teaching and learning process.

Aim to be proactive rather than reactive in your professional learning and in the curriculum planning, implementation and assessment aspects of your work. Yes, listen to the advice of other professionals with more experience, but don't wait to be told, rather initiate your own professional learning approach. Being told does not mean that such advice can be directly transferred into your teaching context; it will need to be transformed by you as you bring your idiosyncratic knowledge and understanding to bear on it. Any new idea or strategy has to be *owned* by you before implementation. The information-acquiring skills identified above need to become unconscious responses to professional learning initiatives; they are the tools of your trade. These skills separate your enhanced and applicable understandings of what is happening in a learning environment from those of someone who just spent time in a classroom. Be prepared to articulate this knowledge and understanding in explaining why what you do is unique and significant.

Summarizing phase 2

The self-monitoring process of your teaching and the students' learning is what you perceive is taking place based on what you are seeing and attentively listening to. Perception is taking what you have observed in these ways and becoming aware that meaning can be attributed and then organized within your existing tentative schema so that on later occasions further clarifying meaning can be attached to it. Observation is more than just noting details about what you perceive and may conceptualize later, to answer questions already formulated. It also involves engaging with your environment, deliberately attending to myriad details and using logic and imagination to provide meaning and visualize possible outcomes. Therefore, in moving into this second phase of the self-monitoring strategy, be aware of what you may be looking for initially that is related to the content or pedagogical initiatives that you highlighted in the rehearsal phase. Use your schematic filters to make meaning of what you perceive. Note this down, and then identify any disruptive influences to your conceptual understandings. Don't forget to include incidents that challenge your professional knowledge and make you a little uncertain. These will require critical review in later phases of your self-monitoring strategy. Acquiring a learning dissonance state will be most helpful in focusing your continuing professional learning. Through focused observations, you will be raising your intellectual understanding of yourself, as the teacher-learner, towards more complex and more readily applicable professional teaching and learning responses.

> When a student teacher's lesson is observed by a mentor, colleague or peer, they should be engaged to focus on the student teacher's identified professional learning initiative. They will also make observations of other incidents or features of the scope and sequence of the lesson, and of the management of learning and learners. These aspects will have been decided in phase 1, and these observations may be included in dialogue towards the end of phase 4.

Phase 3: Individual analysis and interpretation of planning and teaching (immediately post-lesson)

For this phase to be purposeful and effective, you need to find a short time immediately after the lesson – a quiet 10–15 minutes would be sufficient. Any written notes can then be quickly reviewed and any further perceptions about the engagement by you and the learners with your planned lesson can be added. Comments need to be brief – bullet points would work for this purpose. Any incident that appeared to enhance or disrupt the sequence of the learning activity could be included. It may help if the lesson concludes just before a scheduled break or when you were not immediately involved with the group of learners. This immediate post-lesson activity is individually focused and so you would not involve a mentor, colleague or peer in this short phase.

Phase 4: Critiquing – by identifying, analysing, interpreting and theorizing about observational content from phases 2 and 3

You may require up to an hour for this critical review process where you extend descriptive detail of the bullet-point-type notes that you have made. You should then critique the data in order to understand the teaching and learning incidents and situations in the context of your planning and subsequent teaching. By following the earlier stages of the self-monitoring strategy, you will have your intentions adequately detailed in your planning, you will have rehearsed the manner of both the content and the pedagogy of the plans and these will have been implemented in the challenging environment of the classroom. To support this enquiry process, sets of questions are provided to assist you in developing a conceptualizing framework for challenging your perceptions, understanding their implications for your planning and teaching, and changing them into conceptualizations of intent for enhancing your professional learning.

Routinely start any critical review of your teaching with what you perceive to be the positive features of the lesson before considering the areas for more focused development. Once you have reviewed these effective features, you are in the right place for more focused learning enquiry of other issues that you were not so pleased about, and ready to create more positive professional learning responses to them. Always start from a positive perspective. Be pleased with and celebrate your successes, and then anticipate the ways that you can make these professional responses even more effective for you. The development of your relative strengths and how you respond to these will provide the blueprint for your professional development. If you can, make these particular successful ways of operating as a teacher increase in value for you, then the improvement of skills and techniques that you are still a little uncertain about will become less daunting.

The following are relevant questions for your analysis, interpretation and proposed responses to incidents, issues, content and pedagogic ideas and the identified professional learning initiatives. As previously suggested, select those that best suit your individual enquiry process. Don't accept the questions as a process that must be used in their entirety but rather take control of your selection process and make the questions work for you.

Knowing more about and increasing the value and application of your professional attributes

- What aspects of the lesson content, processes and management went well for the learners and for me in the lesson? List three of these successes. Consider each separately:

o Why did this happen in this way for the learners and me?

o How might I further enhance my contribution to this achievement of my learning intentions in subsequent lessons?

o Can this particular strategy, skill or behaviour be used at other times with other subject content?

o How might I adapt or take the intent and structure of this successful implementation into the development of other skills?

- What aspects of the lesson did not go as well as I had anticipated? Again, selecting three such foci will make your review much more manageable and focused. It would seem more appropriate to consider a few of these issues in some depth rather than many, superficially:

    o What have I identified as the contextual conditions that may have influenced the event? What antecedent influences do I perceive that affected this outcome?

    o How might I respond to similar occurrences in subsequent planning and teaching episodes? Will I need to attend to the structure or organization of the skill, or behaviour, to make it better fit with my teaching intentions? Is there a more relevant skill or behaviour that I could now consider that might better meet the requirements of the learning intention?

- Which of my learners appeared to have struggled with the given concepts and processes of the learning?

    o Why do I perceive that this happened in this way? Is there a need for more focused rehearsal on such issues, including relevant management strategies? At what point during the lesson did I perceive that learning, as intended, was happening or not happening?

    o What have I identified as the antecedent and contextual conditions that may have influenced this happening in this way? How might I modify the learning environment so that these influences might not be relevant or significant on subsequent occasions? Would it now be appropriate to focus on such influential conditions during the planning and rehearsal phases of my planning and teaching?

    o How might I now respond to those learners who appeared to have had some difficulties in working with the content or the strategy? Will I need to consider more relevant differentiation in content organization and in the ways that learners will access their learning?

    o How will I respond to this apparent difficulty in my future planning and teaching?

- What unanticipated classroom incidents occurred during the lesson? Be sure to include this question in any of your critical analyses. Such an event, when identified and interpreted, will provide you with significant triggers for your professional learning. Such incidents will come from outside the domains of your planning and lesson rehearsal. Therefore, why they occur will be important in your growing consciousness as an inquisitive teacher-learner.

o Why do I believe this happened? How did I respond? How effectively? What was the outcome of my immediate response? Do I now have any further thoughts about how I could have responded? Why didn't I anticipate this event in my pre-lesson considerations? What aspects of my professional knowledge bases need my focused attention? How might this lead me to focus on a specific aspect of my teaching behaviour?
o How might I respond if similar events occur in other lessons?

If a mentor, colleague or peer is involved in this critical review process as an informed other, it is important that you take control of identifying the significant aspects that you have detected in your teaching. You should suggest ways in which you would respond in subsequent sessions based on your own analyses and interpretations for developing their initiatives for professional learning. The informed other assumes the role of critical friend and clarifier to your theorizing. Their role should be to consider the questions that you have identified to guide the enquiry process, and the creative responses you have proposed to the aspects that challenged you. Once these have been exhausted, there is an opportunity for the informed other to introduce any questions that might identify teaching skills and behaviours that they would encourage you to consider in your analysis in phase 5 of the self-monitoring strategy, and the professional learning agenda. A full discussion of the professional learning agenda will be covered in the following three chapters. The questions suggested earlier will be useful for the partnership of mentors and teacher-learners during both the student teacher-led evaluations and the professional process that evolves to include focused mentor guidance.

Phase 5: Transforming – formulating and justifying initiatives for your professional learning agenda

This phase of the self-monitoring strategy provides the conceptualizing bridge between regular observations and analyses of lesson planning and implementation, and the more formalized and structured critical review, analysis and generation of the on-going individual professional learning programme of the professional learning agenda. From this linking process, professional learning becomes more theory-informed and practice-based as it assumes a state of focused continuity. The modification or introduction of new teaching behaviours, in the form of teaching models and strategies, tends to take a lot of time and practice in varied content areas, in order to consolidate to a point where you will be able to assume executive control of your developing expertise (Joyce & Showers, 2002). Transforming some observations and associated analyses into more permanent PLA initiatives will enable you to continue to include these in your on-going planning and teaching efforts and to monitor your progress over a longer period of time.

After completing your self-observation and analyses in phases 3 and 4 of the self-monitoring strategy, you will have identified a number of professional learning initiatives (maybe three) that you believe are significant attributes for your developing professional expertise and that require continued critical review and analysis. You will have carefully considered your responses to the investigative questioning of incidents, issues and behaviours or skills that were undertaken during earlier phases of this strategy. From your metacognitive awareness, you will have decided on their importance for your on-going professional development. These might be elements of your teaching expertise that you perceive as being successful in achieving your intentions or ones that you believe require focused critical introduction into subsequent lessons so that they too can develop as essential components of your teaching repertoire.

So, after giving yourself a day or so to think further about your analytical findings for observations and analysis, perhaps after a number of further critical evaluations of your lessons, formulate these as professional learning initiatives that you can continue to review and enhance through the PLA process. These will become the cornerstones and building blocks on which you will base and expand your professional development. For this refining process, the following questions will help you to make informed decisions about what to include in the next professional learning exercise. These questions are *cognitive frames of reference* to focus your identification, analysis, interpretation and professional learning responses that have been identified in the earlier phases. You not only need to select the appropriate initiatives thoughtfully, but will also need to reason why you believe each initiative is important to you:

- What new facets of my professional learning have I identified that require focused attention? How have I assessed their relative importance? Why will this be important for both the learners in my classroom and as an initiative for my professional learning?

- What processes, skills or activities will I introduce into my planning, teaching and assessing procedures that will advance my development of this professional learning initiative and my expertise collectively? When will I be able to introduce these variations into my teaching behaviour? Immediately? Gradually? In a sequential pattern? Over the long term?
- Why did I choose this focus on ...? How will this enhance my teaching repertoire and so extend the students' learning? (This is asking you to consider the rationale for why an initiative is important to you. You will see in the following chapters the application of these thoughts and justifications within the *why* cell of the PLA.)
- Later, what am I going to introduce into my teaching repertoire to identify and support my responses to this issue, incident or behaviour? (The responses to this questioning will form part of the information that you provide in the *how* cell of the PLA.)
- What will be my success criteria when assessing the outcomes of my planned responses to this initiative? (The justification and assessment comments that you provide here will relate to the *why* and *progress reviewed* cells of the PLA.)
- How will I record the achievement of my professional learning initiative? (You will have evidence of successful inclusion in planning and practice as a programmatic response identified in the *progress reviewed* cell of the PLA.)
- How will my responses to all of the above continue to sustain achievement of these professional learning initiatives?

As you formalize and hypothesize these initiatives, they will be transformed into your teacher objectives within planning formats, in order to provide guidance for self-assessments in developing professional expertise. As these are introduced into your planning and teaching, their effectiveness in responding to the identified professional learning needs becomes evidence of your enhancing abilities as a teacher-learner.

The review and generative process in phase 5 (transform) of the self-monitoring strategy links the observation strategies and the critical questioning of these into your continuing professional learning. The initiatives identified in these ways will shape your on-going professional learning as you analyse, theorize and generate conceptual frameworks and teaching and learning responses. The schemata are being built and assessed continually by you, for identifying and critically reviewing your theorizing, metacognition, teaching behaviours and practices.

CHAPTER SUMMARY

Through integrating the five-phase self-monitoring strategy with the professional learning agenda, you will be able to theorize about your various roles and generate responses to continuing professional learning within the complexities of the teaching and learning process. These tools support self-regulated autonomous learning. Inquisitive and therefore outstanding teacher-learners are proactive, self-managing and creative learners.

FURTHER READING

Feiman-Nemser, S. (2001) From preparation to practice: designing a continuum to strengthen and sustain teaching. *The Teachers College Record*, 103(6): 1013–55.

The author proposes a framework for thinking about a curriculum for teacher learning. Practice as a site for enquiry about teaching where confusions are turned into questions for extending one's understanding, is considered. Opportunities for teacher learning are situated in the tasks of teaching, planning, enacting teaching, assessing students' involvement and understanding, and in reflecting on teaching.

Mezirow, J. (1997) Transformative learning: theory to practice. *New Directions for Adult and Continuing Education*, 74: 5–12.

This article summarizes the transformation theory of adult learning and explains the relationship of transformative learning to autonomous thinking.

Oosterheert, I.E. and Vermunt, J.D. (2001) Individual differences in learning to teach: relating cognition, regulation and affect. *Learning and Instruction*, 11(2): 133–56.

The study describes individual differences in learning to teach. Secondary student teachers were interviewed about several components of their learning: mental models of learning to teach; learning activities; regulation in general; emotional regulation in particular; ideal self as a teacher; and concerns.

Shulman, L.S. (1987) Knowledge and teaching: foundations of the new reform. *Harvard Educational Review*, 57(1): 1–23.

Shulman responds to four questions: What are the sources of the knowledge base for teaching? In what terms can these sources be conceptualized? What are the processes of pedagogical reasoning and action? And what are the implications for teaching policy and educational reform?

4

THE SELF-REGULATION OF PROFESSIONAL LEARNING – THE PROFESSIONAL LEARNING AGENDA

Having read this chapter, you should have an understanding:

- of enquiry and interpretative thinking skills that will enable you to consider your role and professional expertise
- of how, through the application of a structured enquiry process, effective self-analysis and self-regulation awareness can be initiated and developed
- of the application of the professional learning agenda's enquiry and generative processes that enable you to bring theorizing and practical insights to your teaching role
- that being unsure and uncertain about the how and what of teaching provides triggers for the creation of an effective professional response plan
- of how focused professional learning activities with mentors, peers or colleagues can extend knowledge of both learning content and pedagogy.

Introduction

The professional learning agenda (PLA) offers a systematic, challenging and meaning-making framework for identifying and guiding your understanding of the relevance and comprehensiveness of teacher-learner professional learning about '*what* and *how* to teach'. It is presented in this book both as a range of enquiry questions to help you to interpret and understand your involvement in the complexities of the teaching and learning environment, and as a pro-forma that will help you to systematize the critical review processes inherent in the development of a teaching consciousness.

A rationale follows, with a reasoning, both practical and theoretical, that underpins the creation of this particular approach to managing a stream of evolving teaching consciousness that supports and captures your professional learning. The introduction begins with an exploration of the need for this strategic response. The PLA provides the form and structure that will support and guide your understanding. The following chapters, 5 and 6, identify and explain, in detail, the practical application of the PLA strategy. You are likely to continually move among the concepts of these three chapters as you come to a comprehensive understanding of what this approach is about and its potential value for you in understanding and creating a role for yourself in the complexities of the teaching and learning process. It is hoped that you will also acquire a sense of 'I have read something about this before', which will prompt you to go forwards and backwards through the book, gaining further clarification. This section is not provided as text that is read from cover to cover, as a sequenced story might be. Rather, it provides a responsive set of explanations that, at various times, will trigger your inquisitiveness and challenge you to go back to these chapters. As you find the specific explanation where an idea is first created, an instance of dissonance in what you thought you knew about a particular element of your professional learning may occur, as you interact with this section. It is intended that these instances of uncertainty will require you to work at understanding these disruptions and to resolve the challenges. So use and try out the ideas in these chapters to develop your unique understandings and strategies for creating you as a confident, comfortable and inquisitive teacher-learner.

CONTRIBUTING IDEAS 4.1

In building ideas about a set of new processes, progress comes from challenging earlier understandings.

A rationale for acquiring a personal professional learning strategy

The professional learning agenda format and process presented in these chapters is a comprehensive, analytical and generative learning tool. It allows the learner-researcher to focus on: (i) teaching and learning issues and skills which require further clarification for understanding and application, and (ii) professional attributes which seem to be adequate for purpose but which could be enhanced. As a teacher-learner, you should be cognizant that your professional learning analyses and responses do not necessarily focus only on areas of your planning, teaching and assessing that have been identified as needing attention. You should also be aware of the 'areas of relative strength' that you are bringing to the teaching and learning process. The identification of these professional strengths enables professional learning to be balanced, maintained and enhanced by critical analysis and interpretation, and, subsequently the creation of alternative learning responses to challenge your evolving expertise and the learning of your student group. Further success will become evident from the planning and implementation of these teaching strengths in your teaching programmes for your class group. It will tend to also include a variety of 'not so sure about *this* at this stage' areas of teaching or pedagogical skill development. This dual emphasis not only enables a detailed description of the learning behaviour/skill that is perceived by you as a 'next step' in the sequencing of understanding and response, but also details the critical review process which requires the interrogation, interpretation and synthesis processes that you will apply to an incident/behaviour/event, so as to establish the specific initiating foci for engaging your professional learning.

CONTRIBUTING IDEAS 4.2

A dual focus on your teaching strengths and those teaching and learning aspects that you are 'not so sure about', directs your next professional learning steps.

The PLA process involves a series of enquiry, explanatory, theorizing and creative stages. The PLA pro-forma is a conceptualizing framework for initiating, generating and monitoring changes as they are introduced and explored within your evolving and oft times tentative knowledge and expertise. The generative characteristic of this learning process is the synthesizing of your reviewed interpretations and understandings, and the creation of teaching and learning responses to be added to the teaching programme and subsequently monitored for current effectiveness and possible future enhancement.

Your PLA learning process is challenged and extended over time with increasing intent, purpose and sophistication. Some teaching issues, concerns and behaviours that have been isolated as professional learning initiatives from identified teaching and learning episodes, may be revisited as they trigger further uncertainty because of varying learning environment conditions. A need for a more purposeful and intellectual clarification of the intent and development of your original response will also become evident.

For example, a general intention, 'focus on questioning', becomes more specific and useful if stated as a 'focus on the level of cognitive demand' or 'adapting questioning sequences to promote enquiry processes', and so enables a clarity of pedagogical purpose and response.

This potential re-conceptualization provides for continuing regeneration and application, as the professional learning agenda takes on a more detailed and sophisticated form. It thereby provides a representation of the quality and extent of the sometimes uncertain and tentative nature of the professional learning journey. This depiction within your PLA pro-forma assumes an unfolding of the 'meaning making' and focused teaching and learning responses over time. It is one of the underlying principles that will make the PLA work for the enhancement of your knowledge and understanding, as it shows evidence of how you have attended to such issues in the past. It is considered crucial that this continual opening up of practical and theoretical understandings and reactions is seen as a positive consolidation of on-going professional learning and frees up any negative hindrance or blocking of such development.

The pro-forma of the PLA provides a vehicle for you to record your developing awareness of the critical review and action research processes as you come to understand why you have planned and taught for the class group in these particular ways. What did you plan as content for the series of lessons? How did you decide on the sequencing of content for this group of learners? How effective were these episodes of learning activities in advancing their knowledge and skills? And then, how relevant and effective was the teaching strategy or skill that was used? So, this is you, focusing on your actions of teaching as well as the outcomes that were achieved or in transition through your planned and implemented teaching programme.

CONTRIBUTING IDEAS 4.3

Using the PLA process is a positive experience. It reveals successful and any negative elements and their resolution through on-going professional development.

Using this approach, you will appear to be operating in parallel universes where you will be continually looking over your own shoulder, rather than relying only on the observations of a mentor or informed other when they are available. You are reinforcing the professional state of your evolving inquisitive self.

Teacher-learners have reported in research interviews that initially they hear and respond to the immediate input of mentors or 'informed others' as they create responses that they intend to introduce into their teaching programme (Zanting et al., 2001; Hobson, 2002). Then later, this verbalized guidance, together with their own tentative explanations and explorations, becomes the 'inner voice' that enables them to challenge their actions that ensued during the teaching episode. They are, in a sense, raising their attentiveness and focused consciousness of what is happening in lesson sequences as an outcome of their planning, teaching and managing.

Schön (1987) refers to the initial thinking response as 'reflection-on-practice', which enables a critical awareness of 'reflection-in-practice' to take place more regularly as confidence in the self-awareness process is intensified through focused implementation. The more often that you critically review, through analysis and interpretation, what has occurred in a taught lesson, the more effective this discriminating and modifying process can become, embedded within your actual delivery of the learning experience. The ability to think constructively on one's feet comes from being more penetrative of the surface conditions that exist in the lesson implementation, and enhances your ability to respond to unforeseen situations. You will also find that this preparedness in responding to anticipated problems or incidents that might occur and run counter to the flow of the learning sequence, increasingly becomes something you are able to attend to during the planning phase. In a sense, this is developing a responsive anticipatory set of your critical consciousness as a stage of planning and preparation in teaching and learning (Hunter, 1982).

It is discussed later how you can extend your conceptualization of what peers and colleagues are doing in their interactions with learners, and what you will need to initiate and extend your conceptual, theoretical and interpretative framework for becoming aware of the complexities of the teaching and learning process.

CONTRIBUTING IDEAS 4.4

An anticipatory set of critical consciousness can be developed through (i) attending to potential problems in the learning flow during planning, and (ii) thinking on your feet during lessons.

More explanation follows in the discussions and interpretations of examples of how teacher-learners, like you, might have developed this learning how to learn understanding (see, for example, the PLA examples that are worked on in Chapters 5 and 6). As you become more skilled at and insightful with the analyses and interpretations of your within-lesson and post-lesson reviews, you are becoming an inquisitive self. This state assumes a heightened awareness of how you are working with learners within lesson sequences. You are self-mentoring and self-regulating your professional work. You are becoming a more insightful and responsive self-mentor. You can do this mentoring stuff yourself!

What does the PLA process represent for you?

Developing professional learning partnerships with peers and colleagues can be very helpful in creating such understandings for you when the support and guidance from a designated mentor is not immediately available. More of these parallel interactions will be explored later. The PLA provides a written representation of your critical thinking aloud about:

- your focused and personal responses to the planning, teaching and assessing of initiatives and ideas
- new understandings as they emerge from self-assessment of your teaching
- professional learning initiatives that have been identified after self-observations or observations by, and discussions with, mentors, colleagues and peers.

So, the PLA accommodates your personally focused enquiry of your teaching role, but it is also able to include and respond to guiding ideas from others. Through this critical understanding process, self-regulating your learning of the what and how to teach, you are thereby learning how to learn professionally (see the double-helix model introduced in Chapter 2). It is very important for your continuing professional development that it is not exclusively related to the arranged observations and feed-forward guidance of other professionals. You are becoming a self-regulating teacher by assuming increasing executive control of your investigations, developing understandings of the theoretical and practical implications of your engagement of the teaching and learning process, and subsequent responses.

In this way, you are extending your critical awareness of:

- the significance of these analyses, interrogations, interpretations and focused responses to the complexities of the teaching and learning process
- the translation and transformation of this heightened understanding into the creation of effective classroom programmes.

Throughout, you will be drawing inspiration and knowledge of content organization and the relevant pedagogy, supported by the theoretical and practical experiences of the various learning environments of your teacher education programme, from either university or school settings.

The authority you bring to the enquiry's explanatory and creative phases of the PLA process will have gone beyond the provision of one-off or 'knee-jerk' responses, and will be founded in and connected to your evolving content and pedagogical knowledge bases (Shulman, 1986). You will become increasingly confident in the ever-expanding domains of knowledge and the scientific language of pedagogy inherent in professional learning enquiry. This confidence will enable you to articulate your understandings of the relevance for learners of a particular approach/strategy, and to bring theoretical and research authority to your developing expertise. If you are to move your professional learning along with growing experience, it is imperative that you can hold your own in education discussions of this nature as you use your widening understanding of the language of pedagogy and enquiry to provide both practical and theoretical relevance. This professional characteristic – being able to refer succinctly and with referenced authority to the theoretical and practical principles, and giving examples of an educational issue raised – is most important during employment or higher position interview situations. In informal follow-up discussions with teacher-learners who continued to use the PLA professional learning process in the early years of teaching, it was found that their enquiry, interpretive and generative cognitive understandings have made them more confident in responding to questions from examiners or interviewers in professional career-changing situations.

CONTRIBUTING IDEAS 4.5

In understanding the language of pedagogy and enquiry, you are able to describe to others the practical and theoretical relevance of what you do in teaching, including in career progression settings.

The PLA's enquiry and generative processes, thereby, enable you to bring a theorizing and practical awareness to your understanding of what you are contributing to the teaching and learning interactions in the classroom. Operating in a parallel frame to these practical – and what seems an immediate need for – teaching and learning responses, the intellectual processes being used in this clarifying process will enable you to become increasingly aware of your own learning processes in initiating and generating professional development responses. You are raising your teaching consciousness.

Within a short time of initiating these enquiry and creative approaches, you will find that you are feeling much more comfortable in assuming more direct control of the analysis and interpretations of your planning and teaching behaviour, and the resultant planned responses. The interpretive and generative cognitive frameworks that you are tentatively articulating, at first, will lead to further enhancement of your teaching and learning expertise and to the quality of the learning programmes that you develop for your students. You will grow increasingly confident in your abilities to attend to a teaching and learning incident or episode and to isolate an enquiry focus, as a professional learning initiative (PLI). This initiative provides the beginning focus of your PLA enquiry and synthesis, and enables you to gain relevant insights and understandings through focused interrogation and interpretation.

Your use of higher-order cognitive skills, such as predicting, analysing, evaluating, synthesizing and creating, will make it much easier to develop, apply and engage these processes more frequently. So, even in the early stages of using the PLA's cognitive framework and the associated questioning to comprehend the antecedent and contextual influences of a particular teaching behaviour or its subsequent clarification, the generation of potential curriculum or teaching responses will come more easily to you and become more focused with regular application.

Feeling unsure and uncertain about how and what you will develop in response to particular incidents will recede through having available a plan of response, couched in the language of professional learning. It is very much a cause-and-effect process where the quality and usefulness of an effective response is highly dependent on a commitment to an educationally scientific strategy to overcome the dissonance that might be evident in a troublesome, uncertain teaching and learning situation. A teaching concern about the seemingly inappropriate and inadequate learner responses to your planned teaching programmes does not just go away. It needs to be challenged and to attract the strategies of your evolving professional intellect. If you don't already have a productive professional learning approach to guide your efforts in developing a comprehensive, committed, confident and controlled awareness of how you are becoming an effective teacher-learner, the professional learning agenda will reward your study, trial and evaluation.

The example PLA formats, in general, show that it is your responsibility to identify the particular initiative, idea or behaviour to be focused on; to provide practical and/or theoretical content and contexts; and then to create potential responses that you can introduce into your teaching behaviours. Initially, when using the associated enquiry and interpretative thinking skills of the PLA, you might find that only one potential response comes to mind. This may be fine at an early stage of your developing teacher expertise, but continue to seek possible alternative ways of responding to the perceived need of the identified initiative, isolated from the incident or episode, so that the trialling and evaluating of these other ways will not only add to the range of your teacher expertise but will also further refine your enquiry and generative techniques. You will be enhancing the higher-order cognitive processing that will encourage you to look more deeply into your role, and will be developing knowledge and pedagogical characteristics that you will use later in your professional development to encourage the same attitudes and skills in teachers who follow you.

CONTRIBUTING IDEAS 4.6

Using the associated enquiry and interpretative thinking skills of the PLA, this higher-order cognitive processing will allow you to look more deeply into your role and further your professional expertise.

Throughout this professional learning process, although you will continue to be challenged by teaching and learning encounters in the classroom and school, you will be confident that the new control that you have over your development is well founded in both theoretical and practical domains. Teachers are more than the practice they demonstrate in working effectively in well-managed, focused learning environments. They are inquisitive and are able to self-regulate their contributions to these settings. As they tend to work for long periods of the day without the company of other teachers, they need to become self-sufficient in initiating, maintaining and monitoring their own work through effective self-analysis. The learning processes and products of a PLA-type professional development process provide the vehicle for creating this self-regulation.

Developing awareness and control through focused support

So, what will you need to do to accomplish this awareness and control in learning the what and how to teach processes?

You will need to regularly monitor your emerging content and pedagogical knowledge, understanding and actions within the guided and collegial support frameworks provided by school- and university-based teaching personnel. As well as working collaboratively with these mentors, consider looking for similar involvement with a peer or colleague, that is, another teacher-learner, so that you both engage with this enquiry and generative professional learning process. If you can initiate and develop a collegial, enquiry-based professional learning partnership, then common concerns that you each articulate about your particular engagements with learners can be observed, critically examined and supported. This will encourage both of you to develop attributes of knowledge and understanding and enquiry-guided questioning sequences of the informed other in a mentor-like relationship. The sometimes naïve, clarifying questions that might be asked by a peer or colleague can become the triggers for challenging your critical interrogation and interpretation of the teaching and learning incident or encounter. This assists the careful articulation of the professional learning initiative to which you are endeavouring to respond. It is also an informed other who knows the process that you are trying to implement, even though they might not be considered as a content or pedagogic expert and may be a little short in offering alternative ideas or strategies. It is asking the sets of questions associated with each stage of the professional learning agenda that is significant here, rather than knowing the correct answers to the questions. As neophyte teachers are allocated non-contact time for professional development activities, these collaborative observations and discussions could be timetabled on a regular basis. It is not necessary for such a colleague or peer relationship to be formed within a specific key stage of the primary or secondary curriculum. The enquiry, with its interpretative and responsive processes, will be the common point of professional interest and appropriate to sharing by teacher-learners whether they are involved in primary or secondary education. The colleague or peer who brings a detailed knowledge and understanding of another phase of the general curriculum, or even another subject content area, to the critical analyses and feed-forward discussions after observations will provide another relevant curriculum perspective, be it content or pedagogical. For example, in secondary school, the collaborative working relationship between language and science subject specialists would provide the opportunity for subject-specific pedagogy to be questioned, clarified and possibly exchanged. Similarly, an early years teacher being a colleague of a Key Stage 2 teacher will provide the added advantage of being able to consider the sequencing of content and skills for learners as they spiral across the intervening years. Would it also be profitable for Key Stage 2 and 3 teachers to develop partnerships in this way? Is it worth trying?

CONTRIBUTING IDEAS 4.7

Learning what and how to teach can benefit from collaborative working with mentors and teacher-learner colleagues, sharing in the enquiry and generative professional learning processes.

Name:

Date	WHAT? Professional Learning Initiative (PLI)	WHY?	HOW and WHEN?	Progress reviewed and re-generated - update	Consider linking to any external criteria
	Identify your focus teaching skill or behaviour. Be specific. Consider the antecedent and contextual conditions that influence this specific PLI. See example in Figure 5.1	Explore the significance of this PLI for your own professional learning as well as its effectiveness for students' learning; include possible theoretical, research and practical relevance as drawn from your programme-based studies.	How: Detail process and strategies to be introduced into your teaching repertoire and the students' learning programme. (Be prepared to identify and trial a number of planned responses to achieve an effective way to apply these). When: When will these actions be programmed?	Your responses to the PLI are monitored, evaluated and adapted as required. Identify the sequence of lessons where it would be most appropriate to introduce newly shaped responses and when this will be undertaken. It will be necessary to undertake a sequence of updates as the PLI is reviewed at various times.	For example, Teachers' Standards (England). Identify a standard/criterion that 'best' fits with this initiative. Better to focus on just one.

Figure 4.1 The professional learning agenda pro-forma and column headings explained

Note: The template for this pro-forma is available at ***https://study.sagepub.com/lange***

Many patterns of partnerships for colleagues and peers can be explored as a professional learning process that is established through the enquiry-oriented skills that are being developed. Chapter 5, and then later Chapter 6, explore in more detail the components and strategies of the PLA as an example of a self-regulating process that you can use to identify how you are progressing in professional development about learning to be a teacher.

The PLA pro-forma in Figure 4.1 shows the enquiry cell phases that are associated with the identification, critical review and generative features of a professional learning initiative. Remember, the PLI is the professional learning focus that is extracted from the teaching and learning episodes that you identified as needing attention or continuing development within your teaching and learning process.

What follows is a clarification of each of these phases with associated questioning sequences that can be used to complete them. You will find it useful to continue to review the above pro-forma as you read the following descriptions to aid your understanding of its effective application. In Chapters 5 and 6, we will continue to revisit these clarifications of the cell phases as we interpret and interrogate the teacher-learners' PLA examples, where Bennie, Ayisha and Mike endeavour to build their professional awareness and knowledge.

Using the professional learning agenda pro-forma cells

DATE

This is the date you first decided that you would focus on a particular professional learning initiative. This dated entry will be a useful point of reference when you later review the occasions and teaching and learning contexts where you have organized creative responses to the PLI and incorporated them into your subsequent planning and teaching.

WHAT

'What' is the professional learning initiative that you wish to examine. This can be an idea, skill or resource inherent in a teaching and learning incident or episode; a facet of classroom management or organization; the observation of a specific response from a student, or students, that you did not understand; a 'new' teaching strategy or skill that you want to introduce into your repertoire; a procedure for monitoring students' learning that you feel needs your focused attention, etc. It may be a perplexing issue for you or others. It could just as easily be a behaviour, skill or approach to teaching and learning that you feel you are having success with and want to improve even further; or a perceived 'inadequacy or problem' that needs monitoring with modifications for improving its function or purpose. So, basically, it can be any professional learning initiative that you have identi-fied through the interrogation of incidents in your teaching and learning process, or which may have been raised in feed-forward discussions with mentors or a colleague after an observation and feed-forward session. The term 'feed-forward' is preferred in this book to the more common 'feed-back', as there is a definite intention to move the professional learning response forward to a stage of greater complexity and sophistication, and so enhanced understanding.

Remember that the focus of your 'critical analysis, interpretation and creative response' needs to be specific in its initial description. Your profes-sional learning will be more directed and useful if you target the sub-skills rather than a general clustering of behaviours. For example, instead of identifying and critically reviewing an initiative such as 'develop my ques-tioning skills', it will be most helpful in this self-regulating exercise to focus more specifically on a series of sub-sets of the questioning process – for instance, 'Developing questions to initiate a focused discussion' or 'Developing questioning to promote higher-order thinking by the stu-dents'. In this form, it will provide a more specific professional learning experience for you to engage with. Similarly, 'constructing questions that lead the children through the plenary of their learning session' might also flow from your initial investigation and teaching and learning responses. So, it will be more effective for your critical review if initiatives are identified and considered individually.

Later, you might find that further initiatives will come from this 'ques-tioning domain', as you consider questions that provide 'the structure for the students' concept development', as they come to understand a concept in maths, such as number; or history, such as causality; or geography, such as spatial awareness, and so on. More of this discussion is provided in Chapter 7.

It is important that you 'seek out' the specific facet of your teaching behaviour (or, for that matter, the students' learning behaviour) that is of immediate concern, and then be attentive to how other initiatives will later flow logically from this foundational initiative. All of these professional learning pathways, through critical analyses, interpretation and synthesiz-ing responses, will be significant to your growing teacher expertise. Specifically, these ensuing processes will enhance your personal learning how to learn strategy. As proposed in the model of the double helix of the interlocking and interactive nature of professional learning (discussed in Chapter 2), both the strands of substantive and syntactic orientations will be interlaced and enhanced through your developmental strategy.

This occurs as you move from identifying the PLI to establishing and extending the PLA and providing a creative curriculum or teaching response that can be tentatively introduced into your substantive orientation.

In the context of working directly in the classroom's professional learning environment, it is necessary for these professional learning initiatives to be identified through your self-assessments and critical reviews, though some will enter the critical review through observation and the subsequent 'feed-forward' sessions engaged with colleagues, peers and mentors. It is important that this 'new' professional learning initiative is attended to as soon as practical after such interactions and professional inputs. If it is a concern or a challenge that needs to be responded to, then starting the enquiry process sooner rather than later is a great idea. Make time available at the end of a targeted lesson or at the end of that school day (or, preferably, at your next coffee break) to activate your professional learning analysis, and so seek focused initiatives to guide your continuing professional learning. If you have made brief, Post-it notes on any incident, on the fly, that have challenged you, either positively or negatively, then these will be helpful to focus your later reviews.

We emphasize that the identification of professional learning initiatives should not be restricted to areas of concern or challenge. For the advancement of your professional learning, it may be significant to focus on a skill, technique or idea that will add to the diversity and quality of your planning and teaching repertoire. The development of your relative strengths in responding to the curriculum content, pedagogy and learners' issues will extend the control and confidence that you are creating through your successful involvement in the teaching and learning process (Macintosh & Smith, 1974).

It is important to have a balanced perspective on guiding and enhancing your evolving abilities as a teacher-learner. Concentrating only on the 'not so good' or negative aspects of your role can be stressful, so now is the time to celebrate what is going right for you, and to see how these effective teaching behaviours and strategies can be enhanced and more widely applied in other teaching and learning situations.

Bringing an equilibrium of intent to your critical review and response to your teaching was discussed in the five-phase (REACT) self-monitoring of teaching process in Chapter 3. The identification and celebration of successful processes and outcomes are seen to be just as important for on-going development as the detailing of areas and skills that need attention.

The following are potential enquiry-focused questions to be considered when isolating the characteristics of the professional learning initiative:

- What is the initiative or issue that is specifically identified for attention within a teaching and learning episode?
- Is it part of a cluster of teacher skills or behaviours that will need to be broken down into their constituent parts? If so, what are these? Do these attributes or constituents happen in a particular sequence? If there are pre-requisites, what are they?
- Now that I have articulated these components, is there one that provides the foundation for the sequence of skills or behaviours in the cluster of strategies? How might I decide the order in which I engage these as professional learning initiatives as part of my professional learning?
- What can now be identified as associated skills or behaviours that may become potential professional learning initiatives? So, a mini-programme of initiatives that provides an articulation of the sequence or series of sub-skills, etc., can be formulated. What needs initial attention and can be immediately responded to?

The professional learning initiative you select needs to be specific so that a detailed and relevant analysis and subsequent response can be formulated and implemented. Attention to the constituent parts will enable all facets to be analysed individually, with the later purpose of synthesizing this collection into a more general understanding and application. Be specific and detailed to aid the clarity and extent of your critical analysis, interrogation, interpretation and generative responses.

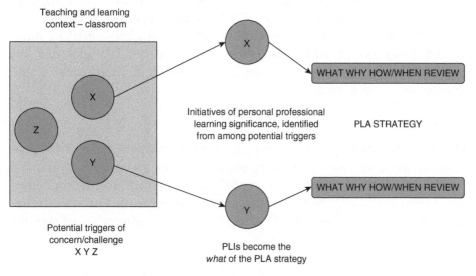

Figure 4.2 Identifying PLIs from a teaching and learning episode

Step 1

A challenging incident that occurred during your teaching and learning process is identified and analysed. It may be relevant to teacher or learner behaviour. It is a disruptor to the normal flow of the scope and sequence of the lesson. It may have produced a negative or even a positive outcome for the teacher and the learners. You may not be able to reach a satisfactory conclusion or treatment of the incident in the immediate context but you will note briefly the uncertainty or positive feedback that you experienced. You will recall that the self-monitoring strategy identified in Chapter 3 provided ways of identifying and considering such incidents.

Step 2

A later critical analysis of the identified incident to isolate a single or cluster of professional learning initiatives (PLIs = 'the *whats*') is then carried out. This then becomes the immediate focus for the critical analysis, interrogation and creativity for development of the PLA strategy – though if you have identified a collective of initiatives, you will need to order and prioritize the PLA treatment.

Step 3

The professional learning initiatives that have been stated are then treated separately, through reasoning, creative and monitoring procedures of the strategy. It is proposed that each PLI becomes theoretically and practically situated (the *whys*) and will generate a number of potential teaching and learning responses (*hows* and *whens*) in the following cell stage. (Note: It is conceivable that a single behavioural (teacher or student) incident could initiate a number of professional learning initiatives. It is possible but unlikely that only one *how* response will enable the desired teaching and learning outcome to be achieved.)

Step 4

This is the monitoring, review and continuing treatment stage of the professional learning process. It is important that you use self-assessment so that feed-forward comments and modifications can be included in subsequent teaching plans. (Note: This too is a cycling-forward process, rather than a cycling-within learning process that risks finishing where it starts!)

WHY

Why is this an initiative that you need to focus on? The answer should *not* be that it is a requirement of a university- or school-based unit of study.

Yes, you will need to consider such directions, but not as initiatives for your PLA that are specific to your personal professional development. You may find that sub-sets of attributes of such tasks could be appropriate to you, so might be included in the PLA enquiry process, after you have applied these in learning sequences.

These enquiry and analysis foci enable you to relate, in a seamless manner, the theoretical and practical perspectives that you intend to bring to the professional learning process of the initiative. This is the professional learning time when you are unpacking the contextual and antecedent conditions and influences of the initiative and finding a place for it within the theoretical and practical aspects of the teaching and learning process, as is relevant to your role.

A questioning sequence that might support this phase of the enquiry process where 'I'm seeking information relative to the identified professional learning initiative' could include:

- How do I get 'beneath the surface' of this initiative, so that I'm better placed to respond in a meaningful way?
- How can I relate the practical phase of this initiative to a research and theoretical understanding of the practical application?
- Now that I have been able to isolate the specific nature of this initiative, how do I place it back in its context of a planned teaching episode?
- What could be identified as the antecedent or current contextual conditions and influences of the identified professional learning initiative? What information needs to be gathered to provide this contextual awareness?
- How can my critical analysis be directed to identifying these influences, individually and collectively? Could my critical analysis, interrogating, interpreting and theorizing clarify these influences and contextual factors, as effective starting points?
- How do I collect, categorize and make inferences from the information I have collected? Do I need to construct and conceptualize this in tabular or concept-web format? How do I organize this information for ease of understanding and interpretation?
- Which of these actions will make for a clearer perception of the inter-relatedness of the attributes of this PLI?
- Once I have produced a cluster map of these attributes, will I be able to make an informed decision on what changes, or modifications, I need to develop? Or, do I need to complete a search of the theoretical literature for advice?
- Should I also review my knowledge and understanding of units of study that have been provided in the academic component of my programme?
- Could I identify a school colleague who has knowledge and expertise in this area of the curriculum or pedagogy?

It is questioning of this nature that first identifies that a plan of action for deepening knowledge, understanding and application needs to be initiated, and, second, a suggested line of enquiry that may guide this aspect of professional learning.

The processes described above consider the significance of the initiative for your personal professional learning, as well as ways of enhancing the effectiveness of your responses for your planning and subsequent activities for students' learning. Don't forget the importance of making summarized references to associated theory and research that might also be relevant to yours and others' understanding of the importance of the selected initiative. Such references with examples will be very helpful when later you may need to offer justifications for the manner and substance of your responses, as you engage in periodic reviews by informed others or supervising personnel.

HOW

How will the responsive learning activities be structured and resourced? At this point in the enquiry, the interpretative and generative process of the professional learning agenda is directly related to the synthesizing of collected information about the PLI, and so provides for the generation of potential strategic responses. It details the processes and strategies to be introduced into your planning and teaching repertoire, and the subsequent learning programme for the students as your direct responses to the identified initiative.

This is the stage where you need to formulate a number of potential responses to the professional learning initiative that has been clarified in both intent and purpose through your consideration of the enquiry questions. These questions are associated with the *what*, of the specific definition of the skill, behaviour or idea, that you see a need to attend to; and with the *why*, as a detailed analysis of the context of the initiative with reference to its practical and theoretical representation. At the end of these phases, you will be sure of what needs to become a focus of your continuing professional learning.

Now that the focused intent of your learning has been established, it is appropriate to decide on the range of potential strategies, which will also involve content and processes from the relevant curriculum domain, for responding to the initiative.

How will you translate your critical analyses and interpretations into actual teaching and learning actions? In the initial stages of this generative process, it is likely that only one possible solution for action will be identified for implementation and, subsequently, for the monitoring of relevance and effectiveness. As you become more comfortable and sure of your ability to control and guide your self-evaluative processes through the associated skills of interpreting, synthesizing and predicting, you will find it much easier to extend the range of options that can be identified as likely pedagogical solutions to your professional learning initiative. Being able to select from a range of potential teaching and learning solutions will provide you with the flexibility to initiate learning processes that seem to best fit the learning environment as you perceive or anticipate it. Because of what you now see as the changing nature of the learning environment, and the monitoring of how the learners are responding to what has been anticipated, this action is perceived as the most relevant strategy at this time and in this context.

At this theorizing and generative stage of selection of the most effective range of strategic responses, you also need to anticipate what might be the likely consequences of your action. In a sense, you are trialling a particular approach but are also cognizant of your reasoning for this selection, and foreseeing the elements in the strategy that might inhibit or extend the learning and involvement that you intended. You are employing a process of critical analysis before the action is engaged so that you are better prepared to respond to possible changes during the implementation if or when they occur. Your review, in the planning phase, your intended planning and subsequent teaching processes may provide a number of options for you.

You have become more adaptable in your teaching as you focus on the nuances of the learners' attention as they work to relate their prior learning to what they are now experiencing. The more effective you become at interrogating and interpreting in your preparation for teaching, the more attentive you become, and so are able to change or modify both the content and the strategies of the learning experience on the run. Thereby, you are becoming more attentive to the nature of the curriculum content and processes and the ways that learners are engaging with your informed, created activities and associated programmes. These preparation and planning strategies will be revisited in a later section where the organization of content and the pedagogy of the taught curriculum are explored (see Chapter 7 on planning and preparation for effective teaching and learning).

A questioning sequence that might support this generative phase of the enquiry process initially could include:

- What has been presented in the subject-content and pedagogy university-based courses that consider this issue?
- What library and internet information bases are available? (You could start with the identified ideas associated with the initiative and then see

if they are matched with research descriptors in journal citation indexes. Or, googling of relevant words/phrases may provide a starting list of possible references that will require a critical sorting process for relevance and application.)

- Are there personnel in the school who have identified expertise in this curriculum content, pedagogy or behaviour area?
- What would I need to have planned before I approach these colleagues? The careful detailing of the issue – why it is significant to my teaching approach and what I have found out that is relevant so far. (It is important that you are seen as a well-prepared professional who has already initiated some knowledge and understanding of the issue, and is now seeking clarification and guidance for the direction of further inquiries.)
- When should I make contact with specialist personnel? By being partly prepared, you present yourself as a teacher-learner who accepts continuing responsibility for your personal professional development but is confident in seeking knowledge and understanding from others.
- Having identified and reviewed possible strategies as 'fit for my purpose' in responding to the professional learning initiative, it is time for their implementation and monitoring. Which strategy will be initially introduced into your teaching programme? Are there pre-requisite knowledge and skills that the learners will require before its introduction? The careful articulation of how this new learning will be added to what is already understood by these learners is important. How will the other associated strategies be prioritized and prepared for introduction into the teaching and learning plans?
- How will I monitor and assess the introduction of this curricula and teaching response into my planning and teaching? It will require a careful analysis of this key lesson. This critical review process needs to be engaged as soon as possible after the teaching of the lesson.

WHEN

When will your developed learning experiences be introduced into the teaching and learning programme? As a sub-phase of the *how* cell on the PLA pro-forma, this focus provides a reference to when you will introduce the strategic curriculum and teaching responses that you have formulated in response to the PLI into your teaching and learning programme. Include a specified time frame within which you will achieve this initiative objective. Your proposed responses to the identified professional learning initiatives may be planned over many episodes of practice. This is included in the *how* of the planning and teaching phases.

Progress reviewed and regenerated – update

After each occasion that you have implemented a strategic response to the PLI within your planning and teaching, it will be necessary to evaluate its effectiveness in meeting your purposes. Your evaluative comments should be recorded together with any consideration of possible changes to that specific trialled response, and with an indication about possible modification that might be introduced to make these new strategies significant for your evolving teacher expertise. You recognize that you may not always have total or immediate success with strategies that you bring into your teaching repertoire. Research into the change processes associated with the introduction of a new teaching strategy or skill found that with many practices, if a complex teaching model is being considered, perhaps ten trials or more need to be undertaken before executive control of the implementation process is achieved by the teacher-learner. So, practice might make perfect, but it is as you bring this practice to your teaching and learning environment, on many occasions, that you are grounding or building from it each time (Joyce & Showers, 2002). Become comfortable with repeated implementation with focused critical analyses and interpretations, and assessments will make perfect.

Development during this professional learning process is recognition that meaningful learning is being achieved by moving on from an initial stage of confusion or cognitive dissonance. It is not a problem if you are unsure in the early stages of the implementation of a new strategy, but through your focus on the development and execution of enquiry-based, theorizing and generative strategies you can resolve such uncertainty (Lange & Burroughs-Lange, 1994).

It can become very stressful and disheartening if a successful resolution is not easily achieved. So, the collection and enhancement of strategies for coming to understand your concerns is very necessary in the early stages of your professional learning. Work with the PLA structure and the collected questions can take some of this uncertainty and related stress out of your work in the classroom. Teaching is a time-consuming, mentally and physically demanding profession, so work clever and use conceptual frameworks that will make your time in school easier to understand and direct.

Connecting with external criteria

The attributes of a successful neophyte teacher are the 'Teachers' Standards' in the UK education system, while in the Australian context, for example, they are identified in the National Professional Standards for Teachers (ITSL).

At various times during your teacher-learner early years on the job, you are required to be evaluated against the statutory requirements of the employing bodies. You will find that if your critical analyses and interpretations of your on-going practice make reference to these in your PLA, you will be better placed to answer questions from supervisors regarding your awareness of and engagement with these standards. Endeavour to identify the standard, or criterion, that best links to a particular professional learning initiative, rather than simply listing the broad standards or criteria. Providing a long list of possible and tangential criteria for your PLI can be confusing and does not demonstrate how you are becoming specific and focused in your professional learning. The starting point is your learning initiative within the personal professional learning agenda that you are constructing. This provides a guide to your awareness of the role that you have in responding to very complex teaching and learning environments. You are seeing how the standards/criteria relate to your work in the classroom and school learning environments, rather than being constrained or driven by these external elements.

Those who have responsibility for the structure and implementation of teacher preparation courses are required to be aware of these external standards of the profession and would have embedded these teacher abilities within the various content and pedagogical strands and units of study of their programme. Therefore, you are more than likely to have developed some initial insights from encounters with your course/programme components. You can expect university and school teaching personnel to also be using such preferred pedagogy in their interactions with your professional learning.

An enquiry-based, interpretative and generative strategy for understanding and reviewing personal, professional learning

Earlier in this section, a blank PLA pro-forma was presented which provided a ready reference to the cell phase descriptions that followed. The following example (pp. 120–1) and others in later chapters will help you clarify the meaning and interpretation of how each of these enquiry-based phases of the analysis and development of the professional learning initiative can be undertaken. They indicate how you, the teacher-learner, may focus on and direct your enquiry, and so generate potential but tentative teaching and management responses, for possible inclusion in your teaching programmes and to form part of your skill repertoire. Questions and discussion elaborate these examples, providing further clarification of the initial and consolidated strategy responses of a teacher-learner. This has been a brief look now at what will provide our learning focus in the following chapters, as we consider the professional learning of Bennie, Ayisha, Mike and others.

Figure 4.3 is an example from Patrick, which includes his response to components of his professional learning using the professional learning agenda cell phases as detailed above.

This is an example of how a teacher-learner, such as you, attempted to initiate a critical review of elements of his evolving professional learning. Note that examples used in this book are presented as illustrative material of work in progress, and are not included as exemplars of a finished professional learning process. Read these thoughtfully and critically, as a way of introducing yourself to thinking about how professional awareness may be initiated in the PLA environment.

CHAPTER SUMMARY

So far, in Chapters 1 and 2, we have identified aspects of theoretical studies that have contributed to the formulation of two interdependent, specific strategies for exploring the conception and application of a personalized professional learning agenda for the teacher-learner. In Chapter 3, we introduced a self-monitoring five-phase REACT process for examining the planning, implementation and assessment of teaching. This was the first introduction of the professional learning focus, as related to the concept of an initiative. This chapter has introduced the self-regulating professional learning strategy of the PLA, which is triggered by the identification of a professional learning initiative extrapolated from a teaching incident you identified as being of interest for furthering your understanding and skills.

In the following chapters, 5 and 6, we review a step-by-step analysis of the processes and procedures that might be undertaken by the teacher-learner as you focus on a professional learning initiative. The work of Bennie, Ayisha, Mike and others are used here. These are realistic examples of teacher-learners' efforts, in critical analysis, interpretation and generation, and provide you with the opportunities to engage with another's efforts in preparation for undertaking these self-regulatory processes yourself. So, treat these as professional learning activities that will help you to further mediate and possibly trigger your evolving professional knowledge and understanding.

Date	WHAT? Professional Learning Initiative (PLI)	WHY?	HOW and WHEN?	Progress reviewed and re-generated - update	Consider linking to any external criteria
	Identify your focus teaching skill or behaviour. Be specific. Consider the antecedent and contextual conditions that influence this specific PLI. See example in Figure 5.1	Explore the significance of this PLI for your own professional learning as well as its effectiveness for students' learning: include possible theoretical, research and practical relevance as drawn from your programme-based studies.	How: Detail process and strategies to be introduced into your teaching repertoire and the students' learning programme. (Be prepared to identify and trial a number of planned responses to achieve an effective way to apply these). When: When will these actions be programmed?	Your responses to the PLI are monitored, evaluated and adapted as required. Identify the sequence of lessons where it would be most appropriate to introduce newly shaped responses and when this will be undertaken. It will be necessary to undertake a sequence of updates as the PLI is reviewed at various times.	For example, Teachers' Standards (England). Identify a standard/criterion that 'best' fits with this initiative. Better to focus on just one.
10 Oct	There is an identified need to differentiate my planning of content and learning processes by responding to the various ways that children learn best, such as: audio, visual, kinaesthetic, and how to effectively progress children's learning by attention to these characteristics	Bruner suggests that when learning a new concept it is relevant to frame the associated activities so that they include enactive, iconic and symbolic orientations. This needs to be kept in mind when planning learning activities, especially when introducing new attributes to the concept in building understanding on prior knowledge. It is important that each of the orientations is introduced through the sequencing of the learning experiences so that individual	HOW: Initially, there will be a need to focus my assessment processes on ascertaining the likely preferred learning orientation of each child in the class. This evaluative understanding will provide guidance in the planning of the scope and sequence of the learning programme to ensure that all learners will have access to the concepts and attributes of the curriculum. ALL learners need to engage with ALL activities. There will also be a need to consider the nature of the questioning strategies that will be used to stimulate, guide and assess the learning that is	The first occasion that this planning perspective was introduced, I observed that there was increased on-task activity by these young learners working with the range of learning activities. Learners were initially directly encouraged to move to the activities that I assessed as a best response to their preferred learning style but were encouraged to 'try' other tasks as well Initially, this has provided positive feedback for the	Teachers' Standard 2: Demonstrate knowledge and understanding of how pupils learn and how this impacts on teaching

Date	WHAT? Professional Learning Initiative (PLI)	WHY?	HOW and WHEN?	Progress reviewed and re-generated - update	Consider linking to any external criteria
		learning preferences are responded to. Therefore, there is a perceived need to include each of these orientations in the various activities of the scope and sequence of the planning process	achieved. For example, after introducing the early phases of this planning process, it may become clear that the plan should include a number of activities focusing on one of the orientations, e.g. 'enactive'. WHEN: On-going aspect of the planning and preparation process. A number of planning patterns will be trialled as my understanding of the right balance for this group of learners is developed. I intend that this will become a strength of my planning	planning process and I will continue to refine the scope and sequence	
14 Oct	Deploy support staff effectively. Improve the learning of the children by giving the support staff clear instructions as to what they should be doing at each stage of the lesson and which children I would like them to be focusing on	There is a need to maximize the use of adults in the classroom and to share teacher expectations with the support staff so that learners can be guided and extended at relevant points of the lesson, e.g. on the carpet, during the main activity or the plenary. At some points during the teaching, the assistant teacher sits and listens. This time could be better spent enhancing the teaching that is being provided so as to ensure the learners make progress in their knowledge and understanding	HOW: + Share the lesson plan, learning intention and success criteria in advance. Allow time for discussion and clarification + Give clear instructions on who to be working with at each stage of the lesson, and what questions to ask in order to support the children's learning. These questions to be provided in lesson plan + Be clear about the AT's responsibilities with particular groups of learners WHEN: On-going during this and subsequent school experience placements	Create a checklist of the tasks that should be engaged in to ensure that support staff have a clear and focused understanding of what is required in the TEAM	TS 8 Develop effective professional relationships with colleagues, knowing how and when to draw on advice and specialist support

Figure 4.3 Patrick's professional learning agenda

FURTHER READING

Feiman-Nemser, S. (2012) *Teachers as learners.* Cambridge, MA: Harvard Education Press.

This is a collection of essays focusing on teacher learning. Arguing that serious and sustained teacher learning is a necessary condition for ambitious student learning, the author examines how teachers acquire, generate and use knowledge about teaching during their careers.

Urban, M. (2008) Dealing with uncertainty: challenges and possibilities for the early childhood profession. *European Early Childhood Education Research Journal*, 16(2): 135–52.

This article argues that the prevailing conceptualization of the early childhood professional is constructed out of a particular, hierarchical mode of producing and applying expert knowledge that is not necessarily appropriate to professional practice in early childhood education. Drawing on the conceptual framework of hermeneutics, the article explores an alternative paradigm of a relational, systematic professionalism that embraces openness and uncertainty.

5

ADVANCING YOUR
PROFESSIONAL LEARNING

Having read this chapter, you will:

- become increasingly aware of the enquiry structure and the professional learning potential of the PLA process

- understand how you can refocus your engagement with professional learning and assume increasing control of this learning

- interpret and review the worked examples of teacher-learners' use and application of this strategy to conceptualize how the process can be targeted to meet your particular learning needs

- develop an appreciation of how your inquisitive self will continue to challenge your evolving tentative conceptual frameworks for determining your teaching role.

Introduction

In this chapter, you will find an example of the enquiry-focused professional learning agenda (PLA) pro-forma. This process and the pro-forma have become a well-used way for individuals to be able to self-regulate and further their own professional learning. With on-going practice, this becomes an increasingly meaningful structure. Worked examples in this chapter and the next show how the PLA can be used to guide and enhance your individualized approach to early and continuous professional learning. With refinement as you learn the intent and acquire the associated critical thinking skills, the strategy can be used to take control of personalized professional development now and throughout a teaching career.

In this chapter, at various times, we review a number of the concepts and associated enquiry processes that were included in Chapter 4. This further consideration of elements of earlier discussions will enable you to extend your developing professional understandings by placing their existence and application within varied conceptual and contextual learning settings. Continual re-aligning of personal awareness has become the case for the authors, and the teachers they've worked with, who, after many years of learning to teach, are still modifying and improving their personal approach to this professional learning process.

The PLA pro-forma provides structure to a process of defining the *what, why, how* and *when* of a professional learning initiative (PLI). It supports your initial focus on identifying a PLI from an incident/context, or series of teaching and learning encounters, within your teaching programme. The *what, why, how* and *when* prompt the questioning of a specific element of a PLI that you have identified from these critical reviews of your involvement in the teaching and learning process. The format initiates and captures your critically analysed responses to this identified initiative. The questions, presented and discussed in Chapter 4, are used to initiate these analysing, interpreting, interrogating and generating responses. It is in the pro-forma process that you are able to review these PLIs and their practical application. The responses you've generated are then reviewed and considered for integration into your on-going professional learning agenda and associated planning process.

The sets of questions identified in the cell phases are not intended to be definitive. They act as associated prompts for you to formulate your personal critical enquiry processes and generation of potential teaching skill outcomes. What is important to consider here is that the response to each of the PLA cell phase descriptions is comprehensive and relevant to critical enquiry within the contextual domains of your current knowledge and understanding. As you extend your knowledge and understanding of the theoretical, research and practical domains of the teaching and learning process, the PLA process will act as a pedagogical strategy enabling you to employ these in your teaching. It also demonstrates the potential for taking your understanding of professional awareness to another level of clarity and comprehensiveness. You will recall from Chapters 1 and 2 that this is a significant process in raising your level of teaching consciousness, as you develop effective theoretical and practical responses to the complexities of the teaching and learning contexts.

Organizing exploration and discussion within the PLA process

The example PLA was developed by Bennie, a teacher-learner, soon after her introduction to the PLA's pro-forma and the associated strategic enquiry processes. She had identified incidents in her teaching contexts that she felt called for developed understanding through critical analysis and the generation of potential content and pedagogical responses. It is more effective for your professional growth if similar incidents that are of concern are brought together into some generic initiatives.

To make effective use of these examples, first put yourself in Bennie's role as the PLA initiator. Focus your learning on the intention and purpose of the particular cell phases of the PLA. These 'cell purposes' are reproduced in the example as a reminder of the descriptions and explanations of use that were detailed in Chapter 4. Bennie's example also includes some clarifying comments about the cell phases as they are developed through her example. In this way, we are working through the example with you, and add our clarifying thoughts and suggestions as they seem appropriate.

To aid your understanding of how this professional learning process progresses, the example includes questioning comments from an 'informed other', to borrow a concept of 'expert support' from Vygotsky (1978: 86). These comments might equally be offered by a supportive mentor or, in collaborative professional learning situations, by a peer or colleague. The comments are there to encourage and support you in conceptualizing and contextualizing the initiative that you have isolated for review. You could consider these comments and questions of the informed other as coming from a more intellectually sophisticated you – your inquisitive self. You will recall that the functioning and critical involvement of your inquisitive self was introduced in Chapter 2. The contributions from informed others in the example are what you might soon be able to bring to the critical analysis and interpretation of your own professional learning.

As you read and interact with this and later examples, ask yourself why the teacher-learner has asked that particular question and then offered that clarifying comment. If you can focus on deepening your understanding of the intention and guidance offered by the informed other, you will be effectively reviewing the self-regulating processes that you can bring to your own, unaided, self-enquiry process. Working in this way, you become more skilful at focusing on those incidents within professional learning that are most relevant to your developing expertise. The initiatives that you identify from these incidents of the teaching and learning process will be isolated and re-constructed with an analytical and creative awareness that you can then bring to the self-regulating process.

This degree of sophisticated conceptualization can, in some ways, mirror what has been presented here as input from the perspective of the informed other. Through critical analysis, you have a way to become more informed about their inherent theoretical and practical influences, and to enhance your own knowledge and understanding of the complexities of the teaching and learning process.

The comments of the informed other are provided here as a way of demonstrating how your enquiry might be refined as you become more sophisticated in interrogating the professional learning initiatives that have been identified. You are, in a sense, becoming the 'informed other' as you take on a role of the inquisitive self in your own self-regulating professional learning processes. As you develop responses to your planning and teaching progress, so will your analytical and generative skills as a PLA user be enhanced. As you grow in seeking higher levels of teaching consciousness, you are internalizing the role of the informed other in bringing an increased inquisitiveness to the interrogation of the PLI and to generating additional potential initiatives. You are adding other levels of cognitive confidence and adaptability as an aware professional operating with purpose within a self-regulating professional learning agenda and processes.

In later examples, you may want to take the opportunity to initiate some supplementary feed-forward comments on the analyses and descriptions provided. Assuming the role of the inquisitive self in critically reviewing someone else's work will help to enhance your own understanding that the analyses and interpretation provided in the PLA enquiry process needs to be easily understood by a reviewer and, subsequently, by the teacher-learner themselves. It is important that you continue to introduce these dual perspectives into your articulation of your professional learning. You should be an analyser and creator of effective responses to your own ideas, as well as the reviewer of your own or someone else's professional thinking.

CONTRIBUTING IDEAS 5.1

Become an analyser, creator and reviewer of the theoretical and practical responses of your professional thinking.

More on using the PLA professional learning process

When this PLA process was earlier trialled and developed with teacher-learners, they found that if comments from the informed other or from their own reviews were inserted directly into their writing, in each phase cell of the pro-forma, it enabled more precise guidance of how their professional learning efforts could be further enhanced. The inserted comments focused their attention on the specific aspect of their analysis and interpretation that needed further clarification. You may find this approach effective when you are considering your descriptions, analyses and proposed changes in the PLA process, or if you are engaging in a supervisory relationship or inducting a mentor, peer or colleague into the 'critical friend' role. A critical friend or an inquisitive self is very relevant when you are reviewing the responses that you have entered in each of the PLA cell phases as you have engaged the critical analysis, interpretation and generative processes. In practice, you might also find it helpful to annotate directly into your text in that cell phase.

In clarifying the intent of each of the pro-forma cell phases in the following example, the informed other's comment has been provided in two forms: (1) a general comment in revisiting the purpose and process of the specific phase being examined – for example, a 'reminder to the reader about the purpose of the *what* cell in the PLA process'; (2) the anticipated comments that might have been made by you, the reviewer, about how you might provide critical analysis comments – for example, 'how an informed other or your inquisitive self might respond to Bennie'.

The clarifying and critical comments are presented in this way, to illustrate how an informed other might contribute to and further challenge the teacher-learner's enquiry findings and the subsequent resolution of the cell phase analysis.

The PLA process captured on the pro-forma provides a structured approach for focusing your enquiry process but can be implemented flexibly because of the varying levels of complexity and sophistication that could evolve in the sequencing of the enquiry-focusing questions. It is likely that in the initial stages of understanding the teaching and learning process, you will feel uncertain about many aspects. You need to accept this as a challenge that can be resolved through enhanced critical analysis and through interpretation of your own practice. There are always answers to what may seem difficult situations in classrooms. The contributing factors, contextual and antecedent influences just need to be identified and carefully sorted through, analysed and interpreted. During your initial trials of this self-focused critical awareness, you may not find the 'perfect' response to the PLI. You should view these intermediary responses as sound at that time but accept that further refinement and creativity will become evident as you develop these professional learning skills. By using the PLA process over time, not only will you enhance your syntactic skills (for learning *how* to learn) but you will also acquire the substantive knowledge (the *what* and *how* of teaching and learning) that brings practical relevance and application to your evolving ideas. It is essential that you anticipate your individual growth process within your professional learning agenda. You may want to refer back to Chapter 2 where the relevant model of teacher professional learning is considered.

The significance of what you record in the pro-forma cells will continue to develop in complexity and sophistication as the higher cognitive levels of the critical analysis process are acquired, applied and reviewed in many differing learning environments. The strength of knowing how to respond to teaching and management challenges is developed through focused application over time. It is important that the exploration of the PLA process is not seen as another 'academic' task to be undertaken and 'ticked off', but rather as entry to a deepening knowledge, understanding and practical, transferable expertise.

In this chapter you will work through the PLA responses from Bennie, and then in the following chapter you will see that other teacher-learners, including Ayisha, take on the role of reviewer and provider of feedforward in parallel to the comments of the informed other. Why not put yourself in the position of the inquisitive teacher-learner and further clarify how you might analyse, interrogate, interpret and generate responses to the example PLIs?

Do you recognize in this example a PLI that you have already identified as being relevant to your own on-going professional development? For example, 'how might you identify and respond to the off-task behaviour of a learner in your classroom?' If this is relevant, how would you critically analyse and interpret this teacher-learner's professional thinking? Questions to ask here may include:

- Would you refine or define this initiative in another way? What attributes would you introduce to further clarify the initiative and the detailed analysis for continuing exploration and application?
- Does it represent a single teaching behaviour or skill, or is it a cluster of behaviours that share common characteristics, functions and, therefore, anticipated outcomes?
- How might you identify and resolve such a cluster of teaching behaviours?
- What research, theoretical and practical evidence and actions might you wish to investigate for their potential inclusion in presenting your reasoned understanding of the teaching and learning context of the initiative?
- Are there any other strategic responses that you would generate for inclusion in your teaching plans and repertoire?
- When and in what ways would you assess the effectiveness of the implementation of these responses, so that modifications could be made?

This review of the investigative processes of the PLI will inform your responses if an alternative strategy or approach or teaching skill development is required rather than a minor change. The information presented in these examples can and should be engaged with, from a variety of professional perspectives.

For your continuing professional learning, you should endeavour to consider the complementary roles you will take on as the developer and implementer of responsive programmes, and also as an enquirer into the planning, teaching, managing and assessing processes. Alongside acquiring substantive understanding of the content and pedagogy of the curriculum, of learning the *what* and *how* to teach, exists the need to continually develop and enhance the metacognitive processes of analysing, interrogating, predicting, evaluating and synthesizing. It is through these intellectual processes that you can constantly enhance your understanding of your role in, and experience of, the teaching and learning environment. Becoming accustomed to adopting these perspectives will empower you to challenge what you now know, and to look beyond this to the next stage of professional learning. You are becoming the critically aware and self-regulating professional.

CONTRIBUTING IDEAS 5.2

Adopt the complementary roles of being both:

- the developer and implementer of responsive teaching and learning programmes

  and

- an enquirer into the planning, teaching, managing and assessment processes.

Worked examples of Bennies's professional learning initiative using the PLA pro-forma

Let us work through an example of PLI identification and critical review. It will be helpful to review this example from both perspectives, as an enquirer of personal professional learning *and* as the informed other or inquisitive self who has taken on a supporting role providing 'feed-forward' comments. The intention of presenting a PLI with the analysis and response of a teacher-learner, juxtaposed with comments about this critical analysis from an informed other, is to reinforce the notion that the teacher-learner can adopt:

Name:

Date	WHAT? Professional Learning Initiative (PLI)	WHY?	HOW and WHEN?	Progress reviewed and re-generated - update	Consider linking to any external criteria
	Identify your focus teaching skill or behaviour. Be specific. Consider the antecedent and contextual conditions that influence this specific PLI.	Explore the significance of this PLI for your own professional learning as well as its effectiveness for students' learning; include possible theoretical, research and practical relevance as drawn from your programme-based studies.	How: Detail process and strategies to be introduced into your teaching repertoire and the students' learning programme. (Be prepared to identify and trial a number of planned responses to achieve an effective way to apply these). When: When will these actions be programmed?	Your responses to the PLI are monitored, evaluated and adapted as required. Identify the sequence of lessons where it would be most appropriate to introduce newly shaped responses and when this will be undertaken. It will be necessary to undertake a sequence of updates as the PLI is reviewed at various times.	For example, Teachers' Standards (England). Identify a standard/criterion that 'best' fits with this initiative. Better to focus on just one.
2 March	Ensure self-accountability for pupils' attainment, progress and outcomes. Be certain that I am moving the children's learning forward and I am being effective in my teaching. Are the children's understandings what I think I am teaching? Adapt my teaching if it is not being effective by attending to relevant planning, teaching strategies and assessment	My experience this week with group work during a numeracy activity. The children appeared not to be grasping the concept of the value of 2p coins; some were counting the number of coins rather than adding up the value. It took me a while to realize the children were not confident counting in twos. I found it difficult to teach all the children at the same time	Focus on the pre-requisites needed for developing an effective lesson. Review this response in the introduction or during the post-lesson assessment session After the self-assessment session, I need to review my plan for the next lesson to see how I need to adapt it to fill in any gaps in the children's learning that have been identified	Progress was made with the formative assessment process, planning and teaching during this week's numeracy session. I produced my plans after the assessment session so that they were created based on learners' acquired knowledge. This will be an on-going process, making sure that I am constantly accountable for pupils' attainment, progress and outcomes	Standard 2: 'Pupils' attainment, progress and outcomes through effective monitoring and assessment' (Note: It is important to provide the concise description of the criterion referred to as it will then continue to provide 'review points' to aid your professional learning)

Date	WHAT? Professional Learning Initiative (PLI)	WHY?	HOW and WHEN?	Progress reviewed and re-generated - update	Consider linking to any external criteria
	If I do not feel that the children are grasping what I am trying to teach, make sure that I am still positive. It is my teaching that needs to be changed and adapted		If I am not confident that the children are grasping what I am teaching, I should discuss their progress with the CT. I should get advice on how to move on their learning or how to adapt my teaching. As well as such discussions, I will also need to understand the conceptual sequencing in the particular subject. How is the conceptual understanding introduced and sequenced for the learners? There is a need to 'match' the learning to the level of learner knowledge and understanding so that the learning sequence can be maintained A more formative focus is to be included in assessment strategies during my teaching sessions so that I can identify and analyse children's learning continuously, rather than just at the beginning and the end of the learning activity Focus on this during this week's numeracy lessons on measuring Also on-going through school experience		

Figure 5.1 Bennie's professional learning agenda

(i) the 'enquirer and self-monitor' roles in the personal professional learning process
(ii) a 'reviewer' perspective of the effectiveness of the ways that a teacher-learner, like you, has managed the critical review process in enhancing their professional learning strategies and expertise.

This revisits and consolidates the tenet that you are a self-regulating professional. In Bennie's example, she initially identified a PLI that is significant to her, and then the pro-forma process prompted the critical analysis, interrogation, interpretation and generation of professional learning responses for potential change in her teaching effectiveness.

Once you have considered the content and processes presented in these responses in the pro-forma cell analyses, you can further engage with these relatively new ideas. After reviewing both the heading descriptions of what is required in each phase cell, together with an analysis of the possible feed-forward comments that have been offered, why not take the opportunity to formulate what you might add to these comments?

Now that you are developing a knowledge and understanding of the enquiry and generative processes that support the critical review and interpretation of the professional learning initiative, what guidance would you propose that would extend and enhance the meaning making that is provided here? Research with teacher-learners shows that the more often they were able to involve themselves in this critical learning process, sometimes with others, both from the perspectives of an analyser/creator and a reviewer, the more attentive and responsive they became to their own professional development (Feiman-Nemser, 2001; Orland-Barak & Yinon, 2007; Zeichner, 2008). As proposed earlier, the internalization of the evolving sophisticated inquisitive self is what you are endeavouring to achieve in controlling and enhancing your professional learning.

Bennie's professional learning story

The following sections provide clarification of the *What, Why, How* and *When* phases of the PLA investigative process. Bennie's descriptions and analysis in each cell phase of the PLA are isolated from the proforma to assist you in cross-referencing as you juxtapose the content of the PLA with the reviewer's comments.

Each phase cell is discussed from two perspectives, including some clarifying comments on the phase cell, re-affirming the professional learning intent of each of the phases of the PLA process, and the comments on the initiative from an informed other, anticipating how a mentor, peer, colleague, and later your inquisitive self, might respond to Bennie. Reviewing these statements will help you focus on the objective of each phase of the PLA process.

The *what*: the professional learning initiative

The initiative is the specific identification of an idea, behaviour or skill that has been extracted from a challenging teaching and learning episode and perceived as needing critical review. It is easier to respond proactively to the teaching initiative you've identified if it is stated specifically and in detail. This detail makes the ensuing enquiry analyses easier to focus and manage. However, it is likely that this specific initiative can be recognized as an example of a generic issue that is impacting the teaching and learning process that could be drawn from a variety of content and skills areas (Figure 4.2 in the previous chapter illustrates this identification process). As you become more proficient in thinking this way, your PLI, in most instances, will be identified as a collective, representative conceptualization of a teaching skill or behaviour that will have application to a number of content areas of the curriculum. It tends not to be subject-content specific as this specificity is more appropriately detailed when you are generating curriculum and teaching responses in the *how* and *when* cell phases. These teaching responses are created and organized for introduction into your planning, teaching and managing repertoire.

CONTRIBUTING IDEAS 5.3

Your personal response to the challenges you encounter, driven by the self-monitored, self-directed and self-regulated professional learning approach, will provide you with a less stressful working environment.

Professional learning initiatives may identify many generated responses for you to introduce over a period of practice before you feel comfortable that the introduced strategy, skill or behaviour is an integral element of your repertoire. For example, if the initiative was concerned with developing an effectiveness in questioning, a relevant PLI might confine the professional learning to a specific type of questioning, such as:

- 'developing questions that assess the current levels of knowledge and understanding of the learner group'
- 'structuring questions to raise the cognitive demand of the learning', for example questions that challenge the learner to analyse, categorize, synthesize, predict, hypothesize and evaluate
- 'asking questions that develop an enquiry process for seeking solutions to a problem'.

These question types highlight a sub-group of the questioning techniques and are much more helpful for your learning than if the PLI merely considered 'improving the quality of questioning', as this is too general for the development of focused questioning sequences, and subsequently for the development of pedagogical responses in your planning of sequences of learning activities.

BENNIE'S PLA EXTRACT – THE *WHAT*

Ensure self-accountability for pupils' attainment, progress and outcomes. Be certain that I am moving the children's learning forward and I am being effective in my teaching. Are the children's understandings what I think I am teaching?

Adapt my teaching if it is not being effective by attending to the relevant planning, teaching strategies and assessment attributes.

If I do not feel that the children are grasping what I am trying to teach, make sure that I am still positive. It is my teaching that needs to be changed and adapted.

How an informed other or your inquisitive self might respond to Bennie

Even a cursory analysis of Bennie's identification of a PLI would identify the compound nature of *what* Bennie has identified for herself. In fact, it contains many initiatives and so should be divided into a number of single-focused initiatives that, individually, could provide guidance for her professional learning. For example, for Bennie, the following professional learning foci would benefit from being clarified and generated into some appropriate teaching and learning responses:

- self-accountability
- guiding pupils' attainment (of curriculum knowledge and understanding)
- effective teaching

- focusing on effective preparation and planning
- adapting teaching to learner needs
- responding to learners' lack of understanding
- developing a positive approach to teaching.

Each of these foci represents significant professional learning initiatives and could provide a valuable professional learning agenda. Each would be well worth considering individually so that a series of detailed critical analyses and interpretations could be initiated.

What Bennie has proposed are appropriate professional learning initiatives to pursue, but presenting them collectively in this manner becomes confusing and counter-productive to providing the clear sequence of professional learning that is required. It does not support the next stage of her understanding for relating professional learning foci to the antecedent and contextual influences, and translating the evolved interpretation and understanding into practical and theoretical forms. The statements about 'self-accountability' and a 'positive manner in the teaching and learning process' are too general in scope, and are most likely to be developed as professional attitudes and values from a range of specific professional learning enquiries and actions. They could contribute to an attitudinal awareness developed by Bennie, as she works through more manageable professional learning initiatives.

The need for specificity in the articulation of the professional learning initiative is essential if the *why* and the *how* phases are to be clarified, interpreted, theorized, researched and implemented successfully. It is important for the enquiring professional to 'keep it singular and simple' (the KISS principle in professional learning) when identifying the initiative, so that a specific yet comprehensive, relevant analysis and generation of teacher responses can be undertaken.

The *why*: significant theoretical research and practical evidence for attending to this teaching and learning requirement

The *why* helps to place the PLI within its contextual and antecedent influences and conditions appropriate to the teacher-learner's evolving teaching and managing expertise. The *why* focus is about grounding the professional learning initiative in specific practical application, and a theoretical and evidence-based research orientation of the broader professional learning context. In creating an interpretative, theorizing and generative conceptual framework, you will be developing your knowledge and understanding so that you can conceptualize the initiative and create responses that can be introduced into your evolving professional awareness. In this way, you can enhance your expertise and respond effectively to your students' levels of learning abilities and needs. The way in which the *why* is elaborated is significant to you and your learners. It increasingly enables you to demonstrate the close relationships and connections that you are identifying between what might be labelled as the theoretical and practical domains of learning *what* and *how* to teach; these comprise the substantive strand of the double-helix model for representing professional learning that we discussed in Chapter 2. The questioning, interrogating, interpreting and generating intellectual processes of 'learning *how* to learn', the syntactic strand of the double-helix model, is what is applied by you to comprehend and make relevant what you regard as your professional strengths and areas that require development. This can be done from focused critical analyses, self-assessments and the feed-forward comments that may be provided by others, in working across the content of the cell phases.

The identification of a PLI requires an attentive teacher-learner to recognize instances where there is a mismatch between what has been anticipated and planned for, and the difficulties indicated by learners that become evident as the lesson progresses. It is from an awareness and critical review of such instances that you will be able to articulate the PLI and the associated teacher objective that will guide your continuing professional learning and planning. A focused response to this awareness was attempted in Bennie's review, though the more theoretical understandings have not been adequately considered. It is this composite picture which is constructed as these insights come together that enables you to recognize the generic source of the students' learning difficulties identified and to address them in subsequent planning and teaching.

A more detailed explanation of this teaching intention is found in Chapter 7 on preparation and planning, and we provide a brief overview here. At this time, it is usual in the curriculum planning process to identify the learning objective, or objectives, that guide the creation of the relevant learning activities for engaging the learners with this particular curriculum goal. Intentions for the learning to be achieved can be formulated to include success criteria. An appropriately constructed 'learning objective' would include reference to the success indicators or criteria that would be achieved by the learners from involvement in the activity. We are proposing that the planning process for a learning activity also needs to include a teacher objective that clearly indicates the skill or behaviour that you intend to introduce or practice, in order specifically to focus your professional learning during the teaching of a particular activity. This teacher objective then becomes the first focus for any critical analysis and review of the teaching and learning process that is undertaken. The professional learning initiative becomes the essence of the teacher objective and, in this way, provides the connection between the outcome of the critical review process of the PLA and the subsequent planning and implementation processes. Such a relationship between the strategic professional learning process, the PLA, and the on-going creation of the teaching plan is essential if professional learning is to become more relevant in contributing to your professional development. This integrated nature of learning to teach was initially recognized in the articulation of the double-helix model in Chapter 2, and is continually reviewed during examinations of teacher-learners' PLAs throughout this and the next chapter.

BENNIE'S PLA EXTRACT – THE *WHY*

My experience this week with group work during a numeracy activity was that the children appeared not to be grasping the concept of the value of 2p coins, so were counting the number of coins rather than adding up the value. It took me a while to realize the children were not confident in counting in twos. I found it difficult to teach all the children at the same time.

How an informed other or your inquisitive self might respond to Bennie

Here, Bennie has basically extended her explanation of the *what* of the PLI. She has provided detail of a specific element of a learning activity in mathematics focusing on number and its application in calculating money transactions. But in this *why* phase of the analysis, the focus needs to be on justifying and qualifying the reasons for identifying the initiative and reviewing any theoretical and practical implications for attending to it. It is where the teacher-learner brings professional authority, her knowledge and understanding to her analysis and interpretation.

The description and analysis provided here by Bennie might be better placed in other phases of the enquiry. A more relevant entry into PLI analysis is required rather than an extension of the description of the *what*. It becomes obvious that the issue for Bennie's review of the *what* is that this phase of the analysis was more specifically concerned with 'adapting the teaching to meet the needs of the learner'. This seems to be a more relevant teaching concern or difficulty that Bennie might focus on. In seeking out the actual initiative that is the concern, Bennie needs to look into the descriptive comments identified in each of the *what* and *why* phases. She has not yet developed an appropriate applicable understanding of the purpose of the introductory phases of the PLA: the *what*, and the *why*, and the investigative processes to be used. The intent of Bennie's PLI really seems to be about being adaptable in developing and managing an effective plan of learning activities. It also implies that she needs to be aware of when and how to respond to changing learner needs as knowledge and understanding are created in a sequence of learning activities. As indicated earlier, there is a continuing need to be specific in isolating what is the 'real' concern of the PLI, in order for you to have a definite focus for the remainder of the analytical and generative phases of the PLA. The initiative requires clarity in purpose and function so as to provide the direction and scope needed for unambiguous guidance for the next *why* and *how* phases of the PLA, and for creating exploratory planning responses across a range of curriculum content areas. Once a clearer initiative has been identified, Bennie needs to seek justification for her selection from the appropriate theoretical and practical perspectives. This cell phase needs to demonstrate that she is aware of the role that an understanding of the relevant theory and research can provide for her further analyses and the articulation of focused pedagogical and curriculum content responses. The professional learning worth of the PLA approach is very much dependent on the melding of the practical and theoretical domains that a teacher-learner brings to their critical analyses and the changes that they make in their planning and teaching roles.

In the teaching and learning activity described by Bennie, the subject content would seem to be about 'differentiating the value of coins' in extending the learners' concept of number. It would be an extension activity of the basic number facts introduced earlier in the planning sequence, for example the development of knowledge of number, such as counting in twos, that would be a pre-requisite understanding for the intended activity for these learners. The learners must be confident in counting in various patterns before the transfer of this numeracy skill to another application, such as the adding up of the value of the coins. An informed other or inquisitive self might prompt Bennie to review whether, and how, number readiness could be introduced into the scope and sequencing of the mathematical content in the planning stage in preparing for such enhanced number learning activities. So, what would be a suggestion of some forward-planning ideas for Bennie?

As well as the specific mathematical concepts described here, development of this awareness of the nuances of the teaching and learning process can be applied in a variety of planned activities across curriculum subject areas. With this focus, a teacher-learner would identify learner needs and learning difficulties, and create a planning formula that will be necessarily flexible in its structure and application. This awareness would equip the teacher-learner with an understanding of how content sequences need to be considered in the planning phase. Once a PLI is rendered into a form that can be managed in this way, there is a much clearer pathway to exploring the reasons why this is occurring, and then how curriculum and teaching responses can be generated to overcome any inadequacies or misdirections in the planning process. Chapter 7 will explore these issues in more detail.

The *how* activities generating phase provides the opportunity to consider this PLI in different curriculum content areas and with a variety of learning activities. In the curriculum planning process, the statements of learning objectives provide guidance for the selection and generation of content and learning activities that might be used with the student group. The teacher-learner will also recognize that reconstituting a professional learning initiative as a teacher objective provides the prompt for introducing changes into the teaching and learning process, and also provides an initial and relevant focus for critical self-assessment of the lesson. A teacher objective provides a clear direction in the programme planning process in terms of what the teacher-learner is to introduce and how they are to do so, and how they can then evaluate the effectiveness of this intervention for the teaching.

The *how* and the *when*

The *how* details the range of potential processes, content and strategies as creative responses to the PLI in the learning programme. The *when* asks: when will these actions be programmed?

This phase is concerned with the generation of creative and relevant sequences or series of learning experiences as responses to the professional learning initiative that has been identified. It demonstrates the teacher-learner's processes for seeking ways to develop personal, professional expertise in planning, teaching, managing and assessing. This phase of the critical enquiry process identifies, in broad terms, both the guidance and nature of the programmatic response to the initiatives. The details regarding the scope and sequencing of the teaching activities in the renewed learning do not need to be extrapolated here and are more appropriately found in the relevant planning documentation. The specific learning objectives, the subject content, the appropriate teaching strategies, the associated resources and assessment procedures will be detailed in medium-term and lesson-planning documents.

BENNIE'S PLA EXTRACT – *HOW* AND *WHEN*

Focus on the pre-requisites needed for developing an effective lesson. Review this response in the introduction or during the post-lesson assessment session.

After the self-assessment session, I need to review my plan for the next lesson to see how I need to adapt it to fill in any gaps in the children's learning that have been identified.

If I am not confident that the children are grasping what I am teaching, I should discuss their progress with the mentor teacher. I should get advice on how to move on their learning or how to adapt my teaching. As well as such discussions, I will also need to understand the conceptual sequencing in the particular subject. How is the conceptual understanding introduced and sequenced for the learners?

There is a need to 'match' the learning to the level of learner knowledge and understanding so that the learning sequence can be maintained.

A more formative focus is to be included in assessment strategies during my teaching sessions so that I can identify and analyse children's learning continuously rather than just at the beginning and the end of the learning activity.

Focus on this during this week's numeracy lessons on measuring; also on-going through school experience.

How an informed other or your inquisitive self might respond to Bennie

Bennie's initial comment identified the pre-requisites for relevant planning: it needs to be effective and responsive. It did not clarify what these might mean and how this focus could be acted on. Though Bennie proposed that this might happen in the introduction or during post-lesson assessment, it does not relate to the *how* and *when* but rather to the *why* of this professional learning analysis. So, the pre-requisites for the planning process need to be identified and considered not here but earlier in the *why* phase. If these pre-requisites for the development of effective planning had been researched and detailed in the *why* investigation, there would be a much clearer indication of how the content and strategies of learning activities would be created. These attributes of effective planning provide the framework that will give purpose, relevance, comprehensiveness and responsiveness to the sequencing of learning activities for these learners. The PLA strategy does not include the detailing of specific lesson content. The PLA's major intention is the articulation of teacher strategies that Bennie has researched and modified so as to fit effectively into the specific learning programme that she develops for this particular set of learners. The subject-specific content of the subsequently developed teaching plan will be melded into the sequencing and structure of the teaching strategy that could then be available to guide content from other subject areas.

Bennie's second comment regarding the self-assessment process and how this information could be used may be more appropriately included in the 'progress reviewed and regenerated' phase. This updating of where Bennie is at regarding her attention to the initial PLI is analysed *after* a teaching response has been introduced and assessed for effectiveness. This discussion could then project the potential application of the initiative in other content contexts and possibly with other teaching strategies.

Bennie's third point focused on her lack of confidence in how the learners access the lesson's content. This too would more appropriately be explored as an element of the cell phase when progress is reviewed and learning activities are regenerated and updated. This confusion seems to be related to her level of confidence in developing a sounder understanding of the scope and sequence of the content of the curriculum, and being comfortable with this awareness. These attributes of scope and sequencing of content are significant components of curriculum understanding which could be developed into a professional learning initiative if considered alongside the later stated concern about the 'matching' of the content sequencing with the development of learners' knowledge and understanding. After relocating such planning process concerns in the 'progress reviewed and regenerated' update discussion, a more relevant PLI could be identified. An investigation of the concept of 'scope and sequence', as it relates to the content, thinking skills and academic skills of the curriculum, will be considered in Chapter 7. Reference is also made in the *what* and *how* phase to; sources of professional assistance that could be available to Bennie. This enquiry and support could occur during the later self-assessment process, when a more deliberate exploration of enhancement of *why* it is significant and relevant to her professional learning, could be undertaken.

CONTRIBUTING IDEAS 5.4

The initiative critically reviewed in the PLA process becomes the 'teacher objective' that guides your professional pedagogical process in subsequent learning activities.

Progress reviewed and regenerated: update

Your evaluative comments on the implementation of an initial response and your proposals for further professional learning for this initiative and its teaching and learning responses are summarized here. You may indicate modifications to be made to the initial response or that a new approach is to be sourced and implemented. The cycle of evaluation and regeneration will continue until you are comfortable with this aspect of your teaching repertoire and have achieved 'executive control'.

The development of a formative assessment process is established in this cell phase. The evaluative focus is to inform and create a feed-forward connection between the critical analysis and interpretation, and the tentative and evolving nature of your professional learning. After the initial introduction of the teaching response into the planning or teaching and learning activities, some teachers have found it useful to use a colour code to identify when they introduced their 'regeneration' responses. This can be helpful when reviewing further developmental responses of a professional learning initiative in the future. This procedure can clearly identify when different responses were introduced into the planning sequence for continuing assessment and review. As it can take many 'practices' of a teaching behaviour or skill to achieve executive control over its application, colour coding enables easy access to the creative thread of how you have effectively implemented the behaviour or skill. This underlines the point that the analysis, interpretation and generation of the professional learning initiative and its associated theorizing are not finished at the completion of the initial assessment. The outcome of your review provides guidance for an articulated teacher objective to be regenerated and reintroduced into future planning and teaching phases. You can recycle this pedagogical response into later preparation and planning occasions.

Professional learning engaged in this way can be viewed as a never-completed activity where continuing growth and challenges are to be both welcomed and planned for. Such a heightened awareness will place you in a comfortable mind frame of confidence with control and competence. So, be patient in accepting what this strategy can offer you, including the potential to challenge and enhance your development as an inquisitive and responsive teacher, who is persistent in cycling and recycling new and updated initiatives and creative responses into their professional expertise.

BENNIE'S PLA EXTRACT: PROGRESS REVIEWED AND REGENERATED – AN UPDATE

Progress was made with the formative assessment process, planning and teaching during this week's numeracy session. I produced my plans after the assessment session so that they were created based on learners' acquired knowledge. This will be an on-going process, making sure that I am constantly accountable for pupils' attainment, progress and outcomes.

How an informed other or your inquisitive self might respond to Bennie

When your evolving expertise is discussed in this phase, you need to identify specifically where progress had been made and where this development might be further targeted and enhanced. Producing guidance for planning as a direct response to this formative assessment approach demonstrates an awareness of how a professional learning initiative is associated with 'matching the planning to the learners' current levels of understanding', which is one of the PLIs that could be extracted from the *what* of Bennie's example. Recognizing that this process of professional learning is on-going should make it clear that you anticipate further trialling of the pedagogical responses to the initiative in other content areas. The connections between the quality of planning and its pre-requisite attributes, and a focus on anticipating potential difficulties, emphasize the notion that the exploration of the professional learning initiative does not finish at this phase but is 'cycled forward' into refining subsequent similar initiatives. A PLI will lead you to generate many more planned learning experiences that will consolidate a skill or behaviour in your own comprehensive teaching repertoire. Though these critical analyses and interpretations are presented in tabular form, there is a definite need for you, as an enquiring teacher, to conceptualize the on-going evolution of your professional behaviours, and hence the need to change the form of the PLI and its associated teaching and learning inputs. Getting into a forward-cycling process where you seek ever more sophisticated and complex understandings of those professional concerns you focus on, will reciprocate with progress in the substantive orientation of learning the *what* and the *how* of teaching.

Connecting with external criteria

In the Teachers' Standards that underpin the profession in England (DfE, 2013), Standard 2 refers to the general criterion, to 'promote good progress – pupils' attainment, progress and outcomes'. A subcategory to this overarching standard considers that the teacher should 'be aware of pupils' capabilities and their prior knowledge, and plan teaching to build in these'. The latter is a more specific reference to what appears in the initiative in Bennie's PLA. The reference made to any standards in this cell phase should be the identification of a teacher aspiration of a single component of a more general category. The standards that are provided in external criteria about teacher competencies are mainly general in nature.

In endeavouring to show the relevance of your critical analyses to such external criteria, you might be tempted to add a long list of standards that may have some, even remote, connection to your identified initiative. A response that identifies such a string of attributes becomes confusing and is not at all helpful. The goal is to be specific and to identify the criterion that most closely matches your focused PLI and to formulate it into a teacher objective. It is also important that you identify only one teacher objective for each initiative, to direct your professional learning and self-assessment at this time. This level of specificity makes your evaluation demonstrably achievable.

The PLI you select must relate directly to your particular issue in developing teacher awareness. The initiative is focused on your individual interpretations and knowledge of the content and learning processes, teaching skills and strategies identified. It is embedded in the curriculum that you are required to adapt or develop to meet the current learning needs and abilities of your students at that specific stage of their learning. Bennie identified the need to 'match' her teaching plan to the current knowledge and understanding of the specific content area.

Identifying the most productive initiative for focusing your professional learning is dependent on your assessment of an observed teaching and learning incident/context. The initiative decided on as requiring professional development review can come from you or from an informed other. As has been emphasized in earlier discussions, the isolated PLI may have been perceived as an inadequate teaching skill or, just as importantly, a strategy or skill that has provided a successful outcome for both the learners and yourself. The genesis of setting the professional learning agenda is focused precisely on your efforts as an enquiring teacher, and relevant to, but not driven by, an adherence to external standards. The locus of control for your professional learning is directly related to your evolving expertise through critical reviews of your actions in meeting the needs of learners, the curriculum objectives and your developing repertoire of teaching behaviours and skills.

Reference made to external criteria in this cell phase of the PLA should include a precise statement of the professional attribute, knowledge, skill or value found in the standard or criteria and not just any numerical code. It is the actual words of the criteria that will reinforce, for you, the meaning of the teacher characteristic that you have decided is significant. It is helpful if a brief description of the actual standard can be summarized – for example, Bennie could write that she is 'considering students' attainment, progress and outcomes through effective monitoring and assessment'. Acquiring this official language will authorize your continuing discussion about your professional development enquiries and actions with mentors and other colleagues.

CHAPTER SUMMARY

Bennie's critical analysis and generation of meaning and response can be enhanced by the effective use of scientific educational language in relating her practical understanding of the professional learning initiative to the theoretical evidence founded in relevant academic reading and involvement in university- and school-based teacher education courses. These connections should be continually sought and referenced. Educational practice and effective teaching are clearly evidence-based in research and theorizing studies that should be understood and used in justifying your involvement in the complexities of the teaching and learning process. Significant and relevant knowledge of your professional domain should be included when discussing planning, teaching and assessing of your professional learning progress, as you engage learners with the prepared learning programme.

So, let's take a moment to review more generally what has been explained through this worked example of Bennie's PLA early in her professional teaching course. In summary, the PLA process and associated pro-forma were not developed to fulfil the role of a 'box-ticker' in responding to external criteria or standards. Rather, they articulate the crucial evidence of the intellectual journey undertaken by the teacher-learner in attending to these dual roles in the classroom context of both 'teacher planner and implementer' and 'enquiring teacher-learner'. It is the constant seeking of excellence in meeting the challenges of a continually changing learning environment and the creating of relevant teaching responses for learners that provide such extensive, personally enriching and rewarding returns for a teaching professional.

FURTHER READING

Feiman-Nemser, S. (2001) From preparation to practice: designing a continuum to strength. *Teachers College Record*, 103(6): 1013–55.

This article is intended to stimulate discussion and debate about what a professional learning continuum from initial preparation through the early years of teaching could be like. It considers the fit (or misfit) between conventional approaches to teacher preparation, induction and professional development and the challenges of learning to teach.

Orland-Barak, L. and Yinon, H. (2007) When theory meets practice: student teachers' reflections on their classroom discourse. *Teaching and Teacher Education*, 23: 957–69.

Student teachers' reflections on their own classroom discourse were analysed to gauge the connections they made between theory and practice. It was concluded that when provided with strategically structured mediation, neophyte teachers were able to reflect at levels beyond technical reflection.

6

REFINING PROFESSIONAL
LEARNING THROUGH REVIEW
AND INTERPRETATION

Having read this chapter, you will have an understanding of:

- the functioning and investigation of the *what*, *why* and *how* phases of a professional learning agenda
- the evaluative principles and interpretative processes used in analysing and theorizing a professional learning agenda and anticipating potential responses
- the application of informed analysis and creative responses to the PLA examples of other teacher-learners.

Introduction

In the previous chapter, you had the opportunity to follow in detail the working through of an interpretive analysis of the professional learning process as developed by Bennie, and to review the potential learning, for you, in engaging with the PLA strategy. Where Bennie's professional learning was identified and understood, the importance was emphasized of clarity and comprehensiveness of the *what*, in clearly establishing the professional learning initiative that would guide the professional learning review process. The *what* establishes the professional focus of the learning you need to engage with if your analysis, interpretation and enrichment are to be effective and professionally rewarding for you.

Later in this chapter, you are taken again through this learning strategy by using examples from Ayisha's professional learning within the PLA framework and reviewing the significance of the clarity of the initiating statement. But, before we explore this critical review of another teacher-learner's PLA experience, we examine a number of examples of how different teacher-learners have analysed the teaching and learning process, and isolated and synthesized the important starting point in this process – the professional learning initiative. It is imperative that the initiative is stated in precise terms so that meaningful and applicable foci can be generated. Clearly articulating the focus will provide you with a more effective starting point in formulating the continuing exploration and enhancement of your professional knowledge and expertise.

We will now look at a series of possible professional learning initiatives; following which we have included an analytical comment examining each one. As you review these discussions, note the advice that you might provide to these teacher-learners to help clarify this focusing element of the PLA. Remember that, in most instances, there may be no 'best' advice that can be offered, but rather considered responses that may be more focused and sophisticated in knowledge, understanding and intent. The advice generated by your inquisitive self is founded in professional learning experiences that have been critically reviewed in a knowledgeable, analytical and generative manner. In this way, professional learning can be conceived as a growth process that moves continually between dissonance attributed to a specific attribute of the teaching and learning process and a possible resolution to this uncertainty by introducing a creative response into your evolving professional consciousness and practice. After considering these PLIs, we then identify and briefly comment on a number of *why* cell responses to review how other teacher-learners have endeavoured to reason and theorize about relating the identified initiatives to relevant theoretical and research ideas and their potential practical responses.

Then, finally, after the review and interpretation of Ayisha's PLA example, a number of *what* statements, together with their associated reasoning, the *whys*, are presented to explore the symbiotic relationship that exists between these initial phases of the professional awareness process. No comments are made in this section as it is anticipated that your reading of these examples will demonstrate how these phases of the PLA strategy are linked and the directions and guidance that they provide for enhancing professional learning. You will start to hypothesize about how you might generate *how* and *when* responses to initiatives that may closely represent professional learning intentions that you might be envisaging for yourself at this stage of your development as a teacher. Remember to generate a range of potential practical responses in this phase, so that you can trial a number of these strategies to establish a 'best fit' for both you and your learning group. The strategy that you decide to use in this context of learner involvement might not be appropriate at another time, so establishing a repertoire of relevant practical responses is effective professional learning knowledge for you. This process of selecting and trying out different approaches will further enhance your ability to make pedagogical choices while you are directly engaged in the teaching and learning process. You will have become more effective in making 'reflection-in-action' decisions (Schön, 1991).

Examples follow of investigation and interpretation of the PLIs identified by teacher-learners like yourself at various stages of their professional understanding and growth. First, the *whats* and then the *whys*, together with the inquisitive self comments, are provided.

How significant is the professional learning initiative?

Review the following teacher-learner responses by preparing your thoughts before considering the comment provided:

Professional learning initiative #1: 'Initiate and enhance the learners' abilities to conceive and ask questions of themselves and each other.'

Comment: This precise statement of teaching behaviour is intended to provide learning opportunities for the students to identify and apply questioning patterns to enhance the quality of the reciprocal learning that might then evolve within the teaching and learning process. This clarity of purpose will support the theorizing processes of the *why*, as it would enable you to focus on a learning process to raise the quality of the interactive and supportive dialogue in the learning environment. In this phase, such a questioning emphasis would encourage learners to ask questions that would further enhance their higher cognitive levels of thinking, and open up the exploration and discussion of the topic issue while limiting the amount of teacher talk and so involve all of the learners in the lesson. In the application phase of the *how* and *when*, this clearly focused *what* might also generate an extension of the 'talking partner's' interactive learning strategy by creating more formal roles, such as being the 'talker' and the 'listener' or 'questioner' in this process. This moves the activity from 'talking *at* each other' to a reciprocal learning engagement.

Professional learning initiative #2: 'Introducing a smoother, or less disruptive and time-consuming, transition between lesson segments.'

Comment: A clear and precise teaching behaviour has been identified within a teaching and learning context that has clear implications for learners' behaviour as well. Transitions provide connections and linkages for learners as they progress effectively and purposefully through the sequencing of the lesson so that the focused objectives of the learning experience are maintained by the learners' on-task engagement. It also provides a focused context for you to theorize about the relevance and applicability of a supportive learning environment and so the potential of the introduction of such a teaching strategy. It would also enable you to investigate, and respond to, learners' movements and interactions during such transition periods and to re-emphasize a commitment to use valuable learning time productively.

Such an emphasis on the significance of 'learning intentions' could de-emphasize your focus on management and initiate a focus of engagement with the learning process. This would introduce a more productive learning atmosphere into the classroom environment. From this defined focus, an awareness of 'time limits' and 'movement pathways' for the re-organization of the teaching and learning environment might be established. For example, the position that you adopt in the classroom setting, as well as learner access to resource materials that are needed at various phases of the lesson sequence, might also be considered. So, the introduction of a learning process response that could be supported by effective management procedures might be appropriate to the initiative rather than a more narrow focus on managing learner behaviour because of inappropriate classroom organization.

Professional learning initiative #3: 'Maintain and enhance the learning opportunities for my students through effective employment of classroom support staff.'

Comment: In the context of the increasing number of adult personnel operating in classrooms, this initiative would provide a number of possible responses. Attention to this professional development process would raise your professional presence as you would be informing and guiding auxiliary staff into a 'partnership' arrangement in the effective implementation of the prepared teaching and learning programme. The support personnel being made aware of the specific timing and nature of the intervention can enhance the quality of learning. Careful induction into the learning process will require thoughtful pedagogical and management awareness by these others that will depend on the exploration and clarification of roles and the insightful understanding of the teaching programme.

Professional learning initiative #4: 'There is a perceived need to refine my questioning strategies by providing learners with "thinking time" and developing an anticipated awareness of their potential responses. Attentiveness to this will focus me on developing more effective responses to the difficulties of understanding and application that might be evident in these learners' responses.'

Comment: A pedagogical context has been established which has then been related to fundamental constituent elements of the questioning pattern. It is also evident that the teacher-learner is aware of the need to anticipate and 'know' the likely responses to the questions posed. It is an awareness of learners' relevant, and also not so appropriate, responses that enables you to make pedagogical decisions about the continuing 'flow' of the lesson sequence. You should attend to this in a 'review phase' embedded in the planning and preparation phases of lesson construction (see Chapter 7). It seems that this teacher-learner needs to be cognizant of such potential 'answers' that either support or are compatible with the proposition being explored. This prepares them for modifying the scope and sequence of the teaching and learning programme where irrelevant, or 'not quite there', responses are offered by the learners. This clearly indicates where there is a mismatch between what they believe is being presented as the lesson content sequence and how such 'new' learning is being assimilated by the student learners.

A reasoned understanding of the *why* of this strategic behaviour will provide you with guidance about the progression or possible review of the learning sequence. This initiative demonstrates that the teacher-learner has become aware of learner inattentiveness that may be more directly related to their own teaching behaviour rather than that of the learners as they struggle to engage with the lesson content. There may be a need to seek more covert, underlying reasons for learners' off-task behaviour rather than to focus on and respond only to the overt behaviour of the learners. The effectiveness of a teaching programme is dependent on its making relevant and numerous contacts with the learners' current knowledge and understanding, and cognitive skills development.

> *Professional learning initiative #5*: 'Providing strategies for increasing levels of student participation in all phases of a lesson. This will ensure that the majority of learners are actively involved in their learning rather than sitting passively listening to me.'

> *Comment*: What would be your analysis of this initiative? How would your inquisitive self analyse and interpret this? These examples, together with the respective comments, should alert you to the need for clarity and precision in proposing the introduction of a teaching skill or behaviour. The comments are intended to show how such precision will enhance the potential of the theoretical and practical reasoning and the subsequent professional learning processes that enable you to be active in your own development. It follows the KISS principle ('keep it simple and singular') that was introduced in Chapter 5. This part of the process is about moving you forward towards more meaningful and supportive professional learning.

Reasoning and theorizing in the *why* phase

In this section, a number of example *why* descriptions are provided that teacher-learners might develop as they theorize and seek reasons for developing professional responses to an initiative they have identified. As well as considering the relevance and effectiveness of the reasoning inherent in the response, you might also take a moment to 'reverse-engineer' the process, i.e. consider what might be the initiative that required the teacher-learner to think and theorize in this way. The *what* and the *why* are intrinsically related to initiating, reasoning, interpreting, theorizing and bringing a professional emphasis to the subsequent generation of *how* responses in later teaching and learning programmes. These examples will be provided without comment, asking you to analyse their relevance:

> *Why example #1*: 'Because teaching assistants are placed in the classroom to support the learning programme, it is important for them to be very clear about the intent of the lesson and overall learning programme, and the specific ways that they can support the learning process. This is especially relevant to learners who are either experiencing difficulties with the learning or who require extended opportunities. It is important that assistants see themselves as important and contributing members of the teaching team and are confident in their knowledge and understanding of the scope and sequence of the learning but also the pedagogical tasks they are to focus on. I need to establish a climate of shared ownership of the learning programme and its processes and ensure the assistants' involvement goes beyond 'crowd control'. Their support needs to be concerned with professional tasks such as the pace of the lesson, techniques to guide and extend learning, the availability and introduction of relevant resources; they need to be able to contribute significantly to the assessment of learners' progress or difficulties in supporting future planning for progression.'

What might be your analysis of the reasoning about the relevance and significance of the initiative underpinning this example? Did you identify the *what* – the PLI that has initiated this reason?

> *Why example #2*: 'It is more difficult for learners to be individually disruptive if they aren't aware where I am in the classroom. So, moving while teaching within the classroom area will help to keep their attention on me. I will also deal with any disruptive behaviour by simply being in that learner's space, touching them on the shoulder, tapping the desk or even just standing by them, other than interrupting my teaching sequence, highlighting the behaviour to the whole class and using my voice when I don't need to.'

What might be your analysis of the reasoning about the relevance and significance of the initiative underpinning this example? Again, what is the PLI that initiated this analysis and reasoning?

> *Why example #3*: 'I need to have an increased awareness of the importance of targets and the recording of learners' progress in association with these. This assessment recording will help me to determine if the teaching plan, the scope and sequence of the teaching, and teaching and learning process were effective. This recording will highlight any common misconceptions and provide guidance for my further planning. To enable this collection and recording of data, I will try to focus on 4–5 learners during and at the conclusion of each lesson. The data will be recorded on a checklist that identifies the anticipated learning outcomes and levels of reaching specific success criteria.'

What might be your analysis of the reasoning about the relevance and significance of the initiative underpinning this example?

> *Why example #4*: 'During my maths lesson, the majority of the learners were listening attentively though passively while a peer answered questions. This not only meant that they quickly became bored, but this individual response also prevented me from assessing the understanding of the group as a whole. In the long term, this could impact on how the learners considered themselves as maths learners, possibly leading to a lack of motivation or willingness to learn.'

What might be your analysis of the reasoning about the relevance and significance of the initiative underpinning this example?

CONTRIBUTING IDEAS 6.1

The focus of the PLA strategy on exploring the *what* and the *why* of a PLI, provides a personal review process that is uniquely pertinent to your teaching and learning awareness.

The story of a teacher-learner's professional learning, as told by Ayisha

The next phase of this exploration of the PLA strategy, for the critical analysis and generation of potential professional learning outcomes, is related to the involvement of Ayisha. In this example, Ayisha is coming to a developed understanding of her role as a teacher-learner as she reviews her engage-ment with actions and interactions within the complexities of her teaching and learning contexts. She appears to be at a later stage of her professional learning, and has internalized and applied elements of the professional guidance that she has acquired as an inquisitive self, as well as the feed-forward comments that she may have received from informed others in professional development activities. But before considering the analysis of Ayisha's example of a teacher-learner's PLA, let us briefly review where your understanding may have reached.

In Bennie's reviewed example in the previous chapter, comments were made from two perspectives. First, there is an analytical comment on the intent of the specific phase of the agenda, using details from Bennie's own critical analysis, and then more specific comments about the relevance of the particular analyses and interpretations to further extend Bennie's pro-fessional learning agenda. In looking at Ayisha's example, there is a specific emphasis on review comments from the perspective of an informed other or your inquisitive self.

This critical review of potential responses to an identified initiative offers you another opportunity to review your understandings and interpretations in respect of someone's developing work on how their professional learning can be interrogated and resolved. There is no definitive 'right answer' to any of the comments that are attached to the discussions of each phase of the ini-tiative. There may be other quite appropriate ways of focusing and engaging an enquiring teacher's thoughts and considered responses. Take time during your reading and interpretation of this section to consider how you might provide clarifying comments from the perspective of your inquisitive self.

It is important that after the critical analysis and interpretation pro-cesses have been carried out, with a number of possibilities identified or created, you look to the 'best fit' response to the particular teaching and learning environment. As has been discussed elsewhere, you must come to accept that there may still be uncertainties during the generation and implementation phases of professional responses and that these should be regarded as normal and welcomed as opportunities for further clarification, carefully considered resolution and, thus, enhanced knowledge and under-standing of the complexities of your teaching and learning environment.

CONTRIBUTING IDEAS 6.2

Learning dissonance that may emerge from the analysis of initiatives in the teaching and learning context contributes to your critical review and to posi-tive professional learning outcomes.

Name:

Date	WHAT? Professional Learning Initiative (PLI)	WHY?	HOW and WHEN?	Progress reviewed and re-generated - update	Consider linking to any external criteria
	Identify your focus teaching skill or behaviour. Be specific. Consider the antecedent and contextual conditions that influence this specific PLI. See example in Figure 5.1	Explore the significance of this PLI for your own professional learning as well as its effectiveness for students' learning; include possible theoretical, research and practical relevance as drawn from your programme-based studies.	How: Detail process and strategies to be introduced into your teaching repertoire and the students' learning programme. (Be prepared to identify and trial a number of planned responses to achieve an effective way to apply these). When: When will these actions be programmed?	Your responses to the PLI are monitored, evaluated and adapted as required. Identify the sequence of lessons where it would be most appropriate to introduce newly shaped responses and when this will be undertaken. It will be necessary to undertake a sequence of updates as the PLI is reviewed at various times.	For example, Teachers' Standards (England). Identify a standard/ criterion that 'best' fits with this initiative. Better to focus on just one.
8 May	Behavioural management techniques need to be more seamless and less disruptive to my teaching during the lesson. This includes refocusing children who are distracted from the lesson sequence To consider the reasons behind children being distracted or not behaving as expected and to react to these influences during the lesson and after the lesson has finished	I am currently using positive reinforcement of behaviour expectations during the lesson, and the children are responding well to this. However, I am having to stop and disrupt the lesson flow in order to speak to an individual child, to remind them of 'good listening', etc. I want to be able to reinforce good behaviour using methods that do not distract from my teaching or interrupt the lesson To improve lesson flow and to allow the primary focus to be on the children's learning	Using other behaviour management techniques that do not necessarily rely on my voice, e.g. tapping on the table next to a child, anticipating behaviour prior to an incident occurring, moving around the classroom to emphasize my presence and make all the children aware that I am there. Could make eye contact with an individual child or use facial expressions (e.g. raised eyebrows) as a behavioural management technique I intend to begin implementing these techniques in the classroom over the coming week and during school experience (1C) and beyond I observe other teachers' behaviour management strategies as well as discussing with teachers the various strategies that they use	This will be an on-going focus throughout SE1C and SE2. Pupils with more challenging behaviour are in my current phonics group, so it is important to be more consistent with behavioural management techniques. Need to implement more sanctions with this group: loss of golden minutes, behavioural forms, taking a minute out of the class, etc., but also to consider if these are actually essential in the lesson: who are they benefiting? During whole-class teaching of numeracy, I felt that my classroom management/lesson flow could have been more seamless. Need to make sure I plan transitions that I	Standard 7: Using approaches which are appropriate to pupils' needs, in order to involve and motivate them

Date	WHAT? Professional Learning Initiative (PLI)	WHY?	HOW and WHEN?	Progress reviewed and re-generated - update	Consider linking to any external criteria
		rather than off-task behaviour Immediate reaction is to blame the child for being distracted or disrupting the class. Other causes could be that the work is too easy/difficult, they are finding the activity boring, my teaching is not effective or there are other problems at school/home. It may be that there is a curriculum content and learning process to be considered about the attentiveness of learners? Considering these reasons may change my methods to manage behaviour and to use approaches that are appropriate to that individual pupil's needs. These considerations will also help me plan future lessons or adapt future teaching strategies	Scan the classroom while teaching (positioning myself so that this is possible) to make sure students are focused on learning that they are to be engaged with Look at all the children throughout the lesson: when are they not focused on the task at hand? What are they being asked to do at this time? Is it an individual student or a number of them that is the issue? Are they distracted at the same time or during different segments of the lesson? What is their behaviour like during other lessons and with other teachers? What are they doing instead of the task? Considering these types of questions during and after the lesson will help me pinpoint the reasons behind the distraction, to enable me to respond appropriately and effectively. If it is often the same children, discuss with other teachers the behaviour management techniques that they use and their effectiveness WHEN: Towards the end of school experience (1B), throughout next session (1C). Particularly when taking over responsibility for whole-class teaching when speaking to an individual child will be a lot more disruptive to lesson flow	am going to use: hand up? 1, 2, 3? Make sure children have stopped and are listening, etc. Need to continue progress on making behaviour and classroom management more seamless. Positive feedback about my lesson transitions; I am becoming more adept at stopping the class and getting the children's attention so I can carry out a mini-plenary or bring them back to the carpet. Consider using other techniques to get pupils' attention: currently using hands up (works with this class but is an issue that learners with backs to you cannot see the signal), use rattle/bell, counting, clapping During lessons, I try to assess pupils' levels of engagement and decide the suitable behaviour management techniques for individuals, e.g. some pupils in my phonics group need firm reminders of expectations and often need sanctions to be carried out fairly and consistently	

Figure 6.1 Ayisha's professional learning agenda

We will now focus on some extracts from Ayisha's professional learning agenda.

AYISHA'S PROFESSIONAL LEARNING INITIATIVE: ANALYSIS AND INTERPRETATION

'Behavioural management techniques need to be more seamless and less disruptive to my teaching during the lesson. This includes refocusing children who are distracted from the lesson sequence.

To consider the reasons behind children being distracted or not behaving as expected and to react to these influences during the lesson and after the lesson has finished.'

How an informed other, or your inquisitive self, might respond to Ayisha

For Ayisha, a number of professional learning statements are identified, including (i) 'the introduction of seamless and less disruptive management techniques' that is associated with (ii) 'considering reasons why children are distracted or not behaving as expected', (iii) 'refocusing on distracted learners' and, finally, (iv) 'ways of responding during and post-lesson'. The professional learning initiative that 'best fits' here would seem to be the reference to 'seamless and less disruptive' teacher behaviour. That is a single and well-defined focus for the critical analysis and interpretation to clarify the initiative and to generate potential ways of responding to this in subsequent teaching and learning sessions. The other possible professional learning statements that were identified here could subsequently be considered as attributes of 'seamless and less disruptive' teacher behaviour and, if so, could then be identified as other single-focused initiatives for later critical review.

The reasons underpinning this behaviour need to be investigated and identified in order to situate this initiative within the theory and practicality of behaviour management. So, these statements might be better situated in the *why* cell phase. As the 'new' *why* review focus, the undertaking of research justification and theorizing and, thereby, considering the contextual and antecedent influences and conditions, it seems to be more specifically directed at this alternative perspective. Also, 'refocusing' and 'ways of responding' are more likely to sit within the *how* and *when* phase. Again, this reminds us that the professional learning enquiry process is to review what is specifically required in each of the investigative phases of determining the *what*, the *why* and the *how* and *when*. Each enquiry focus of the professional learning agenda needs to be adequately reviewed and detailed before you move on to considering the next phase. Understanding the relative intention of each of the enquiry phases is an important consideration. The descriptions on the headings of the PLA pro-forma alone do not provide the clear guidance that is essential if the professional learning enquiry process is to isolate what needs to be accomplished in the phases.

So, let us stay with the statement, 'introduction of seamless and less disruptive management techniques', as the focusing professional learning initiative to guide this component of Ayisha's engagement with her developmental process. It may be appropriate at this point to take a closer look for more relevant placement of the sub-themes elsewhere within the analysing, theorizing and generating strategies of the PLA. It is obvious that there have been occasions (observed and commented on by others, or from self-analysis) when Ayisha has interrupted the flow of her teaching to draw attention to a child's inappropriate behaviour, and she is concerned about the ways that these have become like 'speed bumps' to the sequencing and engagement of the students' learning. So, abstraction of the specific professional learning initiative from the classroom incident is required for the *what* phase of the critical analysis. The need for specificity in articulating initiatives is a point that was raised in Chapter 5 and it is worth reiterating here. It is important to 'keep it simple and singular' when identifying the professional learning initiative, so that a more specific, comprehensive and relevant critical analysis can be undertaken.

AYISHA'S EXAMPLE: THE *WHY?*

'I am currently using positive reinforcement of behaviour expectations during the lesson and the children are responding well to this. However, I am having to stop and disrupt the lesson flow in order to speak to an individual child, to remind them of 'good listening', etc. I want to be able to reinforce good behaviour using methods that do not distract from my teaching or interrupt the lesson.

To improve lesson flow and to allow the primary focus to be on the children's learning rather than on off-task behaviour.

The immediate reaction is to blame the child for being distracted or disrupting the class.

Other causes could be that the work is too easy or too difficult, the children are finding the activity boring, my teaching is not effective or there are other problems at school/home. It may be that there is a curriculum content and learning process to be considered about the attentiveness of learners.

(Continued)

(Continued)

> Considering these reasons may change my methods of managing behaviour and enable me to use approaches that are appropriate to that individual pupil's needs. These considerations will also help me plan future lessons or adapt future teaching strategies.'

How an informed other, or your inquisitive self, might respond to Ayisha

In this *why* phase of the process, Ayisha is providing some discussion of the current context of the professional learning initiative as it is presently operating in the classroom. She refers to the use of positive reinforcement of the behavioural expectations that she has established. Though a concern is expressed about how her 'interjections' about behaviour are interrupting the flow of the lesson's conceptual scope and sequence, Ayisha perceives a need to be able to use approaches to managing and guiding off-task behaviour that are less intrusive and interruptive to the learning sequence. Following on from these comments, she identifies the possible reasons and causes of 'off-task' behaviour. Ayisha's intention seems to be a need to look for appropriate responses that might be used at times during the school day when the learners are not directly involved in learning activities. In a sense, she wants to create an overall climate of positive involvement in and attention to the learning programme with total immersion of the learners in a responsive and cooperative learning environment. For example, she may consider introducing behaviour-directing processes during the class group's movements when entering or leaving the classroom, or during lesson transitions when the learners are moving into various learning group patterns, and identifying incidents for close interaction with individual learners before and after school or during breaks in out-of-classroom settings, such as the playground or the dining hall.

Interestingly, the teaching and learning context that is offered for analysis by Ayisha is now being widened beyond what might be considered as traditional or more direct responses from a behaviour management perspective. There is now a focus on considering how the sequencing of the content of the curriculum and the associated strategies, and the appropriate pedagogy may not be connecting well with the intended learners and, therefore, not responding relevantly to the learning abilities and needs of some individuals in the classroom. It appears from Ayisha's analysis that it is these learners who are inattentive and disruptive and not coping with the scope and sequence of the learning. The professional learning concern inherent here appears to be concerned with the possibility that the initiative needs to be refocused on a curriculum or pedagogical concern rather than simply a behaviour management one. Through recognizing that the management of learners' on-task behaviour is a professional task that she may need to further refine, she is also seeking solutions that go beyond the introduction and application of behaviour modification and re-enforcement processes.

Research studies that look at new teachers' major concerns about their initial years' involvement in school usually cite behaviour management as a significant aspect of the teaching role in managing and guiding productive learning (Rogers, 2000; Broomfield, 2006; Eisenman et al., 2015). The repeated off-task behaviour of learners appears to be getting in the way of the teachers' generation and implementation of effective, interesting and challenging learning programmes. New teachers can be distracted from what they perceive to be their primary role in determining teaching and learning intentions and consider easily observed causes rather than becoming more critically inquisitive of all facets of the teaching and learning environment. There is a tendency to look to respond to the observed behaviour rather than carry out a more critical analysis and interpretation of the contextual and antecedent conditions that might indicate the underlying causes. There is a continual need to 'look beneath the surface', to identify and then critically analyse what is really significant. This can act as the trigger for a professional learning initiative to determine what will lead to a heightened awareness of the teaching and learning process and then to seek more critical responses.

Ayisha seems to have moved her awareness and analysis to a more comprehensive and inclusive review perspective and is seeking and exploring other, not so overt, influences that might be impacting on her teaching. She has decided that most in-classroom behavioural incidents can be related back to inappropriate planning, resourcing and teaching strategies. Though she is still aware that, on occasion, extremes of behaviour can be exhibited by some 'troubled' students, Ayisha appears to be questioning herself: 'Is this observed learner behaviour because there is a lack of programme connectedness with what has "gone before" or does the preciseness in the sequencing of the learning content and process provide uncertainty that leads to off-task or disinterested behaviour?' These perceived issues will further guide Ayisha's critical analyses as she develops a deeper understanding of the interrelated complexities of the teaching and learning environment.

As Ayisha focuses more on the possibility that disruptive behaviour could be traced to the quality of the planning process, this will be a very insightful professional learning activity for her. This professional insight that the 'off-task' behaviours of learners may be a curriculum planning issue, shows Ayisha's growing consciousness of her teaching role. It appears to emphasize planning foci on the selection and sequencing of relevant content, together with the associated and challenging resources that support well-conceived and interestingly presented learning activities. These insights have the potential to become theorizing and generative processes in developing her appropriate learning and management responses. Once Ayisha has found that she is comfortable with the levels of critical awareness that she is able to bring to intriguing and challenging teaching and learning incidents, and is able to identify and respond to the inherent influences, she will find the confidence to guide her future professional learning in these comprehensive ways. Her critical understanding and effectiveness will provide the power and confidence in her syntactic abilities 'to grow' her own professional learning and development as she enhances her substantive knowledge.

AYISHA'S EXAMPLE: THE HOW AND THE WHEN

'Using other behaviour management techniques that do not necessarily rely on my voice, for instance tapping on the table next to a child, anticipating behaviour prior to an incident occurring, moving around the classroom to emphasize my presence and make all the children aware that I am there. Making eye contact with an individual child or using facial expressions (for example, raised eyebrows) as a behavioural management technique.

I intend to begin implementing these techniques in the classroom over the coming week and during this school experience and beyond. I observe other teachers' behaviour management strategies as well as discussing with teachers the various strategies that they use.

Scan the classroom while teaching (positioning myself so that this is possible) to make sure students are focused on the learning that they are to be engaged with.

Look at all the learners throughout the lesson: when are they not focused on the task at hand?

What are they being asked to do at this time? Is it an individual student or a number of them?

Are they distracted at the same time or during different segments of the lesson? What is their behaviour like during other lessons and with other teachers? What are they doing instead of the task?

Considering these types of questions during and after the lesson will help me pinpoint the reasons behind the distraction for me to be able to respond to these appropriately and effectively.

If it is often the same children, discuss with other teachers the behaviour management techniques that they use and their effectiveness.

When – towards the end of this school experience (1B), throughout the next session (1C) [with reference to the following periods of school experience that she will undertake]. Particularly when taking over responsibility for whole-class teaching, when speaking to an individual child will be a lot more disruptive to lesson flow.'

How an informed other, or your inquisitive self, might respond to Ayisha

Strategies to redirect the learners from their off-task behaviours are identified that do not require a verbal interruption to the flow of the lesson, including: (i) tapping of the learner's table, (ii) having a physical presence near the learner, (iii) moving around the classroom, while teaching, to emphasize the teacher's presence, (iv) making eye contact or changing facial expressions (such as raised eyebrows) when communicating 'silently' with the learner, and (v) anticipating an inappropriate behaviour even *before* it overtly occurs.

Except for the last of these, the above strategies seem self-explanatory and would be easy to implement and monitor for effectiveness. The process of anticipating 'inappropriate' learners' interactions with the prepared teaching, as a response to their levels of understanding and needs, is an important concept in the planning process that will be discussed in Chapter 7. Developing an observation skill of attentiveness, a conscious awareness of the many details and interactions that are happening in the classroom environment while engaged in the teaching of the lesson, is an essential characteristic to develop. It is the ability to 'see' and understand the underlying antecedent behaviours or contextual conditions that will enable you to respond almost before the inappropriate behaviour occurs. You will recall that this notion of awareness and attentive listening, together with an extended critical analysis, was explored in Chapter 3.

In reference to the learners and the learning situation, the questions identified as being relevant to the investigative process that might be used by Ayisha could include:

- What are the children being asked to do at this time?
- Is it an individual learner or a number of them that appear to be behaving in this way?
- What are the children doing instead of focusing on the task?

Such questions focus on the contextual conditions of what is being observed and questioned. Other questions include:

- What has been introduced earlier in this learning sequence?
- Are the children distracted at the same time or during different parts of the lesson?
- What is the children's behaviour like during other lessons with other teachers, for instance the music teacher?

These considerations identify possible antecedent states that might be influencing the particular ways that classroom behaviours become overt. The questions and their associated categories of investigation are thoughtfully structured by Ayisha and should tease out the evidence that will be helpful in identifying the reasons why behaviours occur as they do. But, in considering the form of the PLA process, these comments would be more appropriately placed in the earlier section of establishing the contextual and antecedent influences affecting the behaviour inherent in the identified PLI and its sub-themes. If these questions were used to enhance Ayisha's interpretative understanding of *why* the initiative is a necessary addition to the professional learning agenda, then the *how* and *when* responses for inclusion in the teaching programme could be more directly articulated and assessed. Ayisha has to establish a comprehensive and carefully articulated understanding of the initiative in the teaching and learning domain, before she is able to formulate a measured and meaningful programme of strategic responses. That is, she needs to know in detail what she is dealing with and to understand the theoretical and practical implications, before she attempts to go searching for relevant response strategies for her planning.

What is being presented in the *why, how* and *when* phases clearly represents a developing conceptual awareness by Ayisha that can only be further evolved and enhanced by more careful application of the syntactic characteristic of her professional learning approach. You will recall that this label, syntactic, was used earlier when discussing the 'learning *how* to learn' orientation, and was articulated in the double-helix model of the professional learning process, in Chapter 2. It represents the teacher-learner's interpretative, theorizing and generative conceptual framework for critically reviewing professional learning that is based on 'learning the *what* and *how* of teaching' – the 'substantive' orientation. Using analytical and interpretative questioning to investigate beneath the surface of the identified incident of the teaching and learning process and articulating the PLI will ensure that a deepening understanding is generated before Ayisha seeks responsive teaching skills or strategies. Looking for a quick fix by grabbing at an easy superficial solution may stifle or mislead the critical awareness insight that could be available to her professional learning after more thoughtful analysis and interpretation.

CONTRIBUTING IDEAS 6.3

You need a thoughtful interpretation of the context of the learning incident before generating potential professional learning initiatives, a critical reasoning of these and some potential teaching and learning responses.

AYISHA'S EXAMPLE: PROGRESS REVIEWED AND REGENERATED – UPDATE

'This will be an ongoing focus throughout SE1C and SE2 [future sessions of the school experience pattern]. Pupils with more challenging behaviour are in my current phonics group. It is important to be more consistent with behavioural management techniques. Need to implement more sanctions with this group: loss of golden minutes, behavioural forms, taking a minute out of class, etc., but also to consider: if these are actually essential in the lesson, who are they benefiting?

During whole-class teaching of numeracy, I felt that my classroom management/lesson flow could have been more seamless. Need to make sure I plan transitions that I am going to use: hand up? 1, 2, 3? Make sure children have stopped and are listening, etc.

Need to continue progress on making behaviour and classroom management more seamless.

Positive feedback about my lesson transitions; I am becoming more adept at stopping the class and getting their attention so I can carry out a mini-plenary or bring them back to the carpet.

Consider using other techniques to get pupils' attention: currently using hands up (works with this class but issue might be that learners with backs to you cannot see the signal); could also use rattle/bell, counting, clapping.

During lessons, I try to assess pupils' levels of engagement and decide the suitable behaviour management technique for that individual, e.g. some learners in my phonics group need firm reminders of expectations and often need sanctions to be carried out fairly and consistently.'

How an informed other, or your inquisitive self, might respond to Ayisha

This PLI is most likely to be an on-going focus for Ayisha's professional learning. Therefore, the curriculum and teaching responses that she has introduced and assessed for effectiveness in her modified teaching programme and approach to teaching, will provide informed ways in which this initiative will be regenerated for further refinement and application. The initial and, therefore, assessed response is described with suggestions regarding further clarification, such as the implementation of more sanctions with renewed questioning of purpose and outcome highlighted, and asking whether these are actually essential in the lesson implementation, and so on.

Further clarity and preciseness could be brought to this interrogation if the sub-phases of 'progress review' and 'regeneration' were more clearly separated. The generative process needs to go beyond a description of 'considering using other techniques to get learners' attention' to actually enumerating what these responsive strategies might be, as Ayisha extends the strategic responses that she had identified earlier in the *how* and *when* phases. A teacher-learner, after the trialling of their initial responses, would then identify other relevant teaching and learning processes applicable to the PLI. The review and development aspects of this initiative would continue to identify appropriate learning experiences as both the 'learning *how* to learn' and 'learning the *what* and *how* of teaching' become intellectually driven and comprehensive.

The underlying message for Ayisha is the need to *attract* the learner to the interesting and relevant learning that is developed in the well-prepared activity, and *distract* them from engaging in off-task behaviour. The key phrases for Ayisha might become 'attract and distract' rather than 'react and disrupt', when focusing on the learners' involvement in the flow of the learning activity. These responsive teacher actions would be more supportive of her initiative's intent of creating a 'seamless and less disruptive' approach to managing learners' behaviour and attentiveness to the task.

CONTRIBUTING IDEAS 6.4

Plan effective pedagogical responses so as to 'attract and distract' learners rather than 'react and disrupt' the flow of the lesson sequence.

AYISHA'S EXAMPLE: CONNECTING WITH EXTERNAL CRITERIA

Teachers' Standard 7 – Using approaches which are appropriate to pupils' needs in order to involve and motivate them.

How an informed other, or your inquisitive self, might respond to Ayisha

The standard identified in this example is concerned with the ability to 'manage behaviour effectively to ensure a good and safe learning environment' and is probably more specifically about 'using approaches which are appropriate to learners' needs, in order to involve and motivate them'. If these external criteria are important targets to consider, it might be helpful if they were stated, in this PLA cell phase, in concise bullet-pointed references. Though such criteria have been, in most instances, created by external governing bodies, they tend to be stated in very general terms and are not always helpful in identifying the specific and personal professional learning that you may be engaging with. Initiatives guiding teacher behaviours need to be specific if they are to provide clear professional learning pathways. With this understanding in mind, note that some aspects of Ayisha's critical analysis, interpretation and generation of professional learning responses appear to have gone beyond the stated intent of these standards and have sought to personalize and clarify what might be proposed as 'good learning environments' through a series of focused and meaning-making questioning sequences.

Concluding comment on Bennie and Ayisha's examples

While there may be aspects of professional learning that need to be focused on other than those presented in this critical exploration of Bennie and Ayisha's examples, they demonstrate what enquiring professionals might bring to their critical analysis, interrogating, theorizing, interpreting and generative processes. The professional learning that is questioned, clarified and enhanced will take on a personal identity unique to the individual teacher-learner as they conceptualize their current and potential professional knowledge and understanding, their life and educational experiences together with their perception of their role in the classroom. Some questions in the enquiry process might fit better in one particular focus cell phase of the professional learning agenda than another, but the significant characteristic that will be applied by the individual is the understanding that relates to the specific, and sometimes unique, connections that are essential conceptions of their personal understanding. Though every new teacher exists in a wider professional learning community where common skills are required, it is the personal way that such skills are made unique to the individual that is important in this process.

So far, this chapter has revisited the most significant components of the PLA strategy, the articulation of the professional learning initiative (the *what*) together with the personal professional reasoning of the *why*. These components provide the learning focus that is important for your on-going professional expertise.

Further analysis of the *whats* and the *whys*

As the *what* and *why* phases are crucial aspects of the professional learning agenda process, this section will offer an additional opportunity for you to think back over your learning to this stage. We identify a number of *what* statements together with their associated reasoning: the *whys*. As you will have recognized by now, there is a close theoretical and practical relationship that needs to exist between these two elements of the PLA strategy in identifying, maintaining and generating creative planning, pedagogical, managing and assessment responses to the professional issues and concerns raised.

So, critically review each of these pairings and consider how you might add to these to enhance their conceptualization and the reasoning that provides an insight into theoretical and practical knowledge bases for teaching. It is important that you review how these two ideas are related and the ways in which they will influence the creative development of practical teaching and learning responses to the initiatives. An anticipated 'teaching characteristic' reference is included for each of these initiatives that might be helpful if you are relating the initiative to an external criterion.

Example 1

WHAT

'Questioning: Use of further questioning to allow students to extend their answers, references and learning.'

External criteria category: Pedagogy – enabling learners to increase their conceptual understanding.

WHY

'When a student provides an answer, opinion or response, there is a need to allow them the opportunity, through further questioning, to elaborate and explain the point they are making. In this way, I can access their degree of understanding, where their ideas are conceptually and contextually relevant. This procedure is in contrast to my listening to the learner's response and then contextualizing and justifying the response through my own explanations. It may not be helpful for their learning if I "overstate" my interpretation to "better fit" with what I require rather than as a representation of their meaning and articulation.

In addition, subsequent questioning can extend the students' learning as they are being asked to further explain, conceptualize and then justify their current schema of understanding (Piaget, 1964). This interactive teaching approach will enable other learners to enter into the dialogue process and to offer an indication of where their learning "is at". This extending discussion process will provide valuable assessment data for me in the planning of subsequent lesson activities as the content concept and/ or skill is further developed.'

Example 2

WHAT

'Modelling "talk partners": to introduce a model for a learner interaction process for the students that demonstrates that "talk partner" discussions are dialogical.'

External criteria category: Pedagogy – increasing the effectiveness of learner interactions.

WHY

'It is important that "talk partner" interactions are used as a means of creating dialogue and not just as one student talking at another, and are also not a 'time-filler' allowing me to review the lesson intent and sequence before continuing the lesson. To begin such dialogue, I should assign one student the role of the listener (questioner) and the other that of the talker (responder). When asking the talk partners to provide their feedback, the listener (questioner) should be able to provide the points raised by the talker (responder). In this way, I will be able to assess that the students are building their speaking and listening skills. As well as listening attentively to what is being "talked about", the listener will also be required to ask clarifying questions of the talker. Such questions will support the talker in further clarifying the message that they are attempting to give.'

Example 3

WHAT

'To plan for effective group work processes in which students work together co-operatively and are respectful of other group members' participation and their ideas and opinions.'

External criteria category: Pedagogy – maximizing the effect of group work in learning.

WHY

'This initiative is concerned with establishing the "ground rules" for efficient and focused group work behaviour and providing learners with strategies to keep group work response on-track and relevant to the evolving discussion and investigation. Students will be required to work collaboratively with others not only in the school environment but beyond the school gates in later life. It is important that the student learners are involved in the identification and articulation-in-practice of a "set of rules" for guided and effective group interaction. It would be anticipated that the learners would include in their "set", effective group work skills such as attentive listening, respecting divergent opinions, participating courteously and sharing. These are all beneficial life-long skills that serve all of us in the varied communities in which we operate. A community of learners in the classroom cannot exist if the basic means of communication are non-existent.

These skills are learned behaviours and so it is appropriate to focus on encouraging learners to be more aware of how to engage with each other by discussing these behaviours with them explicitly. There may be a further need to display a permanent visual in the classroom that can be referenced and considered often within collegial interactions. This notion that 'academic and group learning skills' need to be emphasized in a teaching and learning programme would indicate that learning objectives may require special lesson sequences that will be as important as lessons prepared to develop skills in maths, English, science, geography, etc. Lessons focusing specifically on skill development for learners will be essential in my programmes.'

Example 4

WHAT

'I will consider introducing into my lesson sequences, learning experiences that actively engage all learners, either through hands-on experience, such as investigations, interactive whiteboard challenges, etc., or visual stimuli, for example videos, flip-charts, pictures, diagrams.'

External criteria category: Pedagogy – considering the nature of the learning focus in activities.

WHY

'There is a perceived need for a more varied teaching approach that will complement both the individual learning styles of the student members and the instances of teacher-talk and associated closed questioning sequences, and writing tasks focusing on the specific content of the lesson. I have found that uninterested or disengaged learners do not usually give their learning attention in predominantly teacher-talk presentations. I propose that relating to these learners through enactive (hands-on engagement, etc.) and iconic (imagery) activities will provide more significant guidance and support for their cognitive development.

Bruner's (1966) three modes of representation (iconic, enactive and symbolic) is an approach to building on the learner's individual learning preference and engagement with discovery learning processes. Engagement with the enactive mode, through experiential learning, helps students to process new ideas and start to form connections with prior and new thinking. They are building on the accommodating of conceptual schemas through the assimilation of these new ideas (Piaget, 1972). The iconic mode of visual representation enhances students' conceptual understanding and progresses their thinking strategies and skills.

The symbolic mode (the language of description and clarification) adds to the enactive and iconic mode, and represents the concept and its understanding in language form. These modes of representation can combine to create and reinforce the attributes and instances of the concept being focused on, and so enhance learners' thinking. References to Bruner's modes of representation of content will provide another conceptual layer to my matching of the content and associated pedagogy to the learning preferences of the students. So, it seems that I have a need to change my planning focus by making my teaching programme responsive to all my learners, and so effectively differentiated.'

Example 5

WHAT

'Behaviour management techniques need to be more seamless and less disruptive to the flow of my teaching during the lesson. This will include refocusing learners who are distracted from the learning sequence.'

External criteria category: Managing learner behaviour – raising awareness of the classroom's learning environment.

WHY

'Currently I'm highlighting positive reinforcement of behavioural expectations during the lesson and learners are responding well to this. However, I am having to stop and disrupt the lesson's flow in order to speak to an individual learner, to remind them of 'good listening'. I want to be able to reinforce attentive behaviour using methods that do not distract from my teaching. The primary focus needs be on the students' learning rather than on the off-task behaviour management. It may be important to develop ways of focusing and increasing my awareness about what is happening in the classroom. It would be very beneficial if I could anticipate inappropriate behaviour prior to it becoming an issue that requires my direct response. Is this a need to raise my levels of attentiveness to *what* is happening in the learning environment and so be better prepared to respond constructively? Is this a planning issue for me, with an identified need to seek more variety and relevance in my selection of associated teaching strategies? Do I need to develop specific intellectual strategies to increase my awareness, my observing and listening skills?'

Example 6

WHAT

'Introduce more open-ended and process- and enquiry-generating questions, such as: What do you know about how this relates to ...? Why do you think ...? How did you come to that conclusion? How might we extend what Thomas has given to us? Are there other ways that we can consider this issue?'

External criteria category: Pedagogy – challenging learners to use self-clarifying questioning patterns.

WHY

'Questioning sequences that require the learners to go beyond just listing facts or providing a basic description of an idea will assist them to become independent and autonomous learners, and scaffold their learning without my having to lead them to the "proposed" answer. This focus will continue to encourage independent thought and ideas. Myhill and Dunkin (2005) found that using a range of questions and focusing open-ended questions enable learners to articulate their thoughts, secure learning and become more independent learners. These questioning sequences can also assist in identifying misconceptions by requiring the learners to explain why they have a particular idea or understanding and to further explore how this specific response has developed. It is also important for me to understand and be able to identify questions that are sometimes labelled "open-ended". What might be the conceptual focus of these question types? What intellectual skills do such questions require of the learners? It is important that these learners develop thinking skills that will include their ability to clarify, classify, analyse, interpret, interrogate, apply, predict, infer, evaluate, synthesize, etc. These are the thinking skills that should be reinforced by my enquiry-focused questioning. Should I also consider the influence that such question processes will have on my collection and interpretation of evaluative information from such learning exchanges?'

Example 7

WHAT

'I need to ascertain learners' understanding of the significant concepts at the introductory phase of a lesson as well as what is required of them before they can engage effectively with the individual or group phase of the activity.'

External criteria category: Ensuring learners' awareness of both the intention and procedure of the learning activity.

WHY

'It is important to have the learners articulate what they have been instructed to do and to review their learning intentions for the following activities. It is important that I ensure that the learners are aware of the specific learning intention and associated success criteria before moving to the next level or phase of the learning experience – that is, what has been taught to them up to this stage of the lesson, what they are expected to do in the following stages, how to do it and how to be successful. This is a way for them to become more confident as autonomous learners. They need to be sure and confident of what is required of them, which may involve a knowledge and understanding that is beyond just a simple statement of 'what am I learning here?' or even 'what are we learning today?' There is a need in the final point of the introductory phase of the activity to establish clear learning pathways for all groups of learners.

The identification of students who appear not to have acquired the learning intention of the lesson's introduction can then be gathered for further explanation before moving to the individual or group phase of the activity. This review session for 'not-quite-with-it learners' will ensure that the class group is 'on task' from the start of the activity phase of the lesson and clearly focused on what is required. If I can introduce these process frameworks, then learning in the classroom will become more effectively directed and achieved. The children need to know what the learning is and, just as importantly, *how* they will accomplish it.'

Example 8

WHAT

'To provide positive feedback to all learners for their contributions during "carpet time" of the lesson [the introductory phase – for this teacher-learner, it takes place on a carpet area at the front of the classroom], regardless of whether they have fully articulated what I might consider to be the "perfect" anticipated response.'

External criteria category: Pedagogy – encouraging learners to engage with all phases of the learning activity.

WHY

'This process is initiated to support learners' awareness of their "self", and so help them feel confident in their ability to share their evolving ideas and to have these "accepted" as contributing to the learning in the classroom. My welcoming of all responses and contributions will also assist in identifying any misconceptions and misunderstandings that should be addressed subsequently. If only learners who are confident that they "know" the right answer are willing to contribute, then many misconceptions may go undetected by me. Many learners may also become disengaged and lack confidence in their own abilities. My creation of a supportive, though sometimes challenging, learning environment needs to encourage all learners to be confident that their "offerings" will be accepted and valued as providing further layers of understanding to the topic of discussion.'

Summarizing the PLA strategy

Chapters 5 and 6 are companion chapters, where we have 'worked through' two examples of PLA entries that have been created by teacher-learners Bennie and Ayisha, as they endeavoured to understand and apply a critical review strategy for self-regulating their professional learning. This is a strategic approach that will support and extend their teaching and management expertise during their teaching sessions in the classroom. You will also see this relevance to your evolving professional understanding if you conduct a PLA-type critical analysis process on any 'new' or challenging idea that you have identified while engaged in professional development learning activity. Intriguing ideas might have challenged you in school or university contexts. Any learning that presents a challenge to you as a teacher-learner in developing professional awareness could be scrutinized using the enquiry and self-generating process of the PLA.

Though we have provided 'feed-forward' comments on each of the efforts of Bennie and Ayisha, we strongly suggested that you can benefit from engaging with the content of the PLA cell phases and the associated questioning patterns of the original investigative and generative responses of Bennie's and Ayisha's PLAs. It is also a useful professional learning exercise for you to provide 'feed-forward' comments relating to each phase's purpose and function, and to imagine how, as the 'informed other' or your evolving inquisitive self, you might consider supporting and guiding their on-going professional learning.

In encouraging you to become further involved in clarifying and refining the professional learning process for your own use, this chapter ends with another example from a teacher-learner, this time from Mike's PLA process. Do your own critical analysis, interrogation and interpretation of what has been presented. As you enter this critical awareness process, try to anticipate how you might develop responses to the professional learning initiative that Mike has identified. What guidance might you offer Mike to support his on-going awareness of his teaching role? The detailed outcomes of your critical analyses and generative responses will, of course, be personal and hence specific to your individual teacher characteristics, values and prior experiences.

This activity further reinforces the dual perspectives that were identified earlier in this chapter – you are both an analyser and creator of effective responses to professional learning ideas, and a reviewer of your own and another's professional concerns and thinking. What is important is the trialling of the questioning processes associated with each stage of the professional learning strategy as an active and challenging professional learning activity to engage with.

Activity: Mike's PLA example for you to work on

THE *WHAT*: THE PROFESSIONAL LEARNING INITIATIVE

'Ensuring that I'm overseeing and monitoring all learning groups that have been established with the sequence of a learning activity, even when I have planned a focused responsibility for one group.'

How might an informed other or your inquisitive self respond to Mike?

THE *WHY*

'When assessing the effectiveness of a recent literacy lesson, I noted that I had been working with a focus group and that, initially, a significant part of my time had been taken up with "getting them started on the task". This had meant that learners in other groups were possibly not supported adequately until later in the sequence of the lesson. I became aware of this about midway through the lesson, and then set my focus group an achievable task to complete as I sought to monitor and support the work of learners in other groups.

After then allocating my time around the other groups, I was able to return to more detailed guiding of my focus group. From this observation, it would seem that a reorganization of my time in providing guidance and support to all groups, including my focus group, needs to be considered.

It would appear that if learners are to gain a sense of the content significance of this particular activity in developing their knowledge and understanding, it is important that I'm "with" them to reinforce this perspective. They must be able to gauge that my direct involvement with them as learners in the learning experience will demonstrate the worth that I'm placing on its importance.'

How might an informed other or your inquisitive self respond to Mike?

THE *HOW* AND THE *WHEN*

'Setting my focus group an initial achievable task that can be completed without my direct involvement while I oversee the "start-up" work of all other groups, is my first strategic response to my concern. For example, while the learners in my focus group are setting up their response sheets to include the learning intention, I will monitor and direct other groups to ensure that they are settled and able to complete the independent or group task successfully. I will need to make this "supportive review path" on a number of occasions during the lesson period.

When: This will be an on-going trial during my future planning and teaching sessions.'

How might an informed other or your inquisitive self respond to Mike?

PROGRESS REVIEWED AND REGENERATED: AN UPDATE

Week 1

'This was a particular area of planning and teaching focus for me during this week. Though I had identified a particular focus group within my lesson plans, I was able to purposefully oversee/monitor all groups within the class. The effective initial setting up of the task for my focus group has enabled this process to continue. I have become confident that I can provide more direct support to all groups. This was evident during my science and geography lessons during which I found that this re-organization provided me with time to rotate efficiently around the various groups during the course of the lesson.'

Week 2

'I now need to extend the purposes of this re-organization as I now find that I'm making insightful observations when overseeing the learning of each group; these observations can be very useful in terms of assessment and so inform my future planning. Groups are now aware of my involvement in their work and tend to be very focused on my interactions with them when I get to their specific group. In a sense, they are coming to expect my interactions with their group and have clarifying questions ready. I need to establish ways of recording information as I move around the classroom (not the same pattern of movement on each occasion) to support learner groups.

Completing an assessment pro-forma or noting down interesting comments or contributions when working with a group, will enable this evaluation development to take place.'

Week 3

'These are organization and assessment strategies that I have been able to develop and refine considerably over the last couple of weeks. Their effectiveness became very clear to me in a recent numeracy activity when I taught without the support of any other adult. I was comfortable in guiding the learning of all groups of learners and provided support to their learning needs as necessary.'

Week 4

'Though not directly related to the monitoring of the learning process of groups, I found that if learners are completing an independent activity, i.e. a mental oral starter, I must ensure that I provide them with the

(Continued)

(Continued)

appropriate amount of thinking time without interruption. It would seem that attending to this "teacher objective" has made me become more aware of the ways that learners are engaging with their tasks.'

Week 5

'Though I have continued my planning and teaching focus on this teacher objective, I find that occasionally my 'all group monitoring' process can be slowed down if I'm seemingly distracted by the needs of one group. This organizational approach will continue to need my close professional learning attention. Should I consider an adaptation to my mini-plenary strategy in some of these circumstances? I have decided to review the introduction of mini-plenaries if, as I monitor various groups, I find that common misconceptions are evident. It will be more appropriate use of my "teaching time" if I have all groups attend to a revised input. I am aware that if some groups are working effectively and don't require the mini-plenary, I could exclude these groups. Is this another PLI that I should consider? Being knowledgeable and therefore flexible about learner needs and only responding as required?'

How might an informed other or your inquisitive self respond to Mike?

CONNECTING WITH EXTERNAL CRITERIA

'I have "situated" my PLI, in the Teachers' Standard associated with promoting good progress and outcomes for learners, with a more specific focus on also being aware of learners' capabilities and their abilities to respond effectively in various learning situations (Standard 2b).'

How might an informed other or your inquisitive self respond to Mike?

CHAPTER SUMMARY

We hope you feel confident to take the opportunity to consider some of the analyses, interpretations and the generation of planning, teaching and managing initiatives raised in different ways and how they may challenge your thinking. We have indicated throughout Chapters 5 and 6 that you should be seeking and sourcing your own unique ways of responding to challenging concerns such as those Mike has identified. It is always helpful to read what another teacher-learner at a similar stage of their professional development might conceptualize about their role. You are not treating such input as coming from an informed other but rather from a peer or colleague who is engaged in similar professional learning contexts to you. You are developing the conceptualizing skills that might be associated with your inquisitive self.

FURTHER READING

Myhill, D. & Dunkin, F. (2005) Questioning learning. *Language and Education*, 19(5): 415–27.

This article describes the classroom observation data in the analysis and illustrates how 'interactive', whole-class teaching is characterized by questions requiring pre-determined answers. It considers the nature of interactivity and the role questions play in supporting and extending students' learning experiences.

Stoughton, E. (2007) How will I get them to behave? Preservice teachers reflect on classroom management. *Teaching and Teacher Education*, 23 (7): 1024–37.

This article examines how pre-service teachers think about disconnections among what they believe about teaching, what they learn in their university coursework and what they observe of behaviour management in school classrooms.

7

THE PLANNING PROCESS

Having read this chapter, you will have an understanding of:

- the key curriculum design concept of the spiral curriculum
- how curriculum design features can be replicated in your planning responses
- planning formats for, and a responsiveness to, differing needs and abilities of specific learners
- developing cognitive planning skills that will enable you to de-construct existing curriculum programmes and create replica teaching plans for your students
- the significance of listening skills in productive teaching strategies and classroom discourse
- the close connections between statements of learning objectives and supportive questioning patterns.

Introduction

The purpose of preparation and planning is to provide a range of interesting and challenging learning experiences which will enable your learners to make connections between what they are being taught, what they already know and the potential to take such knowledge and understanding to a higher level of understanding, application, creativity and affective awareness. The processes for developing interesting, well-conceived and responsive teaching and learning programmes are explored in this chapter through the application of key concepts of curriculum design.

This emphasis on preparation and planning will allow you to progress through your on-going cycle of professional learning. Planning the classroom curriculum forms the essential link for the professional learning experiences that you are undertaking through the processes of identification, critical enquiry and interpretation. In this way, you generate creative responses to your evolving self-conceptualization as an outstanding professional. You are moving through a planning phase, to activity implementation, focused self-observation (REACT), self-regulated professional learning (PLA) to the identification of potential teaching and learning responses. It is a sequence that will enhance your ability to extend students' learning.

Your inquisitive self is created from your need to know and understand, together with the intellectual abilities to use this awareness to enhance both your own and the students' learning. Continue to be inquisitive and challenge yourself to know what is to be learnt in your curriculum and the relevant teaching strategies and skills that will provide curiosity and challenge for your learners. Model for them what you want them to achieve, through self-regulation and commitment to their learning.

The emphasis in this approach to planning recognizes that you are a focused contributor in the curriculum development process. It is important that precise and comprehensive knowledge provides a sound basis for curriculum design and creation. The following conceptual framework is your pathway to this expertise (See Fig 7.1).

How planning can fit your and your students' learning needs: a cautionary tale?

A story from Greek mythology provides a thoughtful metaphor for the approach adopted in this chapter. It sets the scene for your curriculum design and development, and the resultant classroom preparation and planning. It is told that Procrustes, the son of Poseidon, had a stronghold on the sacred way between Athens and Elensis. Procrustes had a peculiar sense of hospitality – he abducted travellers, provided them with a generous dinner, then invited them to spend the night in a rather special bed. He wanted the bed to fit the traveller to perfection. His solution was that those who were too tall had their legs chopped off with a sharp hatchet; and those who were too short were stretched on the bed!

Is there a risk that the way the curriculum is packaged and delivered can feel like a procrustean bed? How can your curriculum planning respond to students with varied strengths and weaknesses, who learn at slightly different paces, varying across subjects? What do you need to attend to if perhaps only half the learners in your class find the median pace of the classroom teaching appropriate to their levels of existing knowledge? What if half the remainder of the class group find the pace too quick, and the other quarter require a higher intensity of teaching and learning progression? What about any variations within each of these sub-groups? Are there still a very few whose learning needs lie outside of these groups?

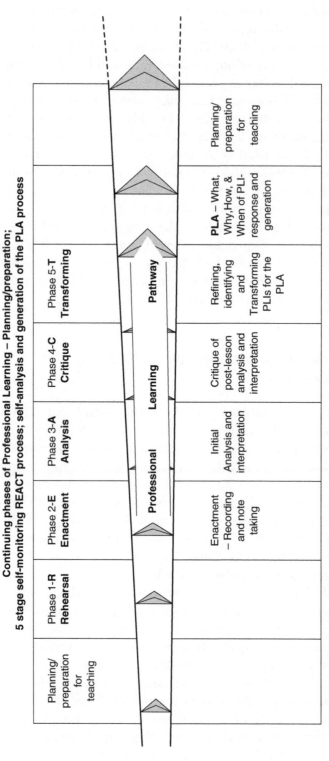

Continuing phases of Professional Learning – Planning/preparation;
5 stage self-monitoring REACT process; self-analysis and generation of the PLA process

Planning/ preparation for teaching	Phase 1-**R** Rehearsal	Phase 2-**E** Enactment	Phase 3-**A** Analysis	Phase 4-**C** Critique	Phase 5-**T** Transforming		Planning/ preparation for teaching
		Enactment – Recording and note taking	Initial Analysis and interpretation	Critique of post-lesson analysis and interpretation	Refining, identifying and Transforming PLIs for the PLA	**PLA** – What, Why,How, & When of PLI-response and generation	

Professional Learning knowledge and processes are increasing through self-regulation, and the developing sophistication, complexity and creativity of the interactions between the perspectives of 'Learning HOW to learn' and 'Learning the WHAT and the HOW to Teach'

Figure 7.1 The expanding professional learning pathway

Refashioning the procrustean bed of an imposed standard curriculum to recognize that the potential of each learner's ability varies, calls for a commitment to tailoring your teaching and responses so that every student can develop to their potential. If your planning of content, its scope and sequencing, and the diversity of pedagogical responses are to be in concert with student needs, then you must go beyond 'the changing of the (work) sheets' and claiming that the bed fits! (There will be further discussion on differentiation later in this chapter.)

How can you develop a curriculum programming process that can adjust the content and pedagogical offerings, through differentiation, to fit students' needs, and so eliminate the categorization of students who don't manage within an inflexible curriculum? The programme preparation and planning strategies that are explored in this chapter will provide you with the tools for focusing and articulating such a responsive classroom curriculum. Therefore, the basic or standard curriculum programme can become a differentiated one.

Curriculum design principles

This section identifies a number of related concepts that will support your planning processes. First, you will need to be able to *deconstruct* the curriculum documentation of others before you *reconstruct* a replica, specifically generated for your student group.

At the start of this reconstruction process, planning begins from the most abstract and complex content elements of the official curriculum. That is a deductive process of starting with the identified curriculum's key ideas and skills. Through this activity, you are identifying the scope and sequencing of the content and process learning activities of your yet-to-be-created learning programme. As your students engage with these programme activities, they acquire their knowledge and understanding through an inductive process. As the programme designer you should plan deductively, beginning with the big picture – the most complex and abstract organizing concepts of the curriculum. This means planning for your students to acquire the specific content inductively as they engage with the learning experiences of your programme. What does this look like? In this learning process, your students are accessing the curriculum programme at the most concrete level of knowledge and understanding, such as facts or basic skills. After identifying and forming connections across information contained in these learning activities, your students will be developing a conceptual awareness of the key idea or concept that you embedded at the start in your planned learning sequence for them.

The adoption of this comprehensive, deductive approach to planning is complemented by the inductive learning processes that you will plan for your students. Carefully sequenced involvement in the learning experience enables a student to increase their conceptual awareness of the key ideas which you have drawn from the official curriculum and on which you based your planning procedure. Your students are being led back along your deductive planning pathway, for their conceptual acquisition of these key ideas, or concepts, in the cognitive domain. Through this process, your learners are being required to go beyond gathering factual content and are moving towards understanding the inherent conceptual structure. To effect this, you need to develop an awareness of the content of subject domains, akin to the working knowledge of an expert in the field.

For instance, Ball and Cohen (1999) argue that prospective teachers must learn content in ways that replicate the ways in which they are expected to teach. Specifically, they suggest the 'development of subject matter that emphasizes the reasoning and "meanings and connections" specific to each field' (as cited in Darling-Hammond, 2006: 194). It is important that you establish this awareness, if your students are to acquire a subject's inherent ideas, meanings and connections. You need to understand that something is relevant, *why* it is so and on what grounds it can be justified. It is just as significant for you as the aspiring expert to have a sense of the influences and specific situations where your acceptance of a curriculum's rationalization can be challenged by your expanding knowledge and commitment.

Grossman and colleagues (1989) proposed three dimensions important to the task of cognitive teaching: (i) central and associated concepts, (ii) organizing principles of the discipline, and (iii) factual information. Their conception of content knowledge emerges through a cognitive process of critical analysis and interpretation that is guided by the substantive and syntactic structures of the subject domain. In this context, substantive knowledge can be characterized as including knowledge of concepts and generalizations, contributing ideas, and facts, and the ways they are conceptually organized. Syntactic knowledge is about the nature of enquiring into a particular subject domain and the intellectual processes through which new knowledge is introduced and accepted in that professional community. It includes knowledge about proofs and the rules of structure (Schwab, 1978). Knowledge of substantive and syntactic structures has implications for 'what teachers choose to teach, and how they teach' (Shulman, 1986: 9). The significance of these curriculum design conceptions was included when discussing the curriculum of professional learning in Chapter 2 (see the double-helix model, Figure 2.1).

Grossman et al. (1989: 30) highlight the importance of syntactic knowledge – the language of common sense and experience. It is a key factor in shaping teaching and its preferred teaching strategies and approaches to the planning and implementation of learning programmes:

> A lack of syntactic knowledge may also seriously limit prospective teachers' abilities to learn new information in their fields. Without a firm grasp of the syntax of a discipline, prospective teachers may be unable to distinguish better, more and less legitimate claims within a field. Teachers may find themselves unable to consider effectively a specious argument, even if they are aware of its dubious nature.

If you are not able to identify and apply the syntactic process within your own study of a subject discipline, then it is unlikely that your students will acquire this key learning process that enables them to establish new knowledge, independently. Their knowledge and understanding will be restricted to the limitations of their taught programme unless they are also able to source the syntactic process from elsewhere.

Shulman's (1986) initial definition of content knowledge was firmly focused on the relationship between how it is possible in an academic, abstract sense to represent and articulate understanding, and hands-on practical skills, by creating ways of representing and formulating the content domain that makes it comprehensible to others. Bruner's theory (1966) about the different modes of knowledge representation – the enactive, the iconic and the symbolic – could also be used to advance an understanding of the substantive orientation of the curriculum.

In review, substantive content knowledge includes the concepts, generalizations, contributing ideas, facts and attitudes and skills of a discipline domain with its explanatory and organizational frameworks, whereas syntactic or process knowledge identifies the methods of enquiry and interpretation in the discipline, and thus demonstrates how its knowledge is generated, tested and justified.

For your students to achieve this, you must have definitive knowledge and understanding of the conceptual structure of all facets of the content and pedagogical elements of the curriculum. Only then are you able, at any time during the teaching and learning process, to place each student's response within the growing complexity of the particular concept of the curriculum. Thus, your focused guidance and support can be directed at continuing the progression of awareness that each of your students requires. Learning of the subjects of the curriculum starts with your level of understanding.

CONTRIBUTING IDEAS 7.1

You need to be a learner of curriculum principles before you can become a designer and constructor of planning for student learning.

Spiralling into complex and abstract understandings

The curriculum design concept – the spiral curriculum – will add significantly to your understanding of the deconstruction and reconstruction process. Any teaching programme that you develop specifically for a student group is best thought of as a mini version of the official curriculum and, therefore, should be constructed as a representative replica of it. So, as you design various time-sensitive planning activities, it is helpful to acquire an applicable understanding of the organizing concepts in curriculum design and planning. You are usually planning to a specific time frame within a school year – for example, for a particular year level, a term, a 5/6-week medium-term plan or a collective daily programme. Each of these curriculum replicas is drawn from your awareness of the scope and sequence of the learning content and associated pedagogy for the specific time frame. Alongside this, you must remain aware of the content foci that are provided in the curriculum for earlier developmental stages as well as of those that follow later. In your initial efforts at planning, you might only be attending to groups of learners with similar teaching and learning requirements. As your ability to match curriculum requirements with learner characteristics is developed and fine-tuned, you will become increasingly comfortable with focusing aspects of your planning on individual students. You have then personalized the curriculum for yourself and the individual learners in your planning group.

The *spiral curriculum* is a description of the patterning and sequencing of the content of the curriculum (See Fig 7.2). This concept is a contributing factor to the deconstruction process and subsequently a design response to your planning intentions and the associated learning experiences. The conception of the spiral curriculum is founded within the cognitive learning theory proposed by Bruner (1960, 1966). He suggested that curriculum design and development would commence with the hypothesis that any subject area of the curriculum can be taught in an intellectually honest and motivating form to any learner at any stage of development. For Bruner, even the most conceptually complex content, if appropriately structured and presented, can be understood by very young learners. Based on Bruner's work, the key principles of the spiral curriculum include the following:

- the learner revisits a theme, concept or skill several times throughout their learning
- the complexity and abstraction of the theme or concept are extended through a focus on relevant attributes with each interaction
- new learning is adapted and absorbed into the knowing context of previous learning.

The benefits of the spiral curriculum perspective include the notion that learning is reinforced and consolidated each time the learner revisits the attributes of the abstract concept. These associated attributes, growing in complexity within this spiral organization, enable a logical progression from simplistic to more complicated knowledge and understanding. In a sense, a layered approach to learning employs the key concept attribute of increasing complexity, embedded in the content samples of a series or sequences of learning activities.

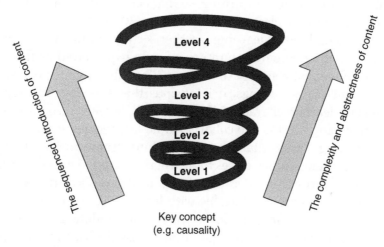

Figure 7.2 A spiral curriculum model

This approach to content organization is applied in most curricula, with key concepts and processes being constant throughout as the sophistication of curriculum learning increases. If you use this perspective consistently during the extrapolation of the subjects of the curriculum, then the identification of content sequences will provide a useful entry into your efforts to differentiate your replica curriculum programme to the abilities and needs of your learners. Some learners will be operating intellectually at varying levels within their key stage, or grade level, while you will find others are better accommodated to modified programmes from earlier or later key stage content and processes.

Conceptualizing differentiation within spiral curriculum design

In responding to varied learner characteristics, the teacher endeavours to create meaningful, relevant learning tasks with an on-going formative assessment focus that enables adjustments to be made to the teaching programme. The manner by which students' cognitive levels are managed usually involves a flexible and changing grouping of learners. Tomlinson (2008, 2014) suggests that differentiation is not a teaching strategy, but rather a way of perceiving and responding to the nature of learning. In planning procedures, this conception can be applied through an approach to content and process design that is in accord with the learner's readiness, interest and articulated learning profile. The concept of differentiation does not presume different learning experiences for each and every learner, but engages a flexible perspective when considering an activity's complexity, the engagement with the activity, the nature of the associated learning resource materials, and the modes of learning, so that each student can experience a *good learning fit* in the classroom (Tomlinson, 2008, 2014).

During the analyses of learning in other sections of this book, the creation of a differentiated curriculum programme is perceived as the normal expected professional response to learners. Though students are ordinarily placed in same-age groupings, it is obvious that this does not represent homogeneous learner characteristics. You will quickly recognize learner qualities that range across age cohorts. Some learners are capable of completing learning tasks that the curriculum frameworks identify as appropriate content and processes for learners two or so years in advance of your year-level curriculum. Because of various delayed learning skills, others might become more comfortable with learning content for students of earlier development and experience. And your middle group may also exhibit learning achievement and potential across the learning spectrum of curriculum content.

As you become increasingly aware of this diversity of ability and potential in your classroom, you should seek advice from school colleagues who possess detailed knowledge and understanding of how you might be able to respond to these varied needs. Special needs support personnel are available, as are those teachers who have developed expertise in providing challenging learning programmes for those who exhibit gifted or somewhat advanced abilities. You may also be required to explore the special education facilities and support in your local area. You need to know where to go for support in providing learning opportunities for these students.

How will you respond to the requirement to differentiate the curriculum content and process and so create diverse and relevant variations in your curriculum programme? The first step is to be aware of the totality of the curriculum subject, its scope and sequence of content, including affective and skill domains as well as the cognitive dimension. Look most carefully at how this sequence is developed over time. You need to clearly identify the minor concepts and attributes, and the tasks that are proposed for these stages. This knowledge of what is seen as relevant conceptual development and associated illustrative activities for the year levels before and after will be most helpful in the next phase of your curriculum programme design process. Remember, the integrity of the content and the matching pedagogy need to be maintained in your planning so that you don't provide watered-down learning activities and resources that are easily recognized, especially by the learners, as having this intent.

The second phase is to focus on the range of learning content of the selected idea or theme and to create your specific scope and sequence chart of this. This is the diversity of content that will be represented in your pro-gramme. You are now ready to consider the teaching skills and strategies, your personal pedagogy, that will enable the students to engage successfully with their learning. As a new teacher, you are extending your knowledge of how your students learn (see Gardner, 1995, 2011). On the other hand, you might find the modes of representation offered by Bruner (1961, 1966) a more manageable process for offering a range of learning within the activity module. Modes of representation are the way in which information and conceptual knowledge and understanding are stored and coded in memory. Rather than being arranged in age-related stages (for example, Piaget, 1964, 1972), the modes of representation are integrated and only loosely sequential as they translate into each other. They can be used effectively to facilitate a student's thinking and problem-solving skills that can subse-quently be transferred to a range of situations (Bruner, 1961):

- enactive representation (action-based)
- iconic representation (image-based)
- symbolic representation (symbol and language-based).

These representations enable learners to construct their own knowledge frameworks and to do this by organizing and categorizing information through these various modes.

As you develop the ability to deconstruct the curriculum and its subject areas, opportunities to introduce a variety of pedagogy and the relevant material, and personnel resources, into your response to learners' character-istics will become evident. So, know the curriculum content that includes and frames the extent of your group's suggested learning, and seek variety in both methods and resources to create meaningful and relevant learning modules and units of study. In short, differentiation is the process of personalizing universal learning goals for groups of students with similar learning characteristics. As such, it is closely related to personalized learning and individualized learning.

Although Bruner was a cognitive theorist, he also endeavoured to put his curriculum design principles into practice with the development of his programme, *Man: A Course of Study* (M:ACOS, 1970). This had a socio-anthropological curriculum approach, with descriptive accounts, simulation and role play, photo-murals, animal studies and anthropological film in the presentation of the sequenced content and associated resources. Key concepts and processes included structure and function; innate and learned behaviour; and cognitive skills associated with observation, developing inferences and generalizations and problem solving. These were continually visited in student learning, with greater sophistication and complexity being introduced through challenging enquiry processes and various knowledge and affective content sample foci. For example, Bruner used content such as studies of animal behaviour (including Konrad Lorenz, 1950 and Jane Goodall, 1969) and the field work of contemporary anthropologists, such as Asen Balikci (1968), in film documentaries following the seasonal migratory cycle of a group of Inuit people, the Netsilik of the Pelly Bay area of Northern Canada.

If you can access a library copy of this curriculum package, you will find that Bruner uses his significant concept of the representation of learning – that is, iconic, symbolic and enactive modes – to provide multiple entry points for student learning within this year-long curriculum. This is also an early curriculum response to providing contexts for individual learning. (See Gardner [1995, 2011] for more on multiple intelligences; also see Taba et al. [1971] for further discussion of the spiral curriculum.)

Having briefly considered the significant concepts in curriculum design and planning, let us now look at how you might use this understanding to prepare a curriculum programme that is directly relevant to your learners.

Deconstructing the curriculum proposals of others

As proposed earlier, your classroom planning involves two critical analytical and generative processes. We now consider the planning process from deconstruction to reconstruction, while being guided at all times by the principles of the spiral curriculum.

Your initial action is interpretative analysis – the deconstruction of official national or local planning documents. These plans might include more specific key learning stages, and long- and medium-term planning proposals and initiatives. Curriculum programmes devised by national or local planners will contain a comprehensive exploration of the sequencing of core concepts and skills over long periods of time. Documentation created by a school or teaching colleagues will have distilled the essential aspects of these societal requirements and placed the curriculum within a school mission statement, specifically adapted for the learners.

It is essential that you focus your initial planning on both these perspectives. Yes, work directly from the local documentation where available, but also ensure that the wider curriculum guidance has been accurately portrayed. An effective implementer of curriculum should understand the design and organizational principles used in the construction of the curriculum and also appreciate the big ideas or concepts that underpin its structure and sequence.

Let us take a moment to define how curriculum content is used in curriculum documentation, and in this book. The content of the curriculum includes: (i) cognitive knowledge and understanding, that is, concepts, generalizations, contributing ideas and facts; (ii) the thinking processes that are used by learners to qualify and extend their understanding through critical enquiry and interpretation; (iii) attitudes and values that are generated through the subject; (iv) social skills, that is, leadership, cooperation, working together, sharing roles and tasks; and (v) the academic skills associated with identifying, differentiating, categorizing and labelling, and constructing information that is applicable to other content areas.

Curriculum content is inclusive of these domains, and care should be taken that your programmes are not confined to the cognitive focus of learning. The affective, thinking processes and social skills areas of student learning need to be directly engaged within planned activities, as these skills do not happen incidentally. The focus of the wider curriculum is more than knowledge and will require all learners to engage effectively in each of the content domains identified above. For example, though the mathematics curriculum will include key concepts such as number (later in the sequence to include algebra), measurement, geometry and statistics, among other topics, it will also address problem solving and data categorization. Key concepts in history will include causality, change and continuity, power and authority, control and conflict, and historical interpretation, though again there will be a focus on developing an empathy with historical periods and significant contributors. We will return to this idea of the conceptual structure of a subject discipline within the curriculum as a process in the discussion on de-construction, later in this chapter.

CONTRIBUTING IDEAS 7.2

To interpret and then create relevant and appropriate learning programmes for students, you must first have an understanding of curriculum design principles and programme sequencing.

The analytical process of a broad range of curriculum documents is focused on:

- *isolating* the explicit and implicit curriculum content (such as concepts, minor concepts, generalizations, contributing ideas, attributes, facts, thinking processes, attitudes and skills), including connections and linkages, and the proposed pedagogical strategies for the implementation of this curriculum programme
- *identifying* the intended student learning behaviours, or competencies, as proposed outcomes of students' engagement with the resourced and differentiated learning experiences that are provided.

Through such analysis, you can acquire knowledge, understanding and appreciation of what is to be taught (curriculum content and associated pedagogy) and for what purpose (learning behaviours and outcomes). This deconstruction process is essential if you are to understand and interpret these appropriately in your planning. This level of awareness will ensure that the programmes you create are in accord with the curriculum emphases and foci of the education system and your school.

This deconstruction process develops through a number of increasingly detailed phases of the evolving complexity of the cognitive content stream, juxtaposed with the key concept and its attributes. In the following discussion, it will be illustrated in a variety of ways. How you interpret this process will necessarily be representative of your meaning making and could lead you to a variety of responses.

The first phase will be for you to identify the structure of the content of the curriculum. For example, for the cognitive content domain, you would isolate the key concepts, the associated minor concepts or attributes, and the processes linked to these to provide syntactic strategies and learning experiences for developing the intended knowledge and understanding. Once you have isolated this conceptual structure at the entry level of the subject curriculum, the next task will be to follow these components throughout the subsequent stages of the curriculum. You will find that as a key concept develops in complexity, abstraction and comprehensiveness, related minor concepts are included. In some cases, key concepts provide the basic foundation of a sequence of learning and can be extended or reinforced to raise the conceptualization to a higher abstract level. This comprehensive knowledge and understanding of a particular curriculum will enable you to place your planning within the overall design pattern. With this appreciation of the overall intent of the curriculum, you will now be more directly concerned with the sub-section relating to the age cohort you are teaching, as well as the content levels immediately before and after this. Let us now consider a curriculum subject area and illustrate how your analysis might be articulated.

Example 1: Adapting a mathematics curriculum in England

Mathematics is an interconnected subject where it is anticipated that students will move fluently between representations of mathematical ideas. Though programmes of study are necessarily organized into apparently discrete domains, it is intended that students should develop powerful connections across mathematical ideas and so develop a fluency in resolving increasingly sophisticated problems. Such acquired mathematical knowledge and understanding may also be applied to science, information technology and computing, geography, biology and other subjects. Curriculum documentation also considers the pace of learning and teaching and suggests that progress will be based on the security of students' understanding and their readiness to progress to the next stage. Your awareness of how students attend to the pace and progression within the subject curriculum will also enable you to recognize and respond to learners who might not reach the proposed levels and who require more prior-stage support. So, what is the conceptual structure of this mathematics subject? Consider the following table that you could adapt to suit other curriculum analyses.

The curriculum analysis in Table 7.1 identifies three levels of cognitive understanding: key concept, minor concepts and associated attributes of learning, and so provides the fundamental organization of a mathematics curriculum. The most concrete level, attributes, provides the opportunity for a statement of general objectives that would then provide a focused framework for the creation of a series of relevant learning activities. The development of a representative table, based on your deconstruction of your particular stage/grade focus, would provide you with a curriculum framework to guide the planning of specific activities for your students.

Table 7.1   Key Stage 1 Mathematics

Key concept	Minor organizing concept	Attributes – including competencies
Number	Place value	fluency with whole numbers
		counting in patterns, reading, writing > 100
		multiples of 2s, 5s, 10s
		language – equal to, more than, most, least, etc.
		identify and represent in objects and pictorially
		number line – patterns in number
	Operations	addition and subtraction, number bonds, one-step problems
		multiplication and division – one step problems, doubling, connections between arrays, patterns
	Fractions	equal parts, half/quarter
Measurement	Lengths/Heights	long/short, tall/short
	Mass/Weight	heavy/light, heavier than, lighter than
	Capacity/Volume	full/empty, more than, less than, half full
	Time	quicker, slower, earlier, later
	Money	recognize and value, denominations, coins/notes
	Measure and record sequence of events	lengths/heights, mass/weight, capacity/volume, time (hrs, mins, seconds, hour/half hour)
	Recognition and use of language	chronological order, dates in sequence
		as for the above measurement areas
Geometry	Properties of 2D and 3D shapes	2D – rectangles (square), circles, triangles
		3D – cuboids (cube), pyramids, spheres
	Position and direction	describe position, direction and movement; include whole, half, quarter and three-quarter turns
Statistics	Tally charts	interpret and construct
(introduced in Year 2)	Block diagrams	sorting categories by quantity
	Simple tables	totalling and comparing categorical data

Following the design principles discussed so far in this chapter, you could create sets or series of clearly situated (with objectives) and defined learning experiences and attach these to the relevant minor concept or attribute. This is now the reconstruction phase of your planning process.

Let us continue with this analysis of a mathematics curriculum, including a focus on the key concept 'number' to enable you to assess how this can provide increasing sophistication in the extrapolation of the associated attributes within a spiral curriculum design. The mathematics curriculum for Key Stage 3 (Table 7.2) continues to identify the subject as being a creative and highly interconnected discipline. The subject is essential to the everyday, critical to science, technology and engineering, and has application in financial literacy and most forms of employment. The identified aims again focus on the need for continuing fluency with the fundamentals of mathematics, and the encouragement of reasoning and enquiry. These intentions emphasize that the solving of problems with increasing sophistication is necessary.

Table 7.2 Key Stage 3 Mathematics

Key concept	Minor organizing concept	Attributes – including competencies
Number	Place value	decimals, measures and integers of any size, order positive and negative integers, decimals and fractions, sets of integers, real and rational numbers
	Product notation and factorization	vocabulary of prime numbers – factor, multiples, common factors, common multiples, higher common factors, lowest common multiples, prime factorization
	Operations	four operations applied to integers, decimals, proper and improper factors, mixed numbers (both positive and negative), approximation
		conventional notation, priority of operations including brackets, powers, roots and reciprocal relationships between operations including inverse operations
	Integer powers	apply real roots (square, cube, higher), organize powers of 2, 3, 4, 5, distinguish representations of roots and decimals approximations
		interpret and compare standard numbers
	Decimals	interchange of decimals and corresponding fractions
	Percentage	interpret percentages, fractions or a decimal, interpret these multiplicatively, one quantity as a percentage of another, percentages greater than 100%, interpret fractions and percentages as operators

This analysis of the curriculum provides insights into how complexity is introduced, not only in the form of significantly more demanding content exploration, but also with minor organizing concepts added in, extending the comprehensiveness of the key concepts. When number is considered and consolidated in complexity in Key Stage 3, notation is extended to include types and powers of integers, with operations to include work with fractions and decimals. It is interesting to note that as the mathematics curriculum bridges from the primary to the secondary contexts, variations are introduced into distinct knowledge domains, even though the conception is of fluent representations and theoretical reasoning with the stated intention of continued competence with increasingly sophisticated problem attention. Key concepts such as number, measurement, geometry and statistics continue to provide intellectual guidance in the development of students' knowledge and understanding. New key concepts, which could be conceived as offshoots of the earlier conception, are included and then subsequently become more complex and challenging, as minor organizing concepts and associated attributes and content samples are engaged with by learners to achieve a higher and more abstract understanding of mathematical concepts and processes.

It is interesting in this discussion to consider how algebra is also introduced as a key concept in the later secondary education stage, as an evolving notational extension of number. Concepts of ratio and probability are similarly introduced that are closely aligned with number, measurement and geometry. The basic key concepts of the initial stages of mathematical development have remained fairly constant, with subsequent more complex minor organizing concepts being elevated in importance. Thus, they can provide for more adaptability and application, for solving higher-order mathematical problems that are identified as residing in other subject domains, such as science, geography, technology, computing, and so on.

This branching and detailing of the increasing complexity of the conceptual structure of the discipline also makes the interconnectedness of the design more observable and relevant. The spiral curriculum design feature is sprouting branch spirals in this advancing conceptual understanding. The clarity of the representation of key concepts remains significant, but the links that can be sought and reinforced within and across the subject domains of the curriculum are also important. In order to develop your appreciation of this interconnectedness, you might want to undertake an investigation of how the concept of space or causality is evident in a number of subject content domains. Space can be identified as a key concept in subjects as diverse as science, mathematics, art, music and movement, the social sciences, and so on. Try to trace the various applications of causality, in history, political science, geography, health and physical education, and other subjects.

The deconstruction process in this example has provided a breadth of understanding of the design concept of the spiral curriculum as it is used to organize the conceptual content of the mathematics curriculum. The key concepts, as the most abstract and complex ideas, have been identified together with the minor organizing concepts and the associated attributes, which identify the students' specific learning. By tracing the spiralling of each key concept from its initial introduction, it is evident that a more challenging conceptualization of attributes is detailed and encouraged at each level of the curriculum. Explicit attention to concepts involves both you and your students in making connections between and among concepts, ideas, attributes, facts and procedures.

Reconstructing curriculum proposals

The next step in the planning process involves reconstructing a new plan, developed from these analysed knowledge bases, together with specific school perspectives. This reconstruction process not only represents your individual expertise and creativity but is also cognizant of the learning needs and abilities of your particular student group. Through an awareness of such knowledge bases, you will have identified the conceptual structure of the various elements of the content domain, but also the proposed pedagogical strategies that will support students' learning of the identified content.

Once you have a detailed understanding of the official curriculum, you are in a much sounder position to consider the manner in which you can match these identified components of the curriculum to the learning abilities and needs of your students. This requires a focused and comprehensive knowledge and understanding of your learners' achievements in the relevant curriculum area. A crucial part of this reconstructing process is in creating sets of objectives that define both the content (of others' plans) and the learning behaviour from previous engagement with the concept or skills and their attributes. You will have identified the learning behaviours, or outcomes, for your specific group of learners through your evaluations and recording of their earlier interactions with the concept and its associated attributes. The sequence of the planned learning experiences can only be safely developed from these two perspectives.

The initial focus in reconstructing a replica programme directly relevant to the needs and abilities of your students is a consideration of the specific attributes and the associated learning outcomes that will provide the scope and sequence of your preparation – for example, in teaching students at a Key Stage 3 level, a further exploration of the key concept number and its minor organizing concept of 'operations', with a teaching and learning focus on the attribute 'priority of operations including brackets'. The conceptual linkages for both your planning and student learning are identified.

You have a defined area of mathematical knowledge and understanding on which to focus your planning of a sequence of learning activities. You might want to consider such a set of related and supportive learning activities as a module, with a focused collection of associated modules providing a unit or programme of learning over a longer planning period. Individual lessons or learning experiences are not isolated items but are rather a part of related planning. The module is a focused collection of related learning experiences that may require careful sequencing for teaching and learning progression, or a series of learning activities that, taken in any order, will enable learners to extend their conceptualization or skill acquisition. The module should be conceived of as the basic unit of planning so that connections are established early in the planning process and then identified by the learning group.

A sequence of lessons for a teaching and learning module and a focused collective of modules provides your planning documentation over a specific time frame. You have identified a general objective that you will break down into more specific lesson-focused learning objectives. It is these specific learning objectives and the relevant learning outcomes that will now inform your planning.

The following description, taken from a Key Stage 2 attribute sample, illustrates the steps that you might follow.

Planning example: Statistics (Key Stage 2 – Years 3 & 4)

Key concept: *statistics*; minor concept: *graphical methods*
Attributes (from minor concept):

- 'interpret and present data using bar charts, pictograms and tables' (Year 3)
- 'interpret and present discrete and continuous data using appropriate graphical methods, including bar-charts and time graphs' (Year 4).

It would appear from these attribute statements that the increased complexity for student learning is the introduction of continuous data and time graphs. Remember, it is the statement of the anticipated intent and outcome of the attribute statement that now provides your planning focus. The mathematics curriculum further identifies specific learning to be undertaken by students in developing knowledge and application of graphing content, including: considering the language used, histograms (bar graphs) – characteristics, x and y axes, grid formation, transformation, translation of data from tables to bar graphs, interpretation of information illustrated, and so on.

Accepting that you have initiated these preliminary investigative processes from the broader representation of the curriculum documentation, the following framework identifies the phases that you might follow in making these curriculum programme documents yours, consistent with your level of understanding.

The emphasis in the following phase descriptions is on a process of planning and accepts the notion that the district or school will have preferred formats for you to adapt. When you use these layout presentations, consider each of the elements and be able to justify their inclusion. For example, if you include a reference to how this learning is related to other subject areas, make sure that this is carefully articulated. Entries in planning documents must have a defined purpose. The written presentation of these documents ensures that such purposes are clearly articulated and appropriately referenced. The details provided need to be adequate and relevant, ensuring that the subsequent implementation is clearly grounded in your preparation. In a sense, your planning and preparation should not be *for show* but *for go*. The following phases provide a quick review of how you might approach this planning process.

Phase 1: Acceptance of curriculum document frameworks (planning) and analyses

Isolate the content structure, the concepts and facts, the thinking processes, the learning processes and skills, and attitudinal development. Your understanding of specific content comes from your interpretation of curriculum documents, the content tables discussed earlier in this chapter. Be very specific in this investigative process so as to focus not only on the key concepts, minor concepts and their attributes, but also on the interconnectedness that you can identify of each attribute as a learning outcome. Look to identify the connections and linkages inherent, inferred or shown within the diagrammatic representations that are created, or in the illustrative representations of the curriculum that you have developed from your own interpretations and understandings. You may find that creating a conceptual web from this description will enable a visual representation of the content, its connections and relevant pedagogy that has been isolated and then abstracted from the planning documents.

Read the available national and school curriculum documents and follow the sequence of the planning processes as they identify how a concept or skill will be developed through focused activities, over time, from one key stage to the next. Alongside this, be able to articulate these concepts and skill attributes in order to link them to your ways of understanding.

CONTRIBUTING IDEAS 7.3

As designer of your teaching programme for your student group, you need to develop a detailed and comprehensive knowledge and understanding of the content and pedagogy of the curriculum.

Phase 2: Writing sets of learning objectives

Sets of learning objectives will guide the sequencing and structure of your planning for teaching; and provide foci for both the specific learning activities that will be resourced to present the content framework identified in Phase 1 and the assessment criteria that will be used to gauge learner achievement. These sets of interrelated learning intentions are identified in a similar way to the content structure above. Specific intentions or objective statements within each set of learning objectives represent the connection that is being sought between the content dimension and the learning behaviour that is anticipated. If the content is focused on the cognitive development and associated thinking processes of the learners, then they will know, understand, apply, analyse, evaluate and synthesize (create) the content that is inherent in and drives the learning activity.

The learning objective has two significant dimensions. These relate to the content of the curriculum subject and to the learning behaviour and outcome that the planner intends the learners to achieve. For example, the following could be identified as guiding a series of learning activities relating to the concept and attributes of statistics identified earlier:

At the end of the set of learning activities, the students will:

- **know** (*the learning behaviour*) the characteristics of histograms/bar graphs in presenting numerical information (*the content*):
  - **list** (*the learning behaviour*) the characteristics of a histogram/bar graph (*the content*)
  - **identify** (*the learning behaviour*) the relationship between data and the forms by which it can be represented (*the content*)
- **construct** (*the learning behaviour*) a histogram from information provided in another form (*the content*)
- **interpret** (*the learning behaviour*) the information provided in a collated form – the histogram (*the content*).

In the listed objectives, a general objective that identifies knowledge is subsequently articulated into more specific learning behaviours, of listing and identifying. The objectives that follow identify an 'academic skill' and also a 'thinking process' from the breadth of the curriculum content. When you are developing evaluation checklists, this specificity is useful in ascertaining the degree to which the intended knowledge of the concept's attributes has been achieved (see Bloom et al., 1956; Krathwohl and Bloom, 1964; Harrow, 1972; Anderson and Krathwohl, 2001, regarding cognitive, affective and psycho-motor taxonomies, and attribute behaviours, that can be used to specifically define students' intended learning).

To enable the students to engage positively with an understanding of their learning processes, you may want to express learning intentions in student-friendly language adapted from the specific learning objectives you have identified. Simplified, student-friendly learning intentions will reflect, in more general terms, the planned programme objectives. It is your planned programme objectives that direct the scope and sequence of the learning activities and not the 'abbreviated' objective for the learners.

Phase 3: Developing and resourcing learning activities and experiences

There are many data sources and websites for accessing a range of activities that can be adapted to match the set of learning objectives that have been identified in each plan. It is important that you initiate your planning from such sets of intentions before seeking a range of learning activities to be planned to meet the differentiated learning needs and abilities of students. Again, Bruner's (1960, 1966) three modes of representation – the iconic, the enactive and the symbolic – could be considered in creating a set of relevant activities. An emphasis on the foundational teaching skills of listening and questioning is explored later in this chapter. The suggested readings, and references throughout, identify teaching strategies and models for teaching, for example concept development, concept attainment, group investigation, enquiry training, synectics, role play and simulation gaming, among many others. You could further research and develop these for inclusion in your teaching repertoire. The suggested readings relating to Joyce (1985) and Joyce et al. (2015) are good starting points for your research.

Phase 4: Assessing the degree to which learning objectives have been achieved

Learning objectives provide the success criteria that form the assessment foci for identifying the actual and potential levels of student learning.

The assessment process usually includes four phases: collection, collation, analysis and your interpretation, as reference information on individual student achievement and potential. Importantly, it also provides feedback for focusing the review process of your planning and implementation of the teaching and learning process (see Black & Wiliam, 2006; Wiliam, 2011). One way to collect, collate and present assessment information is as a checklist, where learning objectives and associated success criteria are column headings of the checklist, with students' names entered as rows. Checks and annotations can be recorded in the cells and your annotated comments regarding the learning attainment of specific learners will enhance your insights into their learning and provide initiatives for subsequent planning.

You might consider the formula, E (evaluation) = A (assessment) + J (judgement), which indicates that you bring professional knowledge and expertise to interpreting and theorizing about the assessment information that you gather.

Sequencing learning activities

The literature on planning for teaching by teacher-learners highlights a need to identify a specific set of experiences that are focused on your evolving understanding and preparation for responding to learning needs (see Blackwell & Pepper, 2008; Norman, 2011; Hudson, 2013). That is, you create a written rehearsal of understanding and awareness that was introduced earlier, through the deconstruction process of what is to be taught and the potential teaching and learning processes that can be used. You must become aware of and monitor the development of the strength of your own planning processes. You must aim to match your knowledge of the abilities and potentials of your specific group of learners with the ideal official curriculum, in ways that are imaginative, supportive and responsive to the group's identified needs and abilities. Your planning needs to be responsive to your evolving need to create carefully sequenced units of study, where the duration of the activity, the extent of the associated content, the complexity of the teaching strategy and approach, and the size of the teaching group are all given due care and attention. There is a professional requirement for careful sequencing and increasing complexity in developing the preparation of learning tasks.

In summary, you should consider in this planning process the

- duration of the planning sequence, at least at a module level of organization
- organization and number of the students to be involved

- organization and presentation of classroom space, and the support personnel
- selection, sequence and connection of teaching content (including differentiation to respond to the variety of learning abilities and needs)
- complexity of the teaching strategy or skill to be used in the learning process
- evaluation of both learner outcomes and the effectiveness of the planning and teaching programme.

Reviewing these requirements anticipates your development of an awareness of the patterns and the interrelatedness of this process. The content structure must be known and understood before starting to plan. The connections that are to be developed by your students should be easily interpreted from a concept mapping of the content and the associated connections. Once the content structure knowledge is secure for you, then it is necessary to clearly identify the level of understanding that is proposed for the students. If the learners are going to be required to apply the acquired knowledge and understanding, then this needs to be clearly identified in the learning objectives. Modular lesson sequencing is the process of organizing several learning experience plans that will be taught consecutively and that relate directly to a topic or theme. The purpose of lesson sequencing is to achieve optimal learning outcomes for your students and to create smooth transitions between lessons in order to meet the stated learning objectives of the learning module, or modules, and the extended unit plans.

Purpose for sequencing of learning experiences

Well-organized and properly sequenced learning experience plans are of benefit to both you and the students, and can generate a smoother functioning classroom where disruptions are minimized. There is less stress for you, and the learning environment is optimized for encouraging student learning. Other benefits to be gained from effective sequencing include:

- *Smoother transitions*: when you can plan what is intended to happen during each learning experience, you will be able to make smooth transitions that encourage the flow of learning for the students. The student benefits as new material is more easily absorbed when presented in an orderly manner that closely relates to what has been worked on before. Your teaching role can be very demanding and requires the development of good organizational skills. The early preparation of resource materials will enable time for a mental rehearsal about their introduction and relevance to the learning tasks.

- *Facilitating the scaffolding of conceptual understanding*: clear goals and sequenced lessons will enable you to anticipate any potential difficulties and problem areas that the students might encounter. Additional support, such as specific exercises and activities, can be garnered to assist students in meeting the challenge of more abstract concepts. Scaffolding the subject's spiralling content enables you to predict the complexity and difficulty of some tasks. Students require resources and insights to draw on if they are to meet these challenges successfully. As students do not progress through the sequencing of the content material at the same rate, in the activity plan you will have differentiated varied sequences to accommodate faster and slower learners – a benefit of having the whole set of modules prepared in advance.
- *Effective organization*: if individuals, or groups, within the class progress through the material more quickly than anticipated, you will be able to move on to more advanced tasks very readily as they are already planned. The converse is also applicable.
- *Future planning*: sequencing lessons in advance will allow you to more closely predict how long you think it will take to cover certain material, and then see how long it actually takes the students to progress through the lessons. You may plan to recycle, with relevant modifications, module plans and unit plans in subsequent years, or for your other teaching groups. You will be able to carry out such revised planning based on self-observations and your evolving experience.
- *Assessment checks*: with module plans and unit plans prepared in advance, you will be able to identify the optimal points for checking the students' understanding of the material and also how best to structure these assessments, that is, an assessment for learning process. Assessment checks are directly based on the specific learning objectives that you have set.

What to remember when sequencing planning

So, in summarizing the discussion on preparation and planning:

- Initially, identify the learning objectives for both the module, unit and medium-term plan as a whole, and those directly relevant to each individual activity plan. The setting of overarching and specific goals assists in sequencing the module's lessons. It also reveals what materials, learning aids and teaching support will be necessary to achieve these objectives.

- Utilize your REACT processes of self-observation to monitor how the students are progressing through the learning activities. Is the lesson sequencing leading the students towards using higher levels of cognition, and applying and justifying their understanding and attitudes through the activities? How can they be supported further with their learning processes?
- Review your modular lesson plans, again using REACT, and evaluate the impact that your scaffolding processes and associated resources have had on students' learning progression. Have you provided the students with the academic learning tools necessary to complete each particular activity of your teaching and learning module?
- Review your assessment processes. Have you designed some evaluative techniques to ascertain students' understanding of the content and resource material? Are these processes and techniques appropriate to the learning group, that is, the needs and abilities of the students as they relate to the content and pedagogy of the modular plan?

In concluding this planning focus, ensure you are using a variety of activities. Assess the activities that you have prepared to make sure that they respond to the learning and intellectual characteristics of the learning group. Determine how you are going to identify and sequence the learning experiences of your module, unit and medium-term planning efforts. You will be able to answer this question as you interact with the professional learning content and pedagogy in the following section. It will provide you with ideas to extend your teaching repertoire.

CONTRIBUTING IDEAS 7.4

Your reconstructed curriculum programme should be carefully crafted and differentiated. Elements are not added to the plan, but rather modifications to match learner needs and abilities are integral to it.

Attentive and responsive listening

As a prelude to exploring questioning skills within structured teaching strategies, we consider the significance and functioning of attentive listening. Listening, as used here, refers to your consideration and interpretation of students' responses within the sequence of a learning activity, as well as carefully attending to what you are saying. Just as importantly, we consider how you can enhance your students' focused listening as they engage with you and others in progressing through your planned programme. The articulation and development of your, and your students', listening abilities is the important first step in creating effective learning. Throughout this book, there has been an emphasis on the professional need for you to acquire and extend ways of increasing your level of consciousness of what is happening in the classroom. Such critical analysis and interpretation of classroom happenings and behaviours can provide meaningful and focused initiatives for your on-going professional learning and supports your evaluative teaching judgements.

A crucial aspect of effective questioning is your ability to listen carefully and critically to the responses that are being provided by your students and the response that these seem to evoke from fellow learners. This enables you to guide an individual's knowledge and growing comprehension, so that it can become more accessible and therefore meaningful to other students in the group. Not only will you be demonstrating interest and expressing that you value their contribution, both verbally and through your body language, but you will also be extending their understanding by further clarifying comments and redirected questioning.

Careful attentive listening is a multi-dimensional teaching skill that you will continually reassess through application in a responsive learning environment. This requires you to situate a particular student's response within their current awareness and to explore how it relates to, and is being accommodated in, the general learning level of the group. It also involves assessing how it contributes to the continuing flow of the scope and sequence of the module. In a sense, you are involved in very responsive decision making as you decide: what will happen now? Where exactly is this specific learner's response taking the flow of the lesson?

How can you extend your level of teaching consciousness? You do this by reviewing the components and influences on learning progress that are inherent in these everyday classroom exchanges. As a professional learning outcome, you will quickly recognize the value of increasing the articulation and development of essential characteristics for all participants in the learning environment, that is, to listen attentively during questioning and responsive sequences. Initially, it may seem that listening and responding are very simple processes, but it will become increasingly evident that these interchanges function at a sophisticated level of conceptual comprehension, where a variety of conditions and influences need to be identified and practised.

A questioning, listening and responding sequence involves the identification and trialling of interconnected teaching skills and a developing awareness on your part. Careful recording of this will enable subsequent critical reviews. It is these reviews that enable you to identify the manner in which you and the students interact and respond. This will eventually become an essential teaching behaviour for you. Intensive analyses of how you anticipate, predict and then interpret the observed learning interactions in these questioning exchanges, will enable you to develop a deepening awareness of the thinking that lies behind students' responses and explanations. You are mining beneath the surface in acquiring critical understandings of learner potential. You are going beyond descriptive accounts and critically seeking deeper and more applicable knowledge and understanding of the complexities in the teaching and learning process.

As has been emphasized throughout this book, it is the attentive and inquisitive teacher-learner who is confident and comfortable in extending their ability to understand and respond effectively to the learning connections that become increasingly apparent in the classroom. As you are able to generate more relevant insights through your focused critical analyses, interpretation and creativity, you come to understand that this enhanced level of teaching and learning consciousness has encouraged and challenged you to seek other pathways for your on-going professional learning. You become progressively more dissatisfied with how you approach troublesome teaching and learning incidents if you are unable to reach an immediate confident and relevant resolution. You will accept, and be professionally challenged by, the uncertainty of this professional dissonance, as a legitimate way of becoming more professional and as crucial to your students' learning (Lange & Burroughs-Lange, 1994).

Your awareness of the significance of attentive listening also has implications for your on-going professional learning. Do you listen attentively during your professional development experiences? Through understanding and applying the REACT and PLA strategies, you are further extending your personal learning processes. How might you enhance these critical review processes to extend your learning situations in classroom and university settings? We will now discuss a number of listening strategies that might challenge your thinking and responses on this learning pathway.

Is there a need to be selective in what you are paying attention to? Is there a need to filter what is being perceived?

Improving information gathering and interpretative awareness skills encourage you to listen with more than your ears, and to make more relevant and grounded decisions. These critical review activities also enhance your ability to respond to students more interactively in the social learning environment of the classroom. Such information skills include the creation of a perception framework, prepared earlier during the planning phase, and, though not inclusive, will help guide your attention to actions, ideas and behaviours that might be significant for you in responding appropriately and effectively to these learners. This can also happen during the rehearsal phase of the REACT strategic process.

As there always seems to be a multitude of behaviours, talking and movement, while you are engaged in the teaching and learning environment, a major challenge to cope with might be sensory overload. During many daily activities, there is a tendency for individuals to develop processes that might be defined as *relevance filters* or *masking templates* that are created to manage and avoid being overwhelmed by the continuous volume and stream of sensory information that is available in a busy and learning-focused classroom. These filtering processes enable the conscious mind to deal with the stimuli and associated information. Once structured and established, filters support and focus your attention on a single task or associated tasks, or on the part of the environment in which you are engaged. In this way, you are able to effectively ignore most of what else is competing for your attention and action. This process of perception was first introduced when the rehearsal and mental image frameworks were discussed in the exploration of the initial preparatory phase of the REACT process, in Chapter 3.

What is filtered, in or out, depends very much on your pre-teaching decision to focus attention on specific aspects of your teaching and learning process that you have planned to introduce or modify. Therefore, in new situations or environments, planned attention to specific features and conditions is an aptitude that you must learn. These changes to your filtering devices and in your professional awareness will be honed over time but in a conscious manner. This level of consciousness will not occur haphazardly but must be planned for and executed with careful thought and assessed judgement. With time and practice, your conscious perceptions can be structures you recognize and accept as signals that represent the planned-for actions and exchanges that are significant in developing a particular response. It is important for you to prioritize these so that you can decide when and where to direct your attention. Of course, you will encounter stimuli that are not directly associated with your planned focus. However, they may be seemingly important insights and will be recognized as *not in this domain* or *at this time*, but still recorded for considered attention later.

In the early stages of self-monitoring the learning environment, you may need to try to maintain your attention on the information that is identified through these focusing filters. In this way, you are provided with lots of opportunities to develop the teaching skills and responses more directly related to your planned-for professional learning. So, staying with the notion of the masking template, you can control the gradual unmasking of areas of the template that allow more varied and equally relevant information about the teaching and learning environment to penetrate your conscious self. You will continue to enhance the quality and comprehensiveness of your expertise through the application of your conceptual skills and associated critical analyses.

What we have been exploring is the relationship that exists between speaker (student) and listener (teacher or fellow student) as responses and discussion points are offered in an interactive teaching and learning experience. This communication is sometimes referred to as *dialogic listening* (see Myhill et al., 2006; Edwards-Groves & Hardy, 2013).

This is a two-way interaction process where teacher and learners endeavour to construct an interpretative meaning from the words spoken. An extended and participatory understanding is acquired through such exchanges where responses are further illustrated by examples, such as descriptive metaphors.

The following ideas and strategies may enhance the productive nature of listening. These complement the discussion of effective questioning, introduced in the following section. Consider the probing and clarifying questions that you might ask that will lead the enquiry process. Note them and check later how they might work for you.

In an effective dialogic process, you should:

- encourage the student to offer more of what they are thinking. Can they provide illustrative examples and clarify the description for sharing with fellow learners? Develop a growing awareness that they are operating in a *threat-free* and *sharing* environment where thoughtful contributions are readily accepted
- articulate your interpretations and share how you are developing, through examples, an understanding of their responses
- paraphrase and feed-forward the current levels of collective understanding and interpretation
- discuss how you arrived at these perceptions and understandings.

This suggested sequencing framework provides for variations to be introduced that further enhance the student group's analyses and interpretations of the responses that are offered and clarified in discussion and in questioning patterns. This emphasizes the sharing perspective of learning.

Improving your listening skills for responsive teaching

It is easy to misjudge listening as a simple, passive task. It requires more than the ability to collect and absorb information from someone else. Listening is a process, and a very active one, that requires focused efforts from the participants. A model of good communication consists of a number of phases represented by the necessary skills of receiving, comprehending and clarifying, remembering, evaluating and responding. Encourage your students to adopt this skill set in their listening activities. *Receiving* is the act of focusing on acceptance of the presented information, whether verbally or nonverbally. Not all communication is given through speech as other senses are also employed in perceiving the information. It is essential that attention is focused, that any distractions are identified and are being controlled or avoided. You may be good at multi-tasking but it is important to demonstrate to the other person that you are committed to the act of listening. Interrupting the speaker is a distraction and, therefore, you may find it more beneficial to the dialogical interaction to practise nonverbal feedback, for example nodding. The focus is on attentive listening, so try to avoid missing significant points that could lead to an incomplete message being received. It is best to leave your response till later.

Comprehending (and so clarifying) is the aim of the listening process and provides the content focus for any clarifying question and response. You have received the information from the speaker and have started to process the inherent meanings. You can extend your understanding by asking clarifying questions or in offering paraphrased interpretations of the message you are receiving. At this stage, you engage in strategies that will enable your conceptualization to go beyond simply absorbing and processing information. You are re-conceptualizing the key elements of a message by first identifying the fundamental points and converting this collection of small details into a more inclusive key idea or theme that has meaning for you. This could be part of a conceptual framework that you have previously developed, that is, you are *remembering*, as you have considered this idea previously. You are making the message more familiar as you relate this new information to existing schema. You will recall that we explored this notion of a categorization of related conceptual information in the earlier discussion regarding the rehearsal process of REACT in Chapter 3.

The next phase is concerned with your *evaluation* of the information that is being offered. Are you starting to prepare your response while still sorting this information as a listener? For example, is the offering, fact or opinion? Is it interpreted or biased and, if so, can you decide the speaker's intent from their message? Now that you have a detailed understanding of the nature of the information being provided, and having identified the key ideas and supporting evidence, you can respond specifically to the other person's statement. Addressing the speaker's points makes it easier for them to transition into a listener role as they focus exactly on the part of their message you are responding to.

This may appear to be a fairly lengthy process, but it tends to happen in an abbreviated time frame. It is important in any classroom communication that you enable both yourself and your students to take control of the listening process to avoid misunderstandings, misconceptions and complications regarding the intent of this significant learning activity.

CONTRIBUTING IDEAS 7.5

Listening is an actively focused process that is enhanced by your skills of receiving, comprehending, remembering, evaluating and responding.

Understanding the teaching skills you will need

What are the teaching skills that you may need to develop? Your repertoire of teaching skills, procedures and strategies is developed as a direct professional response to curriculum content and the learning abilities and needs of your students. While there is not room in this book to explore all of these, the summary below can guide you in accessing the available literature supporting a professional need to provide a specific teaching and learning focus within the planning exercise.

Teaching skills may be categorized into four groupings:

- *presentation skills* include explanations, introductory and closure, variability, modelling, etc.
- skills for *learner involvement* focus on discussion, debates, guided discovery, stimulating enquiry and creativity, *questioning* (our next focus), developing concepts, etc.
- *classroom management and learner guidance* relate to an awareness of learner behaviour, on-task motivation, handling uncooperative behaviour, distracting and attracting attention, etc.
- *small group skills* involve organizing the nature of groups, co-operative group guidance, creating function roles (leadership), and so on.

Earlier, you will have noted some of these teaching skills, described in varying detail as examples of teaching behaviours (in the PLA strategy, in Chapters 5 and 6). The descriptors are also used in the literature for further research of your knowledge and application of these very important teaching procedures. For example, if you have decided in the early planning phase that enquiry-based research will provide a doorway into the content that you have selected, then acquiring the knowledge of this process and its organizational characteristics, and taking advantage of the opportunity to conduct stage-sequenced practices for the students, will be effective planning responses.

Your students will need practice in aspects of a teaching skill or strategy before they will be able to effectively apply it in a learning module. So plan for sequentially introducing the teaching skills identified above, and the more complex teaching models and strategies, into your pedagogy and the learning repertoire of your students. Prepare for them to succeed with any new strategy that you want them to use. Your teaching skills will become their learning skills.

Because the significant and recurring application of sequenced questioning lies within most of these teacher strategies and techniques, an extended exploration of this specific technique follows.

Questioning skills and applications in the learning context

Consider the following scenario: you are in a classroom with students interacting and responding enthusiastically with you and each other. They seem to be eager to answer your and others' thought-provoking and challenging questions. There is excitement and commitment in the air. Then you notice a drop in their participation level and you ask yourself what has caused this. Are they taking *wait time* to let their understandings catch up with what has transpired? You decide to pose another question as a further trigger – some grab onto it and the learning seems to be reinvigorated. The questioning patterns you are using focus on the content of the learning experience. You feel that the students are captivated by the quality and sequencing of the learning. You are comfortable with this unfolding of the conceptualizing sequence and with students seemingly learning from others' contributions as well as your own.

Is this your typical classroom scene or one to which you aspire? How was this intensity of learning enquiry and exchanges planned for? How can you change or develop what you do now to establish an interactive learning environment close to the one described? Let us explore a number of principles and types of questioning and procedures by which you could enhance this active and proactive teaching and learning environment.

Questioning in the classroom

Questions in the classroom are the cornerstone of the educative process and central to the development of thinking and the capacity to learn. They are integral to most learning but may sometimes be overlooked by those new to teaching who are developing their responsive pedagogy. Questioning patterns provide the stimulus for critical thought and deep-level understanding and interpretation. Planned and well-matched questions engage and excite learners. They provide them with opportunities to create new insights and have ideas, and seek relevant connections to the content theme or topic. Questioning has a key role in your planning. Will I need to consciously teach my students how to ask good questions and not just to answer them? Is this an essential condition in creating a *culture of enquiry* in my classroom so that I can encourage relevant independent thought?

Much research into classroom teaching (first recognized in detail by Good and Brophy, 1978, and subsequently by Cotton, 2001; Walshaw & Anthony, 2008; and others) indicates that as much as 60–80% of classroom questioning is based on low order, factual recall and procedural questions.

You plan to create a learning culture of enquiry by the use of higher cognitive questioning aimed at effective teaching and learning progress. To do this, you need to construct questions with precision and then ensure that you are asking the appropriate questions of the relevant learners. In this culture of enquiry, you will be maximizing creativity by encouraging the asking of thoughtful questions that become dynamic focus points for critical involvement and the enriching of understanding. Effective questioning is the key, not only because it makes thinking visible, but also because it brings prior knowledge to the fore, shows specific levels of student understanding and is able to demonstrate reasoning and creative abilities.

The next section discusses the value and significance of questions, identifying what is required of the learner when a question is encountered; exploring questioning methodology; and looking at how to design effective questioning for focusing your learning programme. Throughout the learning process, you should formulate patterns of questioning that demand higher-order thinking, critical thought and interpretation (just as this text is designed to assist you in a similar way).

Questioning strategies

Early in your teacher preparation, you will want to pay close attention to the creation of questioning patterns and sequences that raise the cognitive demand of the enquiry process. For the rehearsal and implementation of your plans, place these questioning sequences directly in the relevant sections of your planning documentation. It is these sequences that provide the scope and guidance of the learning processes.

For example, you may use key questions as representing the content of your planned learning objective. Critical enquiry can be enthusiastically initiated by key questions. Bruner used this approach in his *Man: A Course of Study* (M:ACOS, 1970) social science programme by focusing the content on three questions that were always present, to be reviewed and puzzled over as the students engaged with the various content domains. The questions were:

- What is human about human beings?
- How did they get this way?
- How can they be made more so?

By asking a key question, you can initiate thinking and interactive discussion and so directly engage students in their prospective learning. Framing an activity in the form of a question raises motivation levels and encourages learners to become committed to their learning. They are able to clearly identify the learning objective. You might also consider a Socratic questioning pattern that creates a critical learning environment, probes thinking and so encourages the students to question their knowledge and understanding in a structured way.

> The main categories of the Socratic questioning method would require students to:
>
> - clarify their own thinking about their assumptions and related evidence of their reasoning
> - challenge investigations of other perspectives
> - encourage focused review before offering an opinion
> - validate the initial question.

Regardless of the questioning type you use, it is the *precision* of the question that is key to the quality of the answer and to the subsequent sequence of learning. If your evaluation during the lesson's questioning sequence brings negative vibes about the progress of the learning, don't be reluctant to go back a couple of steps to consolidate or use an alternative sequence in the teaching and learning process. Review and reiteration are at the core of knowledge acquisition as, without these, skills and learning processes become quite meaningless.

Creating a culture of enquiry and participation

Here are some points to consider when creating a culture of enquiry in your classroom as you impress on your students the importance of *everyone* doing the thinking, learning and reviewing throughout each stage of every learning activity:

- Model the ways that a variety of questioning strategies can be used in the classroom. Remind your students that they can say 'Please come back to me' if they need more thinking time, or are unsure, or want to build on the ideas of their peers. Let them know you will *always* come back to them.
- Ensure you and your students have the materials needed to support the learning process, such as means of recording, pencils, whiteboards, dry-erase markers, poster board, computers, tablets or other technology.
- Practise questioning strategies with your students. Repeat these questioning patterns over several phases of your learning programme until they become routine. Give yourself time for expertise to be generated, and for the learners too so that they are better able to accompany you.
- Ensure that thinking time, or wait time, becomes a regular feature of your questioning sequence. This means structuring thinking time of about 4–5 seconds after a question is posed. Don't repeat or rephrase the question before the end of wait time.

The following may be helpful in effective questioning processes:

(1) Give students time to articulate their contribution to the dialogue. Ask probing or clarifying questions if you are aware that they have more to offer. Listen attentively to their words and the inherent meaning. Don't focus on 'hearing' your explanation.
(2) Before sharing, encourage students to illustrate their response to a question with the option for them to extend their opinion later in the activity.
(3) In response to questions, encourage students to apply and synthesize their thinking with individual or group headlines: short, compelling phrases that capture their thinking like a news headline.
(4) Ask reviewing or summarizing questions and require the students to review and add to their notes.
(5) Require students to record their own questions during learning activities or after a question is posed. This categorizing will focus their attention on the types of questions they ask others and on mapping their own levels of higher-order thinking.

Questioning for a specific purpose

Enquiry-generating questions

Effective questions are planned beforehand and could be articulated in your planning. It is helpful to plan sequences of questions that are directed towards guiding your teaching and elaborating and extending students' thinking. Your planned sequences can be identified as initiating an enquiry; engaging in an enquiry; evaluating and interrogating enquiry outcomes; and interpreting enquiry data (see Kuhlthau et al., 2012; Moog, 2014).

As well as raising your consciousness of the cognitive range of the questions and statements you make, your learners also need to conceptualize their thinking. Get them involved more directly in the teaching process as they interact and support the learning of others in their group. Encourage students to pose questions to each other and respond to teacher questions in classroom dialogue and in written conversations with a peer or small group. It is important for them to develop an understanding of the cognitive intensity of these questions.

To intensify the quality of the questioning process, investigate minor strategies that will support classroom dialogue. Consider random distribution procedures in offering questions, develop *thinking threads*, involvement of all learners in the questioning exchange, talking and listening partners, rapid individual responses to posed questions, and the use of recording resources for the sharing of individual thoughts.

Planning for effective questioning strategies

The effective introduction of questioning strategies and patterns into your teaching and learning process requires careful articulation and advanced preparation. While some teacher-learners might be skilled in questioning without preparation and forethought, many find that such on-the-fly questioning inevitably creates phrasing problems. This happens if the questioning patterns are not organized in a logical scope and sequence as intended, or do not encourage or guide students sufficiently to apply the desired thinking processes. Well-conceived questioning strategies and patterns will result in well-conceived learning outcomes. Develop and use questions that will enable your students to use attitudinal responses and skills processes as well as the cognitive understandings that you have identified as part of the learning sequence.

The revised Anderson and Krathwohl (2001) interpretations of Bloom's cognitive taxonomy (1956) present a hierarchical framework for ordering the complexity, from lower to higher, of conceptual understanding and thinking skills. Each level of the student's achievement of the skill is set out below. The revised cognitive taxonomy is a useful device in identifying and classifying questions appropriate to a specific level. Each is applicable to the conceptual understanding and thinking skill acquisition that you are seeking from your learners. This way there will be a direct congruence between your teaching and learning goals for the students and the questions that you formulate to guide the learners in achieving your intentions.

Questions or learners' responsive behaviours are sometimes referred to as lower- or higher-level responses. When this generalizing category is used, lower-level questions are more appropriate to the more concrete levels of the taxonomy where students' recall and understanding are the immediate focus or where you are diagnosing their strengths and weaknesses. If you are encouraging students to think more widely and critically, engaging them in problem solving or discussion activities or requiring them to seek information and patterns of understanding more creatively, then you look to the more complex levels of the hierarchy. As you become more aware of the application of these hierarchical levels to students' learning, you will vary the cognitive level of your questions according to the current learning anticipated.

Phases in planning questioning sequences

The first requirement for effective question planning is to be precise about the purpose for asking a specific sequence of questions. Your stated intention, as an objective, will identify both the content of the learning and the behaviour that you want the learners to achieve. Obviously, the level of cognitive response that is required of them will determine what level of questions you will prepare.

From the scope and sequencing of the content of your curriculum programme, select the specific content that will be the focus for your questioning. You might initially focus on cognitive content and consider the affective domain later in your evolving understanding of the questioning process. Focus your questions on important rather than trivial content:

- Prepare questions that require an extended response or at least an answer that refers to the specific content. Avoid asking questions that can be answered by yes or no, unless you plan to follow up with subsequent questions that further explore students' understanding and application of the learning.
- Regardless of your current expertise as a questioner, it is appropriate to write your key and associated questions directly in your planning document. Completing this task at the planning phase will provide the triggers for your rehearsal phase of self-observation (see the REACT process in Chapter 3).
- Arrange your questioning framework in a logical sequence – from specific to general, lower level to higher level, as a sequence related to students' intended behaviour, as it relates to the content. Or, you might use clusters of questions that echo the sequencing of the content. Remember that by anticipating ways that the activity might be

changed as you teach it, you can be flexible and add additional, or more relevant, responsive questions to replace some of your planned questions. Therefore, spending time in creating and structuring questioning sequences in your planning will have a two-fold benefit. First, having prepared sets of questions will ensure that you ask questions appropriate to your goals and that are directly representative of the content material. They will also provide you with the confidence to introduce responsive variations as aspects of the learning process need to be modified.

- Precise phrasing of your questions will provide clarity of the task for the students. Questions such as 'What about the UK's migration policy?' are too vague and don't offer cues to guide productive learners' responses. 'What did we say about Shakespeare's dialogue?' is too general in developing one specific stream of discussion, but may be helpful if you are seeking to collect a wide range of remembered information which you then intend the students to categorize and label, for example in a concept development strategy.
- Anticipating potential learner responses and the direction that the sequence of learning might take, is a significant aptitude for your professional learning.

Having an anticipatory perspective will develop your ability to be flexible within the learning sequence and encourage students to express their conceptions in their own words. In the initial stages of this learning, it is their descriptions that will allow them to extend the complexity of their later understanding.

As a check for yourself, review the following points to see if they fit with your developing understanding of these aspects of questioning and your rehearsal:

- What are likely to be typical misconceptions that could lead these students to inappropriate answers? Answers might be appropriate if considered within the cognitive understanding of the student at this stage of awareness.
- Will I accept the answer in the students' language or am I expecting the textbook's words or my own terms? If I accept the student's current definition, how do I encourage a response that is closer to textbook forms? The learner's response will indicate their current level of understanding of the content.
- What type of response do I expect from students? A definition? An example? A solution? A suggestion identifying a possible enquiry focus? What will be my strategy for handling incorrect answers?

- What will I do if students do not answer? Should I allow a few seconds before paraphrasing or restating the question? If my questions are thoughtfully prepared, should I trust them to elicit and guide the required learning?

The next section shows why a close conceptual relationship needs to exist among your preparation of well-conceived and clearly identified content; behavioural foci of learning objectives; and the nature and cognitive level of questioning directly related to these. Any questioning sequence that you plan and implement in your classroom has to reflect the intention of your objectives for that learning module. For example, if the learning objectives of your planned learning experiences module are concerned with guiding the learners in an analytic enquiry, that is, at a higher level than remembering and comprehending the specific content, then your explanations and associated questioning should also promote this emphasis.

The summary below is based on the revised version of Bloom's (1956) cognitive taxonomy (Anderson & Krathwohl, 2001). It provides examples of verbs used in objectives and relates them to questioning stems. Only portions of the lowest (*remembering*) and highest (*creating*) cognitive levels are shown here. Your focused research in this domain will provide the content of the 'missing categories' of the taxonomies.

Applying a revised taxonomy of cognitive levels to objective verbs and question stems

The presentation here is adapted to show the close relationship between *what* you are to teach and *how* you might use questioning sequences to enable the learners to attain the stated learning objective. For effective planning, these two aspects of your preparation must be linked conceptually. Guard against a slippage of your intentions when you are considering these related foci in your planning efforts. This procedure makes the identifying of learning outcomes as success criteria flow directly from the stated learner objectives. Evaluative checklists of outcomes will closely reflect the content, process and organization that you have provided for the sequences of your learning objectives.

Level 1: Remembering – knowledge: recall or recognize information and ideas. In preparing learning objectives, you will require the students to:

- exhibit memory of previously learned material by recalling facts, terms, basic attributes and minor concepts, and ideas.

In teaching, for constructing your questioning sequences you:

- present information about the subject topic and cognitive level
- require the learners to process the level of cognitive awareness.

Some examples of behavioural verbs for learning objectives at the recall/ remembering cognitive level include: choose, define, label, match, relate, show, what, when, who, etc.

Examples of question stems for eliciting the identified learning behaviour are:

Who was ...?

When was ...?

Can you name all ...?

What do you remember about ...?

How would you define/recognize/identify ...?

How would you choose ...?

And, for the highest cognitive level – *creating*:

Level 6: Creating – synthesis: Bringing together parts of knowledge to form a new conception and build relationships and connectivity for new situations.

In preparing learning objectives, you require the student to:

- compile information in a different way by combining elements
- create a new pattern or propose alternative solutions.

In teaching with questioning, you will:

- provide opportunities for students to assemble parts of knowledge into other forms/conceptions by questioning for creative thinking and problem solving (relating to the associated thinking processes)
- require students, through questioning sequences, to demonstrate that they can combine concepts to build new ideas for new situations.

Some examples of behavioural verbs for learning objectives at the creative cognitive level include: adapt, compose, construct, design, elaborate, generate, predict, etc.

Examples of associated question stems for eliciting the identified learning behaviour are:

What would happen if ...?

What changes would you make to revise ...?

How would you improve ...?

How would you generate a plan to ...?

The cognitive focus of learning has been partly illustrated in the above, but remember that this is one of three domains of learning that you will want to incorporate into your module and unit plans. The affective domain was presented in a hierarchical taxonomy by Krathwohl (1964) and, later, in the psycho-motor domain by Harrow (1972). You will be able to access similar descriptions of the associated levels of learning. Now that we have demonstrated how the writing of objectives can be closely linked to the creation of questioning patterns for the cognitive domain, you will be able to use a similar layout process in creating your own frameworks for other cognitive levels, and the other two domains. The creation of such referencing frameworks should be an early curriculum development task for you and will provide detailed anchor points for formulating objectives and question writing which you will continually use in all subsequent planning exercises.

To provide a more comprehensive approach to your planning, you could consider providing learning objectives and questioning sequences for two or even three of these domains in your planning modules. Such a diversity of learning will enable you to provide well-conceived and structured learning experiences and will accommodate your planning to a range of learner needs. Using more variation in preparing and implementing lessons will enable your students to create more conceptual networks and pathways, thus enhancing intellectual learning.

CHAPTER SUMMARY

Keeping a learning activity on course can seem particularly difficult. The temptation is to direct your students in a way that may not be entirely consistent with the intention of the teaching strategy because you are not comfortable with allowing too much wandering away from the points that you want to make in the lesson. An image that might be helpful in maintaining the intended sequence of the learning activity or its module, is *tacking*, as in sailing. You adjust your questioning so that you move from side to side through the learning activity, yet stay basically on your intended pathway.

(Continued)

(Continued)

Enable the students to explore ideas away from your intended learning route that are relevant to its forward thrust but be prepared to redirect them as required.

Reassure yourself that because of your careful articulation of both the content and the questioning patterns, you will, at all times, be able to return to the scope and sequence of the lesson. This image may also remind you that to stay on course you need to know *what the course is*, hence the importance of planning sequences based on key questions, and on preparing interesting material relevant to the questions being asked.

FURTHER READING

Joyce, B. (1985) Models for teaching thinking. *Educational Leadership*, 42(8): 4–7.

Joyce proposes that good thinking combines discipline with flexibility. If it is to be nurtured, then that paradox must be mastered and environments created that offer strengths without restriction – that is, environments where cultivation of the intellect is comfortably woven into the study of values, the mastery of information, and education in the basic subject domains.

Walshaw, M. and Anthony, G. (2008) The teacher's role in classroom discourse: a review of recent research into mathematics classrooms. *Review of Educational Research*, 78(3): 516–51.

Current curriculum initiatives in mathematics call for the development of classroom communities that take communication about mathematics as a central focus. The authors critically assess the kinds of human infrastructure that promote mathematical discourse in the classroom and that allow students to achieve desirable outcomes.

Wiliam, D. (2011) What is assessment for learning? *Studies in Educational Evaluation*, 37(1): 3–14.

Understanding the impact that assessment has on learning requires a broader focus than the feedback intervention itself, particularly the learner's responses to the feedback, and the learning milieu in which the feedback operates. Definitions of the terms 'formative assessment' and 'assessment for learning' are discussed.

REFERENCES

Aarts, H. and Dijksterhuis, H. (2001) Habits as knowledge structures. *Journal of Personality and Social Psychology*, 78: 53–63.

Anderson, L. and Krathwohl, D. (eds) (2001) *A taxonomy for learning, teaching and assessing: A revision of Bloom's taxonomy of educational outcomes*. New York: Longman.

Argyris, C. and Schön, D. (1978) *Organizational learning: A theory of action perspective*. Reading, MA: Addison Wesley.

Argyris, C., Putman, R. and McLain-Smith, D. (1985) *Action Science, concepts, methods, and skills for research and intervention*. San Francisco, CA: Jossey-Bass.

Baars, B. and Franklin, S. (2003) How conscious experience and working memory interact. *Trends in Cognitive Sciences*, 7(4): 166–72.

Balikci, A. (1968) *The Netsilik Eskimo*, film series. Newton, MA: National Science Foundation, Educational Development Centre.

Ball, D. and Cohen, D. (1999) Developing practice, developing practitioners: towards a practice-based theory of professional education. In L. Darling-Hammond and G. Sykes (eds) *Teaching as a learning profession: A handbook of policy and practice*. San Francisco, CA: Jossey-Bass.

Bandura, A. (1986) *Social foundations of thought and action: A social cognitive theory*. Englewood Cliffs, NJ: Prentice Hall.

Bandura, A. (1991) Social cognitive theory of self-regulation. *Organizational Behaviour and Human Decision Processes*, 50(2): 248–87.

Bandura, A. (1997) *Self-efficacy: The exercise of control*. New York: Freeman.

Bateson, G. (1987) A theory of play and fantasy. In G. Bateson, *Steps to an ecology of mind*. Northvale, NJ: Jason Aronson (pp. 138–48).

Beijaard, D., Verloop, N. and Vermunt, J. (1999) Teachers' perceptions of a professional identity: an exploratory study from a personal knowledge perspective. *Teaching and Teacher Education*, 16: 749–64.

Berliner, D. (1988) Effective classroom management and instruction. In J. Graden, J. Zins and M. Curtis (eds) *Alternative educational delivery systems: Enhancing instructional options for all students*. Washington, DC: National Association of School Psychologists.

Biesta, G. (2010) Five theses on complexity reduction and its policies. In G. Biesta and D. Osberg (eds) *Complexity theory and its policies of education*. Rotterdam: Sense Publishers (pp. 5–13).

Biggs, J. (1996) Enhancing teaching through constructive alignment. *Higher Education*, 32(3): 347–64.

Biggs, J. and Tang, C. (2011) *Teaching for quality learning at university*. Maidenhead: McGraw-Hill.

Black, P. and Wiliam, D. (2006) *Inside the black box: Raising standards through classroom assessment*. London: Granada Learning.

Blackwell, S. and Pepper, K. (2008) The effect of concept mapping on pre-service teachers' reflective practices when making pedagogical choices. *Journal of Effective Teaching*, 8(2): 77–93.

Bloom, B., Englehart, M., Furst, E., Hill, W. and Krathwohl, D. (1956) *Taxonomy of educational objectives: Handbook 1, Cognitive domain*. New York: David McKay Co.

Bousted, M. (2015) Address given at Association of Teachers and Lecturers Annual Conference, Liverpool, UK, March.

Brandt, B., Farmer, J. and Buchmaster, A. (1993) Cognitive apprenticeship approach to helping adults learn. In D. Flannery (ed.) *Applying cognitive learning theory to adult learning*: 59. San Francisco, CA: Jossey-Bass (pp. 69–78).

Brew, A. and Boud, D. (1995) Teaching and research: establishing the vital link with learning. *Higher Education*, 29(3): 261–73.

Broomfield, C. (2006) PGCE secondary trainee teachers and effective behaviour management: an evaluation and commentary. *Support for Learners*, 21(4): 188–93.

Brown, A. (1978) Knowing when, where, and how to remember: a problem of metacognition. In R. Glaser (ed.) *Advances in instructional psychology*. Hillsdale, NJ: Erlbaum.

Bruner, J. (1960) *The process of education*. Cambridge, MA: Harvard University Press.

Bruner, J. (1961) The act of discovery. *Harvard Educational Review*, 31: 21–32.

Bruner, J. (1966) *Towards a theory on instruction*. Cambridge, MA: Belknap Press.

Bruner, J. (1983) Play, thought, and language. *Peabody Journal of Education*, 60(3): 60–9.

Bruner, J. (1986) *Actual minds, possible worlds*. Cambridge, MA: Harvard University Press.

Campbell, J. and Neill, S. (1994) *Curriculum reform at key stage 1: Teacher commitment and policy failure*. London: Longman.

Carroll, W. and Bandura, A. (1985) Role of timing of visual monitoring and motor rehearsal in observational learning of action patterns. *Journal of Motor Behaviour*, 17(3): 269–81.

Chen, M. and Kuo, S. (2009) From metacognition to social metacognition: similarities, differences and learning. *Journal of Educational Research*, 3(4): 321–38.

Cleary, T. and Zimmerman, B. (2002) Becoming a self-regulated learner: an overview. *Theory into Practice*, 41(2): 64–70.

Cochran-Smith, M. (1991) Reinventing student teaching. *Journal of Teacher Education*, 42(2): 104–18.

Cooper, J. (2007) *Cognitive dissonance: 50 years of a classic theory*. London: Sage.

Cotton, K. (2001) Classroom questioning. In *School improvement research, series 3*. Portland, OR: North West Regional Educational Laboratory.

Crichton, H. and Valdera, G. (2015) Student teachers' perception of feedback as an aid to reflection for developing effective practice in the classroom. *European Journal of Teacher Education*, 38(4): 512–24.

Daniels, H. (2001) *Vygotsky and pedagogy*. Hove: Psychology Press.

Darling-Hammond, L. (1994) *Professional development schools: Schools for developing a profession*. New York: Teachers College Press.

Darling-Hammond, L. (2000) Reforming teacher education and licensing: debating the evidence. *Teacher College Record*, 102(1): 28–56.

Darling-Hammond, L. (2006) *Powerful teacher education*. San Francisco, CA: Jossey-Bass.

Darling-Hammond, L., Wise, A. and Klein, S. (1995) *A licence to teach: Raising standards for teaching*. San Francisco, CA: Jossey-Bass.

Davis, B. and Sumara, D. (1997) Cognition, complexity, and teacher education. *Harvard Educational Review*, 61(1): 105–25.

Davis, B. and Sumara, D. (2002) Constructivist discourses and the field of education: problems and possibilities. *Educational Theory*, 52(4): 409–28.

De Beni, R. and Moe, A. (2003) Imagery and rehearsal as study strategies for written or orally presented passages. *Psychonomic Bulletin and Review*, 10(4): 975–80.

Denscombe, M. (2010) *The good research guide: For small scale research projects*, 4th edn. Maidenhead: McGraw-Hill.

Department for Education (DfE) (2013) *Teachers' standards: guidance for school leaders, school staff and governing bodies*, July 2011, updated 2013. Available at: www.gov.uk/government/uploads/system/uploads/attachment_data/file/301107/Teachers__Standards.pdf

Deshier, D. and Lenz, B. (1989) The strategies instructional approach. *International Journal of Disability, Development and Education*, 36(3): 203–24.

Dewey, J. (1933) *How we think*. Boston: D.C. Heath.

Doll, W. (1989) Foundations for a post-modern curriculum. *Journal of Curriculum Studies*, 21(3): 243–53.

Dudley, P. (2013) Teacher learning in lesson study: what interaction-level discourse analysis revealed about teachers utilizing imagination, tacit knowledge of teaching and freshly gathered evidence of pupils learning. *Teaching and Teacher Education*, 34: 107–21.

Edwards, C. (1995) *Democratic participation in a community of learners*. Faculty Publications, University of Nebraska-Lincoln.

Edwards-Groves, C. and Hardy, I. (2013) Well, that was an intelligent dialogue! *English Teaching: Practice and Critique*, 12(2): 116–36.

Eichenbaum, H. (1997) Declarative memory: insights from cognitive neurobiology. *Annual Review of Psychology*, 48: 547–72.

Eisenman, G., Edwards, S. and Cashman, C. (2015) Bringing reality to classroom management in teacher education. *Professional Educator*, 39(1): 1–12.

Feiman-Nemser, S. (2001) From preparation to practice: designing a continuum to strengthen and sustain teaching. *Teachers College Record*, 103(6): 1013–55.

Feiman-Nemser, S. (2012) *Teachers as learners*. Cambridge, MA: Harvard Education Press.

Festinger, L. (1957) *A theory of cognitive dissonance*. Evanston, IL: Ron Peterson.

Frank, C. (1999) *Ethnographic eyes: A teacher's guide to classroom observation*. Portsmouth: Heinemann.

Fuller, F. (1969) Concerns of teachers: a developmental conceptualization. *American Educational Research Journal*, 6(2): 207–26.

Gardner, H. (1995) Reflections on multiple intelligences: myths and messages. *Phi Delta Kappan*, 77(3): 200–9.

Gardner, H. (2011) *Frames of mind: The theory of multiple intelligences*. New York: Basic Books.

Glaser, R. (1990) The re-emergence of learning theory within instructional research. *American Psychologist*, 45: 29–39.

Goffman, E. (1959) *Presentation of self in everyday life*. Garden City, NY: Doubleday.

Good, T. and Brophy, J. (1978) *Looking in classrooms*. New York: Harper Row.

Goodall, J. (1969) *My friends the wild chimpanzees*. Washington, DC: National Geography Society.

Goodlad, J. (1990) *Teachers for our nations' schools*. San Francisco, CA: Jossey-Bass.

Grossman, P., Wilson, S. and Shulman, L. (1989) Teachers of substance: subject matter knowledge for teaching. In M. Reynolds (ed.) *Knowledge base for the beginning teacher*. Oxford: Pergamon Press.

Gruber, T. (2013) *The acquisition of strategic knowledge*. Chicago: Elsevier.

Habermas, J. (1987) *The theory of communicative action: Lifeworld and system – a critique of functionalist reason*. Boston: Beacon Press.

Hancock, R. (1997) Why are class teachers reluctant to become researchers? *British Journal of In-service Education*, 23(1): 85–99.

Hansman, C. (2001) Context-based adult learning. *New Directions for Adult and Continuing Education*, 89: 43–51.

Harrow, A. (1972) *A taxonomy of the psychomotor domain: A guide for developing behavioural objectives*. New York: David McKay Co.

Hatcher, R. (2011) Professional learning for creative teaching and learning. In J. Sefton-Green, P. Thomas, K. Jones and L. Bresker (eds) *The Routledge international handbook of creative learning*. London: Routledge (pp. 404–13).

Hobson, A. (2002) Student teachers' perceptions of school-based mentoring in initial teacher training. *Mentoring and Tutoring: Partnership in Learning*, 10(1): 5–20.

Holmes Group (1990) *Tomorrow's schools of education: A report of the Holmes Group*. East Lansing, MI: Holmes Group Inc.

Holton, D. and Clarke, D. (2006) Scaffolding and metacognition. *International Journal of Mathematics Education in Science and Technology*, 37(2): 127–43.

Hudson, P. (2013) Strategies for mentoring pedagogical knowledge. *Teachers and Teaching: Theory and Practice*, 19(4): 363–81.

Hunter, M. (1982) *Mastery teaching*. El Segundo, CA: TIP Publications.

Joyce, B. (1985) Models for teaching thinking. *Educational Leadership*, 42(8): 4–7.

Joyce, B. and Showers, B. (2002) *Student achievement through staff development*, 3rd edn. Alexandria, VA: ASCD.

Joyce, B., Weil, M. and Calhoun, E. (2015) *Models of teaching*, 9th edn. Cambridge: Pearson.

Karabenick, S. (1996) Social influences on metacognition: effects of co-learner questioning on comprehension in mentoring. *Journal of Educational Psychology*, 88: 689–703.

Kelaher-Young, A. and Carver, C. (2013) Shifting attention: using learning self-assessment tools during initial coursework to focus teacher candidates on student learning. *Teacher Education Quarterly*, October [online]. Available at: www.researchgate.net/publication/274698447_Shifting_Attention_Using_ Learning_Self-Assessment_Tools_during_Initial_Coursework_to_Focus_ Teacher_Candidates_on_Student_Learning

Kleitman, S. and Stankov, L. (2001) Ecological and person-oriented aspects of metacognitive processes in test-taking. *Applied Cognitive Psychology*, 15(3): 321–41.

Koch, A. (2001) Training in metacognition and comprehension of physics texts. *Science Education*, 85: 758–68.

Kolb, D. (1984) *Experimental learning: Experiences as the source of learning and development*. Englewood Cliffs, NJ: Prentice Hall.

Korthagen, F. (2010) Situated learning theory and the pedagogy of teacher education: towards an integrated view of teacher behaviour and teacher learning. *Teaching and Teacher Education*, 26(1): 98–106.

Krathwohl, D. and Bloom, B. (1964) *Taxonomy of educational objectives, Handbook 2: Affective domain*. New York: David McKay Co.

Kremer-Hayon, L. and Tilleman, H. (1999) Self-regulated learning in the context of teacher education. *Teaching and Teacher Education*, 15(5): 507–22.

Kuhlthau, L., Maniotes, K. and Caspari, A. (2012) *Guided inquiry design: A framework for inquiry in your school*. Santa Barbara, CA: Libraries Unlimited.

Lange, J.D. and Burroughs-Lange, S.G. (1994) Professional uncertainty and professional growth. *Teaching and Teacher Education*, 10(4): 617–31.

Lave, J. (1996) Teaching, as learning, in practice. *Mind, Culture and Activity*, 3(3): 149–64.

Lave, J. and Wenger, E. (1991) *Situated learning: Legitimate peripheral participation*. Cambridge, MA: Cambridge University Press.

Leinhardt, G., McCarthy-Young, K. and Merriman, J. (1995) Commentary integrating professional knowledge: the theory of practice and the practice of theory. *Learning and Instruction*, 5: 401–17.

Lewin, K. (1946) Action research and minority problems. In G.W. Lewin (ed.) *Resolving social conflicts*. New York: Harper Row.

Lorenz, K. (1950) The comparative method in studying innate behaviour patterns. In J.F. Danielle and R. Brown (eds) *Physiological mechanisms in animal behaviour*. Cambridge: Cambridge University Press (pp. 221–68).

Luckner, J. and Nadler, R. (1997) *Processing experience: Strategies to enhance and generate learning*, 2nd edn. Dubuque, IA: Kendall/Hunt Publishers.

Macintosh, H. and Smith, L. (1974) *Towards a freer curriculum*. London: London University Press.

McKay, J. and Kember, D. (1997) Spoon feeding leads to regurgitation: a better diet can result in more digestible learning outcomes. *Higher Education Research and Development*, 16(1): 55–67.

McVee, M., Dunsmore, K. and Gavelek, J. (2005) Schema theory revisited. *Review of Educational Research*, 75(4): 531–66.

M:ACOS (1970) *Man: A course of study*. Alexandria, VA: Education Development Centre, ASCD.

Manning, B. and Payne, B. (1993) A Vygotskian-based theory of teacher cognition: towards the acquisition of mental reflection and self-regulation. *Teaching and Teacher Education*, 9(4): 361–73.

Marchel, C. and Green, S. (2014) Fostering knowledge and skills to teach for diversity: there is nothing so practical as a good theory. *Teacher Education and Practice*, 27(1): 118–137.

Marks, D. (1999) Consciousness, mental imagery and action. *British Journal of Psychology*, 90(4): 567–85.

May, G. and Kahnweiler, W. (2000) The effect of a mastery practice design on learning and transfer in behavior modelling training. *Personnel Psychology*, 53(2): 353–73.

Mead, G. (1934) *Mind, self, and society*. Chicago: Chicago University Press.

Mezirow, J. (1997) Transformative learning: theory into practice. *New Directions for Adult and Continuing Education*, 74: 5–12.

Mezirow, J. (2000) *Learning as transformation: Critical perspectives on a theory in progress*. San Francisco, CA: Jossey-Bass.

Mezirow, J. (2003) Transformative learning as discourse. *Journal of Transformative Education*, 1(1): 58–63.

Moog, R. (2014) Process oriented guided inquiry learning. In M. McDaniel, S. Fitzpatrick, R. Frey and H. Roediger (eds) *Integrating cognitive science with innovative teaching in STEM disciplines*. St Louis, MI: Washington University Press.

Myhill, D. and Dunkin, F. (2005) Questioning learning. *Language and Education*, 19(5): 415–27.

Myhill, D., Jones, S. and Hooper, R. (2006) *Talking, listening, learning: Effective talk in the primary classroom*. Maidenhead: Open University Press.

Norman, P. (2011) Planning for what kind of teaching? Supporting co-operative teachers as teachers of planning. *Teacher Education Quarterly*, 38(3): 40–68.

O'Brien, E. and Hart, S. (1999) Action learning: the link between academia and industry? *Educational Research*, 41(1): 77–89.

Oosterheert, I. and Vermunt, J. (2001) Individual differences in learning to teach: relating cognition, regulation and effect. *Learning and Instruction*, 11(2): 132–56.

Orland-Barak, L. and Yinon, H. (2007) When theory meets practice: student teachers' reflections on their classroom discourse. *Teaching and Teacher Education*, 23(6): 957–69.

Piaget, J. (1926) *Language and the thought of the child*. New York: Harcourt Brace.

Piaget, J. (1952) *The origins of intelligence in children*. M. Cook (trans.). New York: International University Press.

Piaget, J. (1964) Cognitive development in children: Piaget development and learning. *Journal of Research in Science Education*, 2(3): 176–86.

Piaget, J. (1972) Intellectual evolution from adolescence to adulthood. *Human Development*, 15(1): 1–12.

Piaget, J. (1977) *Development of thought: Equilibration of cognitive structures*. Chicago: University of Chicago Press.

Ponte, P. (2010) Action research as a tool for teacher professional development. In *International Encyclopedia of Education*, 2nd edn. Oxford: Elsevier (pp. 540–7).

Reid, A. and O'Donoghue, M. (2004) Revisiting enquiry-based teacher education in neo-liberal times. *Teaching and Teacher Education*, 20(6): 559–70.

Richardson, V. (1990) Significant and worthwhile change in teaching practice. *Educational Researcher*, 10(7): 10–18.

Rogers, B. (2000) *Behaviour management: A whole school approach*. London: Sage.

Rogoff, B. (1995) Observing sociocultural activity in three planes: participatory approximation, guided participation, and apprenticeship. In J. Wertsch, P. del Rio and A. Alvarez (eds) *Socio-cultural studies of the mind*. Cambridge: Cambridge University Press.

Schön, D. (1987) *Educating the reflective practitioner*. San Francisco, CA: Jossey-Bass.

Schön, D. (1991) *The reflective turn: Case studies in and on educational practice*. New York: Teachers College Press.

Schwab, J. (1978) Education and the structure of the disciplines. In I. Westbury and N. Wilkof (eds) *Science, curriculum, and liberal education: Selected essays*. Chicago: University of Chicago Press (pp. 229–72).

Shulman, L. (1986) Those who understand: knowledge growth in teaching. *Educational Researcher*, 15(2): 4–14.

Shulman, L. (1987) Knowledge and teaching: foundations of the new reform. *Harvard Educational Review*, 57(1): 1–23.

Shulman, L. and Grossman, P. (1988) *Knowledge growth in teaching: A final report to the Spencer Foundation*. Stanford, CA: Stanford University Press.

Smith, L. (1967) The micro-ethnography of the classroom. *Psychology in the Schools*, 4(3): 216–21.

Spiro, M. (1992) On the strange and the familiar in recent anthropological thought. In M. Spiro (ed.) *Anthropological other, or Burmese brother*. New Brunswick, NJ: Transaction Press.

Stoughton, E. (2007) How will I get them to behave? Pre-service teachers reflect on classroom management. *Teaching and Teacher Education*, 23(7): 1024–57.

Taba, H., Durkin, M., Fraenkel, J. and McNaughton, A. (1971) *A teachers' handbook to elementary school social studies: An inductive approach*. Reading, MA: Addison-Wesley.

Thomas, N.J. (1999) Are theories of imagery, theories on imagination? An active perception approach to conscious mental content. *Cognitive Science*, 23(2): 207–45.

Tomlinson, C. (2008) *A parallel curriculum: A design to develop learner potential and challenge advanced learners*. Westlake Village, CA: Merrill Educational Center/ASCD College Textbooks.

Tomlinson, C. (2014) *The differentiated curriculum: Responding to the needs of all learners*, 2nd edn. Westlake Village, CA: Merrill Educational Center/ASCD College Textbooks.

Torbert, W. (1991) *The power of balance: Transforming self, society and scientific inquiry*. Newbury Park, CA: Sage.

Urban, M. (2008) Dealing with uncertainty: challenges and possibilities for the early childhood profession. *European Early Childhood Education Journal*, 16(2): 135–52.

Van Eekelen, I., Boshuizen, H. and Vermunt, J. (2005) Self-regulation in higher education teacher education. *Higher Education*, 50: 447–71.

Varela, F., Thompson, E. and Rosch, E. (1991) *The embodied mind: Cognitive science and human experience*. Cambridge, MA: MIT Press.

Vermunt, J. and Vermetten, Y. (2004) Patterns in student learning: relationships between learning strategies, conceptions of learning, and learning orientations. *Educational Psychological Review*, 16(4): 359–84.

Vygotsky, L. (1978) *Mind in society: The development of higher psychological processes*. Cambridge, MA: Harvard University Press.

Vygotsky, L. (1981) The genesis of higher order functions. In J. Wertsch (ed.) *The concept of activity in Soviet psychology*. Armonk, NY: M.E. Sharp (pp. 144–88).

Vygotsky, L.S. (1986) *Thought and language*. Cambridge, MA: MIT Press.

Vygotsky, L.S. (1987) Thinking and speech. In *The Collected Works of L.S. Vygotsky, Volume 1: Problems of general psychology*. New York: Plenum Press (pp. 39–285). [Original work 1934]

Walshaw, M. and Anthony, G. (2008) The teacher's role in classroom discourse: a review of recent research into mathematics classrooms. *Review of Educational Research*, 78(3): 516–51.

Weber, K. (2001) Student difficulty in constructing proofs: the need for strategic knowledge. *Educational Studies in Mathematics*, 48(1): 101–19.

Weinberger, E. and McCombs, B. (2003) Applying learner centred practices to high school education. *Theory into Practice*, 42(2): 117–26.

Wheatley, W., Maddox, E. and Anthony, W. (1987) Enhancing education through the use of mental imagery. *Reading Improvement*, 24(3): 150–62.

Wiliam, D. (2011) What is assessment for learning? *Studies in Educational Evaluation*, 37(1): 3–14.

Williamson, D. and Morgan, J. (2009) Educational reform, enquiry-based learning and the re-professionalisation of teachers. *The Curriculum Journal*, 20(3): 287–304.

Wood, D. (1998) *How children think and learn*, 2nd edn. Oxford: Blackwell.

Wood, D., Bruner, J. and Ross, G. (1976) The role of tutoring in problem solving. *Journal of Child Psychology and Psychiatry*, 17(2): 89–100.

Young, M. (2014) Powerful knowledge as a curriculum principle. In M. Young, D. Lambert, C. Roberts and M. Roberts (eds) *Knowledge and the future school curriculum and social justice*. London: Bloomsbury Academic (pp. 65–88).

Zanting, A., Verloop, N. and Vermunt, J. (2001) Student teachers' beliefs about mentoring and learning to teach during teaching practice. *British Journal of Educational Psychology*, 71(1): 57–80.

Zeichner, K. (2008) A critical analysis of reflection as a goal for teacher education. *Educational Sociology*, 29(103): 535–54.

INDEX

Added to a page number 'f' denotes a figure and 't' denotes a table.